Nelles Guides

... get you going.

AVAILABLE TITLES

Berlin and Potsdam
California
Crete
Egypt
Florida
The Caribbean: Greater Antilles,
                Bermuda, Bahamas
The Caribbean: Lesser Antilles
Hawaii
Hungary
India North
India South
Indonesia-West
  (Sumatra, Java, Bali, Lombok)
Kenya
Morocco
Nepal
New Zealand
Spain North
Spain South
Thailand
Turkey

IN PREPARATION
(spring '92)
Australia
Brittany
Cyprus
Mexico
Munich
New York
Paris
Provence

For your information:
Nelles Guides are also available in German, French and Dutch.

MOROCCO
©Nelles Verlag GmbH, München 45
  All rights reserved

First Edition 1992
ISBN 3-88618-385-8

Publisher:	Günter Nelles	**Cartography:**	Nelles Verlag GmbH, München
Chief Editor:	Dr. Heinz Vestner		
Project Editor:	Berthold Schwarz	**DTP-Exposure:**	Printshop Schimann, Ingolstadt
Editor:	Bernd Peyer, Bernadette Boyle	**Color**	
Translation:	S. Braun, E. Goldmann, Ch. Grimm, R. Rosko	**Separation:**	Priegnitz, München
		Printed by:	Gorenjski Tisk, Kranj, Slovenia

MOROCCO

First Edition
1992

TABLE OF CONTENTS

FEATURES

GUIDELINES

LIST OF MAPS

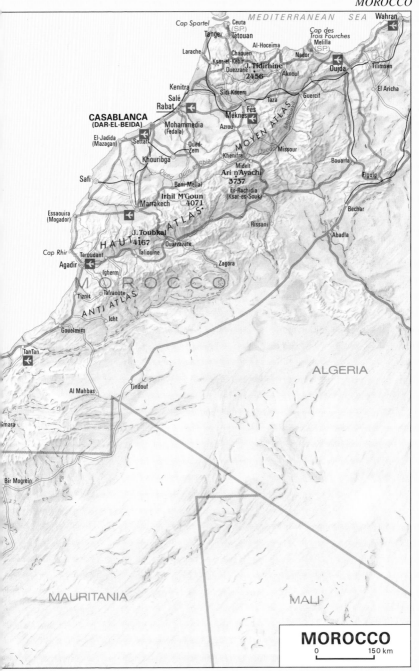

MEDITERRANEAN SEA

Wahran

Cap Spartel
Ceuta
(SP)
Tanger
Tétouan
Cap des
Trois Fourches
Melilla
(SP)

Larache
Al-Hoceïma
Nador

Chaouen
Ksar-el-Kebir
J. Tidirhine
2456
Aknoul
Oujda
Tilimsen

Ouezzane
Taza
Guercif
El Aricha

Kenitra
Salé
Rabat
Sidi Kacem
Fès
Meknès

CASABLANCA
(DAR-EL-BEIDA)
Mohammedia
(Fedala)
Azrou

El-Jadida
(Mazagan)
Settat
Oued-
Zem
Khenifra
Missour
Bouarfa

Khouribga
Midelt
Ari n'Ayachi
3737
Figuig

Safi
Beni-Mellal
Er-Rachidia
(Ksar-es-Souk)

Irhil M'Goun
4071
Bechar

Essaouira
(Mogador)
Marrakech
Rissani
Abadla

Cap Rhir
J. Toubkal
4167
Ouarzazate

Agadir
Taroudant
Taliouine

Igherm
Zagora
MOROCCO

Tiznit
Tafraoute

ANTI ATLAS
Icht

Gouelmim

TanTan

ALGERIA

Al Mahbas
Tindouf

Bir Mogreïn

Smara

MAURITANIA
MALI

MOYEN ATLAS
HAUT ATLAS
Oued Oum er Rbie

MOROCCO
0   150 km

7

A BRIEF HISTORY

Stone-age skeleton finds near Casablanca and Rabat testify to the fact that there were inhabitants in Morocco millions of years ago. Some 40,000 years ago the region was fertile enough to sustain Palaeolithic hunters and gatherers before they were supposedly displaced by more sophisticated Homo sapiens. Archeological finds in the area of Berkane in northern Morocco show that our intelligent forefathers even carried out brain surgery at this very early period in the history of mankind.

About 10,000 years ago North Africa's heavy rain falls stopped at the end of the Würm ice-age, the youngest of the four European fluctuations in the Pleistocene glacial epoch. When the summer rains stopped, the forests in southern Morocco disappeared and, as time went by, the desert sands encroached more and more on the High Atlas.

Groups of early stone-age hunters and gatherers followed the river upstream as far as its source in the Atlas Mountains in search of game. Petroglyphs on the walls of Wadis (Draa, Oued Akka) and in the vicinity of alpine meadows (Oukaimeden, Yagour) show the different kinds of animals that were hunted: elephants, rhinoceroses, ostriches, panthers, mouflons, gazelles and buffaloes. When livestock breeding started about 7,000 years ago, the earlier hunting stage depicted in the rock petroglyphs gave way to the pastoral period. There are many depictions of cattle dating back to this age.

The forefathers of the Berber tribes living in present-day Morocco probably

Previous pages: Agadir-watchman in Irherm n' Ougdal. Moorish ornamental design in Fès. Berber assembly in the south. The High Atlas Mountains – barrier to the desert. Left: Merenid sanctuary mosque in Rabat.

came from western Egypt during the period around 3000 B.C. By 1200 B.C. Phoenician traders had established fairly important settlements near Melilla, Tétouan, Tangier, Larache and El Jadida. These settlements were in turn taken over by Carthaginians after 814 B.C.

Following their victory over Carthage in 146 B.C., the Romans first exacted tribute from the Berber kingdom of Mauretania before integrating it into their Empire in A.D. 42. The agricultural and olive-oil producing province *mauretania tingitana* together with the Roman towns of Tingis, Lixis, Banasa, Volubilis and Sala were thus established in the region we now know as northern Morocco. Germanic Vandals conquered the Roman North African provinces in A.D. 429, but their reign was finally brought to an end by Byzantine troops in A.D. 533.

The year A.D. 632 marks the death of Islam's prophet, Mohammed. In 647 an army of Arab Moslem invaders clashed with Berber tribes in the region we now know as Libya. Farther west, in what is now known as the Algerian Aures Mountains, the warriors had to contend with the hostile forces of Jewish Berber queen Kahina. In 682 Arab conquerers under the command of *Okba* reached the Atlantic and marched as far south as the valleys of Sous and Ziz where Berber tribes then forced him to retreat. During a second invasion from 703 to 711 the Arab leader Moussa was successful in his attempts to convert the hostile Berber tribes in northern Morocco to Islam by promising them an adequate share of whatever was to be taken in future raids.

In 711 Moussa sent his personal slave, the Berber Tarik, with some 10,000 Berber horsemen across the Straits of Gibraltar to Christian Spain. Their rapid conquest of the Iberian peninsula triggered off a feeling of envy among the Arabs and soon the Berbers realized that the promises of equality for all non-Arabs willing to adhere to the Koran were not being fulfilled. In 740 the North African Berber tribes eventually revolted against the Omajad caliphs residing in the town of Damascus, joining forces with the dissident Shiite sect of the Kharedjite.

In the year 788 Idriss, a direct descendant of the prophet Mohammed, landed in Tangier and was readily accepted by the members of the Aouraba Berber tribe as their leader. He, Moulay Idriss I, established the first, though regionally bound, dynasty on Moroccan soil. This dynasty, however, already started to disintegrate after the death of his son Idriss II in the year 829. The newly established Idrissid city of Fès developed into a bastion of Moorish culture. Its Kairawine Mosque soon became a major center of learning. In the 10th century Spanish Omajads, Zenata Berber from the East, Iraqi Abbasidians and Tunisian Fatimids battled against one another in contention for the Idrassic heirloom. By 1050 fierce tribes of Arab Beni Hilal were scourging the Moroccan plains and eventually drove out the Berbers who settled from there into the Atlas Mountains.

In the 11th century the Tuareg Sanhadja tribe, which dominated the caravan routes in the Sahara, proclaimed Koran scholar Ibn Yasin their leader. He taught the desert fighters the orthodox Islamic principles of the Sunnites in a holy order *(ribat)* based in the Sengal River region. From then on the Sanhadja Berbers called themselves *al murabitun* (Men of the Ribat = Almoravids).Their leader, Youssef ben Tachfin established the city of Marrakech in 1071. The Moslem emirs of Spain, whose cities had attained a high level of civilization, called upon the camel-riding tribes of the Sahara for support against the Christian Reconquista in 1085. The Almoravids came, conquered and remained. In the year 1107 they ruled from Valencia to Lisbon, from Granada

Right: Gazelle, sheep or cow? A neolithic place of worship in the Anti-Atlas.

to Timbuktu and from the Atlantic Ocean to eastern Algeria.

In 1122 A.D. the preacher Ibn Toumart incited the Masmouda Berbers of the High Atlas to wage a *jihad* (Holy War) on the Almoravids for worshipping idols and also for their corrupt ways. By 1146 the Masmouda, who called themselves *al muwahiddun* (Believers of the One = Almohads) had conquered Marrakech and, by 1160, Algeria, Tunisia and East Lybia, as well as the principal cities in Andalusia. Their victorious leader Abd el Moumen proclaimed himself Calpih of Seville in 1162. His grandson Yakoub al Mansur defeated the Christian army of Castille at Alarcos in 1195. The arts and sciences flourished during this great Moorish period. The Koutoubia Mosque was erected in Marrakech, the Hassan Tower in Rabat and the Giralda in Seville. In 1212 Yacoub's son lost the Battle of Las Navas de Tolosa against Castillian King Alfons VII, however; a fatal blow for Spanish Islam, from which it never quite recovered.

As of 1213 the Merinids, Zenata Berbers from the East, attempted to take over the Almohad dynasty. They took Fès in 1248 and conquered the entire Maghreb region by 1269. After settling in the towns the nomads contributed a great deal to Moroccan city culture. Morocco's most beautiful Koran schools was built by the Merinid sultans Abu el Hassan (1331-1349) and Abu Inan (1349-1358). Many learned Jews and Moslems came to the north of Morocco in the wake of the Spanish Reconquista. The sultanate of Fès profited greatly from this new influx of Moorish-Spanish culture.

The succeeding Beni Ouatta Berber dynasty of the 15th century was already so weak that Portugal was able to establish itself as a naval power in the slave and gold trade in Moroccan waters off the coast of Ceuta, Tangier, Asilah, El Jadida, Essaouira, Agadir and Sidi Ifni. In the year of 1492, the Spanish conquered

Granada, thus putting an end to almost 700 years of Islamic rule over Andalusia. They occupied Melilla in 1497 and Ceuta in 1580, and remained there until today.

The Saadian Sharifs, descendants of the Prophet, who had come from Arabia to the Draa Valley, declared Holy War on infidels. With the exception of El Jadida, the Portuguese were forced to leave their Atlantic strongholds. The young Portuguese king Sebastian perished in a bloody battle at Ksar el Kebir at which two Saadian sultans also fell. Ahmed el Mansour (1578-1602) emerged as the victorious new ruler. He was able to stop the Ottoman Turks in Algeria. His profitable assault on the gold-trading city of Timbuktu earned him the byname of *ed dehbi* (The Golden One). The Saadian tombs in Marrakech remain a testimony to the opulence of El Mansour's seat of residence. Anarchy became widespread following his death, though. The pirate republic of Bou Regreg was founded in Rabat in 1609 by Moors who had been expelled from Spain.

The Moslem Brotherhoods of various *zawiyas* (orders) run by Sheikhs worshipped as *marabouts* (local saints) sometimes fought on the same side as, and sometimes against the successive sultans. Religious leaders, in their bid for power, frequently encouraged fanaticism amongst Moslems. The disruptive effect this had on the country was to last until the early 20th century.

In the year of 1640 Moulay Ali Sherif, the Alawi descendant of the Prophet, gained power in Tafilalet, situated at the end of the important caravan route through the Sahara. The ablest of his sons, Moulay Ismail (1672-1727), proclaimed Meknes as the new sultan's residence and secured Alawi rule of Morocco, which continued until the present. Moulay Ismail is remembered as a great, if ruthless ruler. His most brutal weapon against rebellious Berber tribes was his 15,000-strong equestrian bodyguard of black troops. Arab mercenary tribes like the Oudaia in Rabat also served him. Christians held captive at his

command by the pirates of Rabat and Sale were set to work building Moulay Ismail's strongholds. They also brought him handsome sums of ransom money. Ismail left some 500 sons. After his death the country collapsed into a state of anarchy with a never-ending dispute over the rightful heir to the throne. Ismail's grandson Sidi Mohammed ben Abdallah (1757-1790) managed to gain control of the trading routes once again.

The 19th century marks the beginning of European imperialism in North Africa. A weak Turkish governor made it easy for the French to take Algeria in 1832. Very soon, however, the Algerian Kabyle Abd el Kader Berber tribes started an armed struggle against their infidel aggressors. The Moroccan sultan, Moulay Abd er Rahman (1822-1859), supported this Holy War from the very beginning. The French took revenge by attacking Essaouira and Tangier; the Moroccans

Above: The sons of Israel returned home – ruins of a Jewish Casbah in Todhra Valley.

were forced to hand over Abd el Kader who had fled to the region in 1847.

The energetic sultan Moulay Hassan (1873-1894) spent most of his time trying to subdue the rebellious Berber tribes who were still settled in the remote and inaccessible Atlas region. This region became known as the *bled es siba*, the rebellious land, in contrast to *bled el makhzen*, the loyal region.

Moulay Abd el Aziz was a mere boy of 14 when he ascended the throne in Fès in 1894. His government was in debt and dependent on the good will of Parisian banks. More and more tribes rebelled. The French took advantage of the situation and began to occupy the region beyond Casablanca. In 1911 the new sultan, Abd el Hafiz, who forced his incapable brother off the throne, was being held under siege by Berbers in Fès: he made a grave mistake when he called on the French for help. By way of the Protectorate Treaty of 1912 they dispossessed him of the largest part of his kingdom – the region south of the Loukos River.

North Morocco became a Spanish protectorate on Nov. 11, 1912, and Tangier an international free trading zone. The Europeans divided their North African territory among themselves. The envious Germans who had secured mineral prospecting rights were compensated with territorial gains in their colony of Cameroun. The English strengthened their hold on Egypt and the Italians were permitted to colonize Libya.

The French Resident General, Lyautey, became the most powerful man in the country. He made Rabat the new capital, and by creating separate European neighbourhoods in all the larger cities he was able to preserve the old *medinas*.

In 1923 Abd el Krim declared an Islamic Republic in the Rif Mountains and almost defeated the Spanish in 1925. His rebellion was eventually crushed by colonial French troops, however.

Thousands of French *colons* (settlers) poured into Morocco during the following years. Grabbing the country's most fertile regions, they set up modern farms. A sophisticated infrastructure with harbors, roads, railways and reservoirs was established, primarily to serve the economic interests of the French: exploitation of minerals, farming crops for export to France, and establishing a secure market for French industrial products.

The infamous French Foreign Legion was brought in to keep the remote tribal regions under control, which they did until 1934. In the High Atlas the Goundafa, Glaoua and M'tougga Berber tribes collaborated with the Protectorate rulers and as a reward were allowed to extend their power to the oases regions in the south. The Glaoui governor of Marrakech, Thami el Glaoui, forced the French to send well-liked sultan Mohammed V into exile in 1953 because of his outspoken support for the Istqlal independence party founded in 1943. This triggered off mass demonstrations, violence and counter-violence. The French

saw no way out except capitulating and allowing his return. On Nov. 16, 1955 he declared independence and proclaimed himself king. By virtue of birth he was a sharif, a descendant of the Prophet, and as *amir al mumin* he was entitled to call himself "Ruler of the Pious".

Mohammed V died in 1961. He was succeeded by his son Hassan II, who had already crushed a rebellion in the Rif Mountains in 1959 and believed in ruling the country with a strong hand. Today, King Hassan II has full power over the constitutional parties as well as the power to dissolve parliament, which he did in 1965. Student unrest was stamped out by the army in 1965. In 1971 and 1972 the army attempted a coup but failed.Until today, hundreds of political prisoners are still under arrest from that time.

The Green March of Nov. 6, 1975 when 350,000 unarmed men marched into Spanish Western Sahara, turned public attention away from social and economic problems and a new surge of patriotism finally moved Spain to withdraw from its colonies. Franco was on his deathbed at the time. Moroccan soldiers occupied the north, Mauretanian military the south. 165,000 Sahrawis – more than half of the people living in Western Sahara – fled to Algerian Tindouf. Guerrilla fighters of the Polisario resistance movement fought a long battle against King Hassan's pro-western troops. Moroccans occupied the southern half of the Sahara in 1979 after the Mauretanians pulled out. A plebiscite on the future of the former Spanish colony is due to take place in January 1992 under UNO supervision.

King Hassan II was in a precarious situation during the 1990/91 Gulf War. He sent 1,300 soldiers to support the U.S., whilst the majority of his people supported Iraq. Many lives were lost during the December 1990 riots. In February, 1991, hundreds of thousands demonstrated against the West and social injustice and autocratic rule in Morocco.

GEOGRAPHY

The widespread belief that Morocco consists entirely of desert that is inhabited mainly by camels is a gross misconception. The Atlas Mountains prevent the Saharan desert sands from spreading to the Atlantic and to the Mediterranean so that the arid region only begins beyond the sheltered Atlas slopes, the sandy desert in the south and the steppe in the east. The northwestern part of the country even offers farmers fertile earth.

From a distance, the numerous snow-capped mountain peaks offer a splendid contrast to the green central *meseta* region, west of the Middle Atlas. The Arabs call this part of the country *jezira al maghrib*, the Island of the West. It is bordered by Atlantic beaches in the west, and by the Rif Mountains in the north, the Middle Atlas in the east and the High Atlas in the south. The Sebou, Oum er Rbia (Mother of Everything Green) and Tensift river are never dry – and water means life in North Africa.

The majority of Moroccans live in this region. Particularly the four ancient royal cities Rabat, Meknes, Fès and Marrakech, as well as Casablanca with its population of recently over three millions, are situated here. Phosphate mining on the Khouribga Plateau, the sardine industry in Safi, the modern irrigation farming enterprises of the Rharb, Sais, Tadla and Haouz plains and tourism – all contribute to Moroccan economy. Four international airports, Atlantic ports, railways and major roads emphasize the growing economic wealth of the region – wealth in comparison to the larger but still less developed southern region.

Over the past 300 million years, the entire African continent has moved closer

Left: Jebel Saghro is one of the geologically oldest mountain ranges in Morocco.

and closer to Europe. The Rif, the Middle Atlas and the High Atlas mountain ranges were created by this gigantic movement in the earth's crust. In fact, from the geological point of view Africa begins in the southern region of the Anti Atlas, near Sidi Ifni on the Atlantic, and stretches northeastwards as far as the Draa River beyond the dormant Jebel Siroua volcano with an elevation of 3,304 meters.

The Anti Atlas dates back to the Precambrian so that the effects of changing climate conditions over this vast period in time have created intricate relief-like formations. The highest peak of all is Adrar n'Aklim at 2,531 m. Oval granite blocks stand out in this arid mountainous region, which has an annual rainfall of 250 mm. Barley crops often yield a very poor harvest in this part of the country. The entire region is just sparsely populated by *shluh* Berbers. Centuries ago, the barley crop was usually stored in vaste *agadires*, granaries made of stone.

The thorny Argan tree, with its oil-producing fruit which look very similar to olives, flourishes on the slopes of the Anti Atlas. This hardy Moroccan tree can survive for hundreds of years even in this harsh region. Otherwise it merely grows in the bordering Sous Valley orange plantation region in the north and in the neighbouring western High Atlas region. The cactus-like Euphorb plant is resilient enough to defy even the scorching rays of the relentless desert sun. Gazelles, mouflons and lions have become extinct, but there are still quite a population of venomous snakes and scorpions.

Akka and Tata, oases on the southern edge of the Anti Atlas are Morocco's remotest agricultural outposts. Beyond this, on the lower course of the dried up Draa River, the apparently endless *hammada* (stone desert) begins. Its black-colored stones make it one of the world's most hostile deserts. Temperatures can reach up to 70 degrees centigrade on the surface of the dark rocks. The drastic drop in

temperature during the night causes the rocks to break apart so that stone particles are blown about by hot desert winds and eventually turn to dust.

The upper reaches of the Draa stretch 150 km along a date-palm oasis in which the first signs of African vegetation become evident. Dark-skinned *haratin*, descendants from slaves, as well as the enclosed mud-hut villages (*ksour*) remind the traveler of the actual proximity of Black Africa. In the past, it took no less than 56 days by camel to cross the Sahara from Zagora to Timbuktu.

East of the magnificent Draa Canyon the Anti Atlas gives way to the barren mountains of Jebel Saghro (up to 2,544 m in height; rich copper and gold deposits). In the north it is bordered by the long-stretched-out, magnificiently palm-lined Dades River oasis. The sun-dried mud *kasbahs* (strongholds) and the *tighermatine* (fortresses) in the valley present a

Above: The Middle Atlas mountain range is domain of nomads tending sheep and goats.

picturesque view before the imposing backdrop of the 3,000-m High Atlas.

A little farther eastwards, the Saghro Mountains are threatened by encroaching desert sands. The over 100-m high Erg Chebbi sand dunes, one of the main tourist attractions in Morocco, are situated just beyond the Tafilalt Oasis, where the last drops of the Ziz River slowly evaporate. Even here one can still find black *khaimas,* the tents of nomadic Berbers. The nomads' camels graze peacefully on the *hammada* pastures (with no more than some 100 mm rainfall per year).

The hardiness of the nomads enables them to overcome the hardships of desert life. It is the *asabijja* ("tireless strength of the desert tribes") that a long time ago made it possible for them to conquer the Maghreb and half of Spain during the Moroccan Middle Ages.

The 700-km long High Atlas mountain range with its snow-capped peaks - four of them over 4,000 m – gorges, oases, forests and desert-like plateaus is certainly the most impressive of Morocco's mountain regions. The Western High Atlas, with peaks reaching 2,000 m, are just beyond Agadir, the prosperous Atlantic seaside resort which has become so popular over the years. The indigenous Arghan trees and a few holmoaks grow well in the reddish mountain *hamri* soil. There are also some extensive Berber-thuja forests in this region.

Jebel Toubkal in the Crystalline High Atlas to the east is North Africa's highest mountain at 4,167 m. This area, in which barit, manganese and antimony deposits are found, is becoming increasingly popular with trekkers and skiers. Neighboring Jebel Oukaimeden (3,273 m) with its lifts and resorts is a favorite mountain with downhill skiers. Generally, it is snow-covered well into the month of March. In the remote protection of mountain river oases, the *shluh* Berber have managed to retain their ancient hill-farming culture even to the present day.

The Central High Atlas embraces a region more than 300 km long and 100 km wide, between the Tichka pass in the west and the Talrhemt pass in the east. River oases are found on high ground. There are many monkeys, eagles and leopards in this remote part of the country. Berber-thuya, cedar, oaks and juniper grow here. Atlas cedars cover the slopes of the 3,737-m Ayachi Massif in the northeast.

Irhil M'Goun (4,068 m) and Jebel Azourki (3,690 m) in the Central Atlas' heart are ideal for trekking. The spectacular Tessaout, Titflout and Arous gorges are popular for trekking, climbing and, more recently, for canoeing. The magnificent gorges on the mountain's south side, along the upper course of the Dades and Todhra rivers, can be reached by bus.

The *Beraber* tribal region lies to the east of the M'Goun Massif. The semi-nomadic Berber tribes leave their villages in spring with herds of sheep and goats and set up camp on higher grazing ground.

To the east of the High Atlas, the country becomes more and more arid and flat, finally giving way to the Tamelelt plain. The Algerian frontier lies beyond the Figuig oasis which, interestingly, features artesian wells.

The Middle Atlas begins in the west, on the edge of the *meseta*, as an Atlas plateau with heavy rainfall. Its highest peaks are 2,000 m. It sometimes snows well into April in these parts. This almost uninhabited region is used manily for grazing and forestry. Among its many scenic attractions are the impressive Ouzoud waterfalls and the Bin el Ouidane reservoir, which irrigates the lemon and sugar-beet plantations in the Tadla basin. The Aguelmane Azigza (1,800 m) stands amid dense Cedar forests. Semi-nomads like to set up camp on the mountain slopes. Mishlliffen, the *Fassis'* (citizens of Fès) ski resort is situated on the slopes of Jebel Hebri (2,036 m). In the northeast, Jebel Bou Naceur, the highest peak in the entire Middle Atlas, reaches 3,340 m. In the east, there is a very steep drop to the some 400-km long Moulouya river valley, a green strip in the bordering arid grassy plain. Jebel Tazzeka (1,980 m) in the north is a national park, and a considerable attraction with its deep caves and evergreen holmoak forests.

The Rif mountain range stretches beyond the historic Taza Gap, once a place of great importance. The impressive Jebala Mountains meet the Atlantic in the west, at Tangiers. They are lined with beautiful beaches with silver sands near the Mediterranean coastal town of Smir-Restinga.The Central Rif mountain range starts further east, at Chefchaouen. Its highest peak is Jebel Tidiquin at 2,450 m. It rains almost as much here as it does e.g. in the Bavarian Alps – up to 2,000 mm a year – so that cedars and oaks grow well. *Rifi*-Berber farmers cultivate hemp illegally in the remote valleys near Ketama. The steep northern face of the Central Rif adjoins the cliffs of the rocky Mediterranean coast. The lower East Rif marks the beginning of an arid steppe region.

MOROCCAN LIFE

People

Who are the Berbers? Perhaps it is easier to describe where they live. Nowadays they settle in villages – just rarely in tents – in the mountains and oases of North Africa and Egypt, as far as Mauretania. The Sahara is also part of Berber country. The dignified *Tuareg,* the last of the desert horesemen, live primarily in Algeria, Niger and Mali. They are related to the *Beraber* nomads of southeastern Morocco (*Sanhdja* group). The independent *Kabyle* live in the Rif Mountains in northern Morocco (*Zenata* group). The Shluh (*Masmouda* group), hardy farmers and clever merchants, settle in the western region of the High Atlas and in the Anti Atlas. At 40 percent of the total population, Morocco has the highest concentration of Berber among the Maghreb states. Berber tribes were exposed to much foreign influence, so they are no longer a homogeneous group.

Many *Shluh* of Tafraoute in the Anti-Atlas actually look more European than some Southern Europeans do. On the other hand, some members of the same tribe have the features of Black Africans. The Berber language belongs to the Hemito-Semitic language group, of the varity spoken in the Middle East. A 14th-century Moroccan historian claimed that the Berbers are descendants "of Cane, the son of Ham, the son of Noah".

As far as the Romans were concerned, all Africans were *barbari* (Greek *barbaroi* = bearded). The nomads in the region beyond Carthago were probably identical with the *Zenata* Berber tribe, who were greatly feared as opponents or admired as legionaries and gladiators.

Left: El Haij Yussef, a pious Shluh-Berber from the upper Dades Valley.

The Romans seemed to have gotten along better with the *mauri* (Greek *amauros* = dark) who settled in the Roman province of Mauretania and were probably related to the sedentary *masmouda* Berber.

But there had been foreign influence long before the Romans came to North Africa. Black Africans, probably from Ethiopia and Ghana, made their way across the Sahara to the Draa Valley in 5000 B.C. As of 1200 B.C. Phoenicians and Greeks also had contact with Berber tribes. Jewish settlements in Morocco date to the 6th century B.C.

Roman influence had a lasting effect on Berber culture. The brooches worn by Berber women date way back to Roman times, as well as the ornate doorlocks and the *Shluh* word *almu,* meaning summer pastures. The *ksar,* a walled-in village, has its origins in the Latin *castrum.* Roman Christians spread their religion throughout North Africa. Saint Augustine was a converted *Zenata* Berber.

Some of the fair-skinned Moroccans are descendants of the German Vandals who came to North Africa in the 5th century A.D. The first of the Arab invaders who came in the 7th century did not bring their women with them and thus often took Berber wives. Sultan Idriss II, son of Moulay Idriss I, descendant of the Prophet, was the progeny of a mixed marriage in the late 8th century.

Though the Berber did not fully adapt to Arab customs, they did convert to Islam – even the *Sanhadja* Berber of the Sahara. This tribe established the Almoravid dynasty in the 11th century and subjected the Arab empire in Spain after having conquered the *Masmouda* and *Zenata* tribes of Morocco. Thus the sophisticated Moorish culture, which had flourished in the Iberian peninsula since the Arab conquest in 711 B.C., obtained an additional cultural element in its mélange of Arab, Berber, Jewish and Spain-Christian traditions. Morocco was in turn influenced by the rather refined Moorish

urban culture, especially in the 13th century when educated Moslems, mainly Arabs and Jews, fled to Morocco from Andalusia in an attempt to escape the wrath of the Christian Reconquista. More than 3 million people arrived in Morocco by 1610. The Sephardic Jews were given their own quarters in so-called *mellahs*. Many of them became advisers to the sultan in banking, commercial and administrative matters. The Berbers were in power from the 11th to the 15th century – the so-called *Sanhadja* (Almoravids), the *Masmouda*, (Almohads) and the *Zenata* (Merinids) succeeded one another.

An increasing number of *Beni Hilal* Arab nomadic tribes made their way to the fertile Maghreb plains after the 11th century. The Arabs drove the indigenous tribes north into the mountains, but also mingled with the Berbers living in the river oasis region.

Left: Berber women in the High Atlas mountains wear no veils. Right: Morocco's greater south is a diverse racial melting pot.

Arabs have been on the throne in Berber country ever since the 16th century. The Arab Sultan Moulay Ismail "bred" a special troop of Black retainers in order to suppress rebellious Berber tribes. The dark-skinned *Haratin* in the south are the progeny of the Sultan's soldiers and the thriving slave trade of those times.

The greatest foreign influence exerted on the Berbers since the Arab invasion in the 7th century came in 1912 with the signing of the Protectorate Treaty, which brought northern Morocco under Spanish rule and almost all of the remaining part of the country under French rule. The French sent its notorious Foreign Legion to keep "peace" among the Berbers. To do so, they did not hesitate to use bombs and poison gas against the rebellious tribes. After the Foreign Legion French settlers occupied the most fertile regions. The Protectorate rulers favored the Berber leader El Glaoui, who in turn brought the tribal democracies in the south under the heavy yoke of feudalism. Most of the famous *kasbahs* as we see them today were constructed in the 20th century as strongholds for the small, but powerful, Glaoua Berber clan.

French politicians were partial to Jews in the administration and, true to the "divide and conquer" policy, consciously promoted a rift between Arabs and Berbers – especially in linguistic and legal matters. They failed, however, because the Islamic bonds proved too strong. The Catholic church even planned to christianize the Berbers.

Following the declaration of independence in 1956, most of the 250,000 Jewish residents left the country in fear of being persecuted. Among them were many successful businessmen with Spanish origins, as wells as Jews from southern Berber and Arab regions. The majority of the Spanish and French population also left after independence. Hundreds of thousands of job-seeking Moroccans have departed for Europe since then.

Language

Official language is Moroccan Arabic – a variety of classical Arabic. It is the mother tongue of 60% of the 25 million Moroccans and spreading, due to its use in schools, official places and the media.

Although only 5 % of the population have Arab origins, Arab culture has strongly influenced the mainly Berber population. In the Atlantic basin between Tangier and Essaouira, Arabic dialects spoken by the Arab nomads who came to the region in the Middle Ages predominate. That is why the *Regulbat* nomads of the West Sahara – once feared as caravan robbers – now speak the Arabic *hassani* dialect. Urbanization has accelerated the trend to speak Arabic. In large cities with their Arab *medinas* and French *villes nouvelles*, most Berber children soon forget their tribal mother tongue. Nowadays, only 40% of the Moroccan population are able to speak one of the four Hamito-Semitic Berber languages: *Zenatia, Tarifit, Tashelhite* and *Tamazirt*.

These different languages, or rather dialects, conform roughly to the geographic regions of the land. The descendants of the Masmouda, the Shluh in the western High Atlas and in the Anti Atlas, speak *Tachelheit*. Today, it can also be heard on regional radio stations and on music cassettes. *Tamazirt* is spoken by the Beraber, descendants of the Sanhadja, particularly in the eastern parts of the Middle and High Atlas and in the bordering steppe region. *Tarifit* is spoken in the eastern Rif mountain area by the descendants of the Zenata, appropriately named the Riffis. *Zanatia,* spoken by the Beni Quarain and Ait Segrouch in the eastern part of the Middle Atlas, is a closely related dialect. Shluh, Beraber und Riffis, however, are hardly able to communicate with each other in their respective Berber dialects. They have to use Arabic as their *lingua franca* – if they are able to speak it at all, that is. Unlike their Tuareg cousins in the desert, who even developed their own alphabet, the Moroccan Berber never had a script of their own. A number of Berber

comments on Islamic law written in the 15th century in Arabic and today kept in the Tamgroute Library near Zagora still bear witness to this.

Only very few visitors to Morocco can speak a word of Arabic, let alone any of the country's Berber dialects. One will find, however, that Moroccans who have significant dealings with the tourist population are able to speak at the very least a smattering of English. Those who have command of French will get by almost anywhere as much of the country is bilingual (a relict from the last colonists). Spanish frequently can also be very useful, especially in the old Spanish protectorate zones around Tétouan, as well as in the Rif area and in the extreme south.

At school, all subjects are taught in Arabic for the first two years. Thereafter French is also used. For political reasons, the Berber language is not taught at all at

Left: Visitors to a mosque wear no shoes.
Right: Koubba, the holy tomb, is the symbol of Morocco's popular Islam.

school. The Arab ruling classes insist on regarding Morocco as a purely Arab nation, despite the fact that well over a third of the country's total population has little or even no knowledge of Arabic. But this language is spreading at an increasingly rapid rate. Television plays an extremely important role in promoting Arabic, making it accessible as well to young Berber girls who are unable to attend school. As pious Moslems, the Berber tribes revere Arabic as the sacred language of the Holy Koran. And, according to the teachings in the Koran, the holy book should never be translated because it is sacred.

In spite of their history and the social appearances the Berbers do not regard themselves as an underprivileged and exploited minority group. In neighboring Algeria there was a lot of political unrest in 1980 following the refusal of the Arab authorities to allow a Berber poetry recital in Kabylei. The UNESCO has been funding an Encyclopédie Berbère since 1984, and by so doing, also the study of the different Berber tribes.

Religion

The major part of the Moroccans are Sunni Moslems. They adhere to the Malekite school of law and observe the Five Pillars of Islam: 1. *shahada* (the belief that there is no God other than Allah, and that Mohammed is His Prophet), 2. *salat* (prayer five times daily), 3. *saum* (rigorous fast during Ramadan), 4. *zakat* (the giving of alms to the poor), 5. *hadj* (pilgrimage to Mecca).

Converting the peoples of the Maghreb to Islam was not entirely a one-sided or perfectly successful affair. In their mostly remote regions, the Berbers were able to retain much of their pre-Islamic religious cult, which focussed worship around individual local saints. The *ulema*, actually a collective name for Koranic scholars from the Karaouine University in Fès, condemned the worshiping of saints – also derived from the Jews, Christians and Animists – as contrary to the principles of Islamic teaching.

The *koubbas* (holy tombs) have become an integral part of the landscape. In the Moorish part of the country they are whitewashed, partly tiled, domed buildings, square in shape. The tombs of important sharifs (descendants of the Prophet) frequently have pyramid-shaped roofs made of green glazed bricks. The countryside to the south of the High Atlas is studded with holy *marabouts*, ochre-coloured mud constructions on which the dome narrows to a cone at the top. In graveyards of poorer villages sometimes the graves of *agurram* (Berber saints) are marked distinctively by a low stone border around the grave.

Mountain peaks, caves and springs can also be sacred to the Berber. A female mythical figure, *lalla todhra,* is revered as a spring saint in the gorge of Todhra. Formerly this was a Berber cult site, but nowadays Arab women from the northern towns also come to the shrine to be blessed with spring water.

Despite strong protest from Koranic scholars, a shrine revering a woman in the form of a holy tree still exists in the Rif mountains: the *lalla zeitoun* (Holy Lady Olive Tree). Wells and prominent trees, quite often situated next to holy tombs, still serve as living reminders for pre-Islamic fertility symbols.

Koubbas belonging to miracle healers are often visited by the sick, even though Morocco has modern medical facilities. Some *marabouts* are consulted for infertility problems, others for eye ailments or psychological disorders. The main thing is to fall asleep at the tomb. Allegedly, the remedy is then revealed in a dream, which can also, for instance, instruct the person to visit seven more holy men.

Even peace-makers – blood feuds were common in the Atlas – were elevated to sainthood. Scholars could also become *marabouts* posthumously, such as the much visited mausoleum of the founder of the library and Koran school in Tamegroute, Sidi Mohammed Abdallah ben Nasser, shows.

Courageous missionaries spent much of their life spreading or reviving Islam in the desert and mountains regions. For this purpose they often established a *ribat*, or holy order, and in the Maghreb region they were consequently referred to as *murabit* (or *marabout* in the French spelling). Two such preachers were of great historic importance. Ibn Yasin persuaded the *Sanhadja* Berber in the Sahara to embark on a *jihad* (holy war) in the 11th century, which took them as far as Spain. The *mahdi* (legal adviser), Ibn Tumart, encouraged the *Masmouda* of the High Atlas to take up arms in a religious war against the *Sanhadja* in the 12th century. Both preachers were able to instil the feeling of *asabijja* in the Berber, the fearless courage in the face of death which enables an individual to endure the hardships of war and to sacrifice his life for any religious cause.

Left: Magic ornaments protect the bride from evil. Right: Gold jewelry is the husband's gift to his wife after the wedding night.

A *marabout* crisis began in the 15th century and lasted until the 20th. Several sheikhs of powerful *zawiyas* (religious orders), such as the leaders of the Moslem Order of Ouezzane, were temporarily more influential than the sultans. The king's secret police nowadays keeps an ever watchful eye on all the religious fanatics. Anyone wearing a beard ("The Prophet's Beard") is already suspect.

Sufis, Islamic mystics from the East, introduced trance rites to the Maghreb holy cult at this time. The rituals, which take place at the annual *moussems* (pilgrimages to holy tombs), do not comply at all with Koranic teachings. The Assaoua, followers of Sidi Aissa, who is buried in Meknes, willingly eat live snakes and sheep, lick burning embers and walk on sharp knives. By engaging in such rites, they hope to achieve a closer relationship to all that is sacred.

The most sacred of the sharif-marabouts is Moulay Idris I, descendant of the Prophet and founder of a dynasty. For prestige purposes, Berber holy men and entire Berber tribes frequently claim they are descendants of Mohammed. Even sharifian bloodlines, however, are no longer a guarantee for prosperity. Today, there are many beggars among the Idrissids. Entire villages in the Draa valley claim to descend from Mohammed, in which case the place names are preceded by the titles *shorfa* or *m'rabtin*.

Baraka
– Blessing, Happiness and Security –

Baraka allahu fik is a polite way of saying thank you and means: "May the blessing of Allah rest upon you." In rural Morocco the welfare of the individual still depends upon the fertility of family, pastures and herds. Without *baraka* (the power of blessing) crops die off, the family is deprived of sons, the king is assassinated and life is full of pitfalls. *Baraka* is a heavenly blessing and because holy men have more influence in heavenly matters, even more so after their death, the needy visit their *koubbas* (tombs). Stones, rags or combs containing bushels of hair, all of which are thought to have magical powers, are sacrificed at the *marabout's* tomb.

The king, who rules as *amir el mumin* (Ruler of the Pious), is especially in need of *baraka*. Hassan II, who survived many attempted assassinations, is said to have a great deal of it. The magical powers of a *marabout* can be passed on to his sons. In this way pilgrims' donations, often generous, remain in the family. Selling good luck charms made of copper and silver, said to protect those that wear them from evil spirits, is a lucrative business.

Protection from the Evil Eye

The Berbers believe that the evil eye of witches or wizards can cause infertility or even worse. For this reason, Berber women protect themselves by tatooing the body orifices most exposed to the evil

eye and against malignant spirits known as *gnuns*. Very vulnerable are the nose and mouth, and accordingly the chin is decorated with magic designs to keep away evil spirits. Variations of the *siyala* (palmtree) are popular designs for the chin. The date palm is the most widespread symbol of fertility throughout the Orient. A five-pointed cross between the thumb and index finger is said to ward off infertility. The magic signs are scratched slightly into the surface of an infant's skin. A bride's hands and feet are painted with *henna* (a red vegetable dye). This is thought to bring luck. Black eye make-up known as *khol* makes the eyes sparkle and thus keeps the somber spirits away. Silver studs on head-scarves serve exactly the same purpose. Red corals, amber and silver worked into headbands, earrings and necklaces are also believed to frighten away evil spirits.

Lucky ornaments often adorn jewelry, household goods, walls and carpets. They usually have a geometrical form, the base of which is a lucky number. Numbers generally are important in this religious form. The depiction of human images had already been condemned as idolatry by Mohammed. Three, four and five are thought to be very lucky numbers. A bride receives a gift of jewellery from her future husband, the value of which is agreed upon before the wedding. The triangular shapes often seen on massive silver bracelets worn by Berber women are also said to protect them from infertility. A triangle pointing downwards symbolizes femininity, one pointing upwards stands for masculinity. Superimposed, they take on the shape of the Star of David found on the doors of synagogues. Four symbolizes worldly happiness. Two squares form the octagonal shapes often found on carpets and mosaics. Five (*khamsa*) is thought to be an especially lucky number. A five-pointed cross even decorates the Moroccan flag. "Fatima's Hand" – Fatima was the Prophet's favorite daughter – is worn as a golden amulet or painted in red *henna* next to house doors to bring luck.

The geometrical designs found on lots of the Arab-Moorish buildings frequently depict foliage and other forms of plant life. Arabesques are reminiscent of Dionysos' grape vines, a Greek symbol of fertility. Their entwined tendrils symbolize eternity. Unlike Christian art, Moorish art does not tell a story, but has a meditative function and strives to emphasize the omnipresence of Allah.

Calligraphy was and still is an Arab speciality. Koranic verses in rounded or angular *(Kufic)* script are interwoven with arabesques on stucco overlays decorating the walls of mosques and palaces. The *Kufic* description of Mohammed's *baraka* on a decorative medallion, reminiscent of a Greek labyrinth, is often found on wells, above city gates and on palace portals.

Right: Red coral, amber and silver are the adornments of Shluh-Berber women.

Women between Islam and the Modern Age

Around 622 A.D. Mohammed formulated new Islamic laws on family matters that were to give women more rights than they had ever had previously. Infanticide was forbidden, and daughters were given the right to inherit their fathers' property. Until then, this right had been strictly reserved for male descendants. They were also entitled to a proper marriage contract protecting their rights throughout marriage, and they were promised sexual fulfillment by their husbands after marriage. The right to divorce was also introduced at this time.

Seen within the context of 7th-century Arabia, these laws were actually quite progressive. Mohammed certainly had a great passion for women, so much so that after his ninth marriage Allah had to reprimand him through verse 33 in the Koran: "In future, you are not permitted to take any more wives, neither are you allowed to replace your present wives with more beautiful ones". Owing to this, the prophet allowed the common people to have up to four main wives, thus making it possible for married men to marry their brothers' widows. This provided an important source of financial security for widows and fatherless children, as a great number of men lost their lives at this time in the *jihad*. Four main wives, however, did not suffice the caliphs, sultans and pashas. Luckily, the Prophet made no mention of the number of slaves a man was entitled to have. Moulay Ismail, for instance, is said to have had as many as 500 women in his harem in Meknes. This could never happen in 20th-century Morocco. According to the Koran, every woman is entitled to a gift from her bridegroom – usually jewellery. In wealthier families, this could be a belt made of one kilo of gold that remains the wive's property even after divorce. The majority of Moroccans are, not surprisingly, mono-

gamous. The way things are, they simply couldn't afford a single wife more.

"Men are superior to women because of what Allah bestowed upon them, and because they give them (the women) their money. "Righteous women are obedient and avoid temptation during (their husbands) absence... The obstinate... are punished..."(4th verse). "... and that she shall cover her bosom with a veil and only expose her charms to her husband..." (24th verse). According to the Koran a man is obliged to provide a comfortable home for his wife and she is obliged to remain chaste throughout her married life. Although Moroccan law states that the man is the sole breadwinner, high unemployment often means that the man is dependent on his wife's earnings as well. Morocco's divorce rate is extremely high, and divorced mothers are not always able to adhere to Islamic principles when looking for work.

Fathers still arrange marriage contracts for their daughters, especially in the rural areas. Brothers are still responsible for safeguarding their sisters' good reputation, and they have to make sure she remains a virgin until marriage – a difficult undertaking in a large, bustling city like Casablanca. A man's reputation demands that his wife behaves in a reserved manner at all times when in public. For this reason, women in the *medinas* cover their faces with the *litham* (veil) and their heads with the hoods of their *jellabah*. But an increasing number of Moroccan women, especially those living in the city areas, are no longer prepared to veil themselves after marriage. Moroccan women are exposed, and indeed even partial to the latest fashions, displayed in French women's magazines. Furthermore, education and birth control are often the key to a woman's independence.

Educated women are quite happy to have less children so that they can take up a career outside the home. But the illiteracy rate remains high among the female population, however. Farmers' daughters work at home from a very early age in rural districts. And very often, only the

33

sons attend school. As the male members of the family are expected to support their parents in their old age, it is obviously more important to educate them.

Political decisions are made by men and birth control is condemned vociferously by fundamentalists as being contrary to the principles of Islamic teaching. Left-wing politicians reject birth control as an imperialistic plot against the Third World. Women do not always have the time to think about complicated issues such as these. They find it easier and less time-consuming to take the pill or some form of herbal medicine.

Whilst emancipated students in Rabat or in Agadir attend lectures in mini-skirts or sunbathe topless, a Berber woman in the Rif Mountains might be reprimanded by her husband if she doesn't dress in a modest fashion. In the High Atlas a man might even reject his wife if he thinks her

Left: Medersas almost always testify to the splendor of the Moorish culture. Right: On the "road of the casbahs".

honor has been tarnished by an exchange of glances with another man. It is important to bear this in mind when taking photographs in the remoter areas of Morocco. *Shluh* Berber women in the south and *Rifi* women in the north wear a *haik*, a large head-scarve that also covers the shoulders, rather than the veil worn by Arab women in the cities to protect themselves from a stranger's glances.

The semi-nomadic *Beraber* women in the southeast are not as conservative. Like their Tuareg cousins in the Sahara, they are not veiled. Women here are an essential part of the labor force. Men couldn't afford to leave their wives at home, and even if they could, their wives would never agree to it. The women in this region do not tolerate polygamy either. The older and more democratic tribal law overrides Koranic law on women's issues and on all matters concerning the elderly. Women in this region even work in the nearby markets selling traditional cosmetics. In the Rif Mountains there are also markets run solely by

women. These were established in 1920 when the men were fighting in the war against Spain and were unable to go to the market themselves.

Divorced Berber women can pick themselves a new husband at the famous Ait Haddidou marriage market which takes place each September in the Imilchil district in the Central High Atlas. Some women come every year. The Ait Haddidou men are beginning to boycott this pre-Islamic tradition, however, because of the high divorce rate mainly initiated by the women.

Architecture

Contrary to popular opinion, the Arabs did not design the blind alleys in the *medinas* in order to confuse non-Moslem tourists. Their main purpose is to allow the residents a certain amount of privacy. Houses in the old town have no windows. Those wandering into this part of the city might leave even more quickly than they came. Strangers are not welcome here.

They could blemish a woman's good reputation! But visitors are welcome in the *souks* (market places, also called bazaars) and in the craftsmen's quarter. Only the *kisseria*, the bazaar with expensive silks and brocades, is closed at night.

There is usually at least one mosque with a Koran school in a neighborhood. Moslems go to a *hammam* (Turkish bath) as part of the Islamic tradition of cleanliness. Young girls with trays balanced on their heads sell *khobza*, freshly baked flat bread. Decorative public wells supply each neighborhood with water. The largest building in each city is generally the Friday Mosque. Men congregrate here each Friday for midday prayers.

All Moroccan mosques have a courtyard and are designed according to the Prophet's unpretentious atrium house in Medina. Palace courtyards are laid out as *riad* (courtyard gardens), which the Islamic belief that paradise resembles an oasis garden in full bloom. In keeping with this belief, there is a running fountain *(sadirvan)* in the outer courtyard

35

(*sahn*) in front of every mosque. This leads into the *haram* (prayer hall), at the far end of which stands the *kibla* (prayer wall) containing the *mihrab* (prayer alcove) pointing towards Mecca. The *minaret* is usually situated on the *sahn* side and is square, in keeping with Almohad tradition. Almohad architects calculated the height of the minaret according to the following rule: height = five times the length of the foundations. Although non-Moslems are generally not permitted to enter mosques, they can get a rough idea of what the Karaouine mosque in Fès looks like by stealing a glance through the open doorway.

Every visitor to Morocco should look at at least one *medersa* (Koran school). The Attarine and Bou Inania in Fès or the Ben Yussef-Medersa in Marrakech were built in the 13th century and are highlights of Islamic architecture and artistic design. The *tolba* (scholars) at the theo-

Above: This new farm house is made of mud and Spanish reeds.

logical school are taught in the courtyard, which usually has a marble fountain in its center. Theprayer hall is containing the *mihrab*. Intricate Moorish artistic designs in marble, colored fayence mosaics, stucco and cedar carvings decorate the walls. The students'living quarters on the first floor are, in contrast to the rest of building, very Spartan indeed.

Islamic brotherhoods congregate in a *zawiya*, which usually embraces a holy tomb, a mosque and a Koran school, and is named after a *marabout*.

In comparison to the elegant Moorish buildings in the cities, the sun-dried mud constructions in the south seem indeed rather archaic. Workers sing in rhythmic harmony as they stamp down the mud between wooden planks. Birds like to build their little nests in the spaces left by the horizontal planks. Nevertheless, the walls have proved to be quite durable. Wooden beams made of palms and silver poplars support the mud roofs. As these beams are not very wide, the rooms are mostly relatively small.

Former Berber feudal rulers' stronghold residences in the south are called *kasbahs*. The most significant examples of these – displaying ornamental supernatural defence symbols – are situated in Telouet in the High Atlas, in Taourirt and in Tiffoultoute near Ourzazate, as well as in Tamdaght in the Assif Mellah Valley. Not only did the *kasbahs* keep the farmers in the fertile oasis regions under control, but also monitored the gold, salt and slave caravan routes through the Sahara. Kasbahs generally contained slave quarters. The *kaids*, tribal chiefs, and the *khalifas*, the ruler's representatives, have long since abandoned their feudal strongholds. But descendants of slaves, *haratin*, sometimes still live among the ruins.

Rich oasis farmers live in residential complexes called *tighremt*. This type of sun-dried mud building can have up to four storeys. It is square in shape, usually with four towers and an inner courtyard. Illustrations, particularly phallic symbols adorn the walls and towers on the battlements, symbolizing masculine virility. It is customary to cover these symbols with old pots. This is done to keep evil spirits away that might endanger people, animals or crops. The most beautiful of the inhabited *tighermatine* (residential complexes), sometimes reminiscent of Yemenite multi-storey sun-dried mud buildings, are in the Dades and Draa valleys, along the "Kasbah Route".

A *ksar* (plural *ksour*) is a fortified walled-in village, built of sun-dried mud and bricks, of the type found in Ait Benhaddou in the Ouarzazate region and in Tinsouline in the Draa Valley. A number of *tighermatine* can also be found within the village walls. The *ksar*-gates display elaborate decorations believed to ward off *gnuns* (evil spirits).

The main gate is usually situated in the east, next to the village mosque. In the past otherwise welcome visitors were compelled to sleep in the vicinity of the gates – after all, they may have been spies

from hostile tribes. Up until 100 years ago, when the *Kaids* of the *Glaoua* clan assumed power, the *Ksour* were ruled by the *jemaa* (male assembly) in a fairly democratic fashion. The Berbers thus have an appropriate name for themselves: *Imazirhen*, "the Free". Once the population exceeded 500 and it became more difficult to reach unanimous decisions on important issues, a new *ksar* was established within view of the old. This is how the rows of picturesque *ksour* in the Ziz and Draa oasis regions arose.

Agadir, or *irherm*, are the communal granaries found in the High Atlas and Anti Atlas, usually in secure positions, high above the *Shluh* Berber villages. Each family owned a space in the *agadir* where they could store their grain and tools under lock and key. Decoratively carved locks kept thieves away and colored door designs protected the grain from evil spirits. An *amin* (a trustworthy villager), chosen by the village council, spent his entire life keeping guard at the entrance to the storage house.

These *agadir* were also used by Berber farmers as fortifications against the hostile attacks of nomadic tribes and thus became symbols of Berber independence. For this very reason they were destroyed by the *Glaoua-Kaids,* who extended their feudal powers to the south with the help of the French at the turn of this century.

A truly impressive *agadir,* made up of a great number of compartments and still in use today, is in the village of Tasguent in the Anti Atlas, 60 km east of Tafraoute. It is open to the public. The communal granary in Irherm n'Ougdal (along route P 31, about 20 km south of the Tichka Pass) is also worth a visit. This square-shaped *irherm* was constructed merely of stamped mud and, because of the harsh local climate, covered with a timbered roof. Although the tribes have lived in peaceful co-existence since 1933, local farmers still guard their granaries against possible attack.

AGRICULTURE IN TRANSITION

Morocco is, for the most part, still an agrarian country. In cultivating the soil, the Moroccan farmers have created a cultural landscape as well with an aesthetic charm (an indispensible touristic asset), which comes to light in the form of several colorful folklore festivals: the Almond Blossom Festival in Tafraoute, the Date Palm Festival in Erfoud, the Rose Festival in El Kelaa des M'Gouna and the Cherry Festival in Sefrou.

Today, approximately two thirds of all Moroccans make a living from agriculture. There is, though, a wide range of occupations in this field: from the goatherd, whose animals climb to the top of the *Arghan* trees in arduous search of food; to the agricultural engineer, who develops computer programs at the University of Rabat for the automatic fertilization of export-bound strawberries. A "farmer" here may be a man who resides in Casablanca and flies on weekends to his irrigated *domaine* in Beni Mellal to inspect his tangerine plantation, or the tenant farmer who, despite the fateful recurring years of drought, tries to cultivate barley with his mule and wooden plough on the neighboring dry and hilly countryside. High-tech and medieval farming methods exist side by side – the result of European expansionism in the 20th century.

Tradional Dry Farming

Farming without artificial irrigation is only possible in regions with more than 400 mm of rain per year. For the most part, this area stretches in a half-moon shape from the north side of the High Atlas mountain range and from the west

Left: Citrus fruits are the most important Moroccan agricultural export product.

side of the Middle Atlas range out to the Atlantic, with the Mediterranean bordering to the north. Apart from large modern farms, this is where one will witness the wooden ploughs pulled by mules or even by camels still being used in the cultivation of barley and wheat.

The prophet once said: "The most wretched sound on earth is the braying of a donkey." He may have been right, but the advantages of 1.5 million donkeys outweigh this one unflattering characteristic by far. The donkey is unsurpassed as a draught animal on steep and terraced slopes. Its food grows in the backyard, it fertilizes the fields with its waste, and it has constant four-wheel drive. In contrast to its four-wheeled, diesel-guzzling rival, the donkey does not pack down the soil, and the archaic plow it pulls does not destroy the soil's natural composition (as does the deep-biting motorized plough). It thus helps to conserve the earth's moisture – a doubtlessly weighty argument in favor of a farming method otherwise regarded as antiquated.

Herbs grow wild in the barley fields, and in the springtime tourists enjoy their beautiful blossoms. Still, these plants are not yet considered weeds to be destroyed with a chemical mace. They are handpicked by the farmers' daughters and are an important source of nourishment for dairy cows. The state now recognizes the importance of this traditional farming method *(bour)* for grain production and, therefore, even plans to promote it with tax exemptions in the near future.

Traditional Animal Husbandry

The hard drought-years of 1980-1984 forced many livestock-breeding nomads of the south to give up their particular social and economic way of life. In times of drought, these nomads (descendants of the dynastic Berber tribes of *Sanhadja* and *Beni Meri*) raided the sedentary oasis farmers for grain. As the proud camel,

sheep and goat herdsmen they were, they despised the *fellahs* for their abasing work in the fields. The days when camel-riding nomads raided villages, though, have been over since 1934, when French legionaires put down the last nomad uprising against the detested protectionists in Jebel Saghro.

When herds of livestock perished in the drought of the early 1980's, there were merely two alternatives for the nomads: To live in their tattered *khaimas* (tents) on the outskirts of the villages and depend on charity, or to move to the ghettos in Casablanca and Rabat, where at least drinking water was consistently available. During these crisis years, the government was also forced to limit the mass slaughter of rams during *id el kebir* (sacrificial offering), the ritual celebration of Abraham's offering. The meager pastureland of the arid steppe is to be im-

Left: Rural livestock breeders rival the nomads. Right: Water is a precious commodity in southern Morocco.

proved in the future, with support from the Food and Agricultural Organization of the United Nations, by the planting of drought-resistant shrubbery.

For ages, the lush meadows of the Atlas mountain range have been the summer destination of the nomadic tribes. The southern tribes, such as the *Ait Atta* of Jebel Saghro, move to the High Atlas in spring. The *Beni M'Guild* put up their tents in the Middle Atlas during the hot season, then move northwest in the winter for their sheep to graze the stubble fields of the wheat growing region. But then, in the course of time, many tents become huts and the eternal wanderers begin to settle down. Even the village farmers have long been enlarging their own herds, thus disputing the traditional grazing rights of the nomadic tribes. The resulting overgrazing, together with the felling of firewood by herdsmen, has turned large areas into steppe lands. If overgrazing and indiscriminate felling continue to deforest and erode the mountains, catastrophic flooding from the rapid flow of winter rains will occur in the lower regions. Nomads and farmers kept approximately 16 million sheep, 5 million goats, 3 million cattle and 50,000 camels in 1990. Due to religious reasons, the meat from 9,000 pigs is destined for the stomachs of Europeans only. In all, animal husbandry makes up one third of the country's agricultural net product.

Traditional Irrigation Methods

The arid regions, which the French called *maroc inutile* (useless Morocco), lie primarily south of the High Atlas and eastward of the Middle Atlas. To the leeward side of the mountains, precipitation falls below that magical figure of 400 mm per year minimum. Here agriculture is only possible with the help of intricate irrigation systems. The availability of precious water is by no means unrestricted. A *douar* (village), a family or even a person can inherit, sell or lease water rights. For example, the amount of water available for someone to water his crops could be measured by the time it takes for a punctured bucket to sink in the village reservoir. When this happens, the water is cut off to that person and it is then someone else's turn. This is in fact the way water is distributed in the village of Oumesnat in the Lower Atlas. *Seguia* is the name of a slightly raised water canal running parallel to a river, the most common irrigation method in Morocco. An *arhour* is a well from which water is drawn up by camels or mules. A *nouria* (water-drawing wheel) is of Mesopotamian origin and was brought into the country by the Arabs. An especially picturesque *nouria* can be seen on the road from Fès to Volubilis. It draws water from the Mikkes River for the olive groves. At the Imi n' Tanoute Pass in the High Atlas there is a another interesting, horizontal *nouria* with a wooden drive wheel and shaft, and a chain of buckets drawn by mules.

The mile-long chain of earthen piles formed by underground *khettaras* along the edge of the Rheris Oasis in the southeast looks like a row of giant molehills. Long ago, and under dangerous working conditions, slaves dug our these shafts running 30 m deep and carrying groundwater from the foot of the nearby mountains to the *ksour* (settled and fortified villages). Even the Saharan *Sanhadja* Berbers, who founded Marrakech in the 11th century, set up *khettaras* along the Haouz Plateau to supply the city with water from the Atlas Mountains. Consequently, Marrakech is rightly designated as the northernmost oasis. Typical spring water oases are found along the southern edge of the entire Anti-Atlas (as in Fam el Hissn), whereas Figuig Oasis on the southeastern border to Algeria is served by artesian wells.

The lifelines of southern Morocco are the river oases of Ziz, Todhra, Dades and Dra. Beyond the High Atlas Mountains, the sun scorches the land from March to November, causing considerable evaporation. To compensate this loss, the oasis farmers have resorted to storey farming. Fig trees, apricot trees, pomegranates and henna bushes grow under the shade provided by date palms; below them grains, vegetables and forage plants thrive. Even the summer heat is mostly bearable in these small plotted gardens of Eden. The scourges of this man-made paradise are the locust, the date-palm abiod fungus and, particularly, the periodically re-occurring droughts. Dams built in 1972 on the upper reaches of the Ziz, Dades and Massa rivers have not quite sufficiently remedied the problem of water scarcity.

Age of Protectorate

The *colons* (French settlers), who came by thousands to Morocco after the signing of the Protectorate agreements of 1911, had no qualms about acquisitioning land. They ignored for the most part the traditional common property rights of the tribes – land claims and private property in the European sense were unknown to Berber and Arab. The *colons* thus acquired the most fertile soil in the best agricultural areas. The Sais Plateau between Meknes and Fès, the Tiffa Plateau near Berkane, the Tadla Plateau between Beni Mellal and Kasbah Tadla, the Haouz Plateau near Marrakech, the Sous Valley, as well as the tribal areas of Abda, Doukkala, Chaouia, Zemmour and Rharb near the Atlantic coast were thus colonized. During the 45 years of the Protectorate, the French and Spanish claimed ownership to more than one million hectares of land; and on this land they produced durum wheat, rice and oranges for export, as well as wine for their own domestic needs. 13 large dams were built between 1929 and 1956 along the water-abundant rivers of the Middle Atlas mountain range. The dams guaranteed water for ir-

Right: Donkey and archaic plow are still typical implements of rural farming.

rigation, and thus high agricultural production, they protected against flooding and provided electricity.

Land Reform

After a series of uprisings and revolts, the Moroccan people gained independence in 1955. Ever since then they have been demanding the redistribution of the *colons'* lands and a land reform, but they have only been moderately successful so far. It took until 1973 for the last of the French holdings to be expropriated. To this day, despite peasant uprisings, only one third of the land was distributed to the landless. The remaining two thirds have been divided up between the state and its closely allied upper class. The big-time absentee landlords of today acquired the land inexpensively shortly before it was expropriated from the French.

The question of land reform is still a potential source for social conflicts. Big-time farmers (only one tenth of the population) own more than half of the farmland and the lion's share of the irrigated, and thus most productive fields. Three fourths of the *fellahs* (peasants) have to make do with plots smaller than two hectares called *bour,* and their only source of water is rain. Frequently such small holdings are again divided through inheritance. In the Rif Mountains, for example, sometimes each limb of a single tree may have a different owner!

Khammessat

The landless tenants have the hardest lot, and approximately 40% of the rural families belong to this group of people. In the traditional tenant farming system, *khammessat,* the tenant *(khammes)* receives only one fifth *(khamsa = 5)* of his harvest. The remaining four fifths go to the owner(s) of the land, seed, plough and draught animals. Even the water from springs, wells or canals can have an own-

er who demands his share of payment. The use of a tractor or fertilizer can cost the tenant farmer so much that his yield dwindles to a tenth of his harvest. The *khammes* therefore often lives at the subsistence level, and his family is dependent upon additional income from labor on large farms. These, however, are making more and more use of modern machinery. A single combine harvester, for instance, puts 100 harvesters using sickles out of work. The economic gain for the farmers with modern equipment does not necessarily pay off on the national economic level because migration from rural areas to the cities has intensified social problems. This is especially evident in such places as Marrakech, Fès and Casablanca, where most migrants end up.

Agricultural Politics

To prevent depletion of the short supply of foreign exchange and to feed a population growing at the rapid rate of 2.6% per year, agricultural policies have aimed to reduce dependency on expensive, imported food commodities. The staple foods in the Moroccan diet are: *khobza* (a round, flat loaf of bread made from barley); *couscous* (semolina gruel); *tajine* (a stew made from vegetables, meat and olive oil); *thé à la menthe* (green tea with mint and plenty of sugar), as well as sardines. Therefore, the cultivation of wheat, barley, sugar beets and sugar cane is especially encouraged. Alfalfa and corn are raised to increase milk and meat production, and sunflowers deliver an affordable oil. The fertilizer required for this purpose can be produced on a long-term basis since Morocco has over two thirds of the world's phosphate reserves. Small farmers should also be able to enjoy the benefits of modern agricultural inventions and, therefore, equipment sharing is being set up. The foreign exchange needed to import tractors must be provided not only by the phosphate industry, but also by credit transfers from Moroccan employees in Europe, by tourism and by agricultural exports. The ex-

port of citrus fruits, spring vegetables, nuts, stone fruit and, last but not least, strawberries brings in more than US$ 350 million annually. In addition, the coastal fisheries deliver about US $ 300 million in sardines for export.

Presently, Morocco's primary market is the European Economic Community (EEC). Moroccan association with the EEC is based mainly on its close economic ties to France, which stem from the days of the protectorate. The export of *maroc*-oranges and of spring tomatoes, which are grown in long rows of plastic-covered greenhouses along the Atlantic coast, today suffers from the competition created by new EEC members like Portugal, Spain and Greece.

In their search for new markets, the export strategists have discovered Saudi Arabia and the former Soviet Union. A future source of foreign exchange could

be new exports such as avocados, pecans, artichokes, or asparagus. Banana plantations in the Tensift and Sous valleys, however, are primarily there to cover domestic needs. The apples from the cooler Middle Atlas region are becoming a favorite at the *souks*. Frowned upon by the state, but profitable and rich in tradition, is the cultivation of *cannabis indica* (Indian hemp) in the Rif Mountains. The dried leaves are smoked as *kif* and the concentrated resin used as *hashish*. Officially, the cultivation of drugs has long been prohibited, and volunteers from Europe serving in Morocco are instructing the *Rifi* (people of Rif) in the cultivation of alternative products. The illegal export of *cannabis indica* at night across the Mediterranean to Europe is, however, flourishing as ever.

Modern Irrigation and Agriculture

The most ambitious project in modern irrigation is currently being conducted on the Sebou River, in the northwestern part

Above: The weekly souks even nowadays are vital news exchanges. Right: Dams secure water for irrigation.

of Morocco. By the year 2005, 13 dams will have been built between the river's source in the eastern Middle Atlas and its mouth near Kenitra on the Atlantic. More than 200,000 ha of farmland will then reap the benefits of a consistent water supply and flood protection. In Rharb on the lower reaches of the Sebou River, impressive results have already been attained in a pilot sugar cane project started in 1980. Sugar cane has proven to be an uncomplicated plant for the *fellahs* to cultivate. The government also subsidizes sugar cane planting, and attractive prices as well as transportation to newly-built sugar refineries are guaranteed.

In contrast, the southern Massa project, 25 km north of Tiznit on the Massa River, has failed pathetically. With the aid of US $ 240 million in foreign capital, the fringes of the Euphorbian dry steppe region (only used intensively as poor grazing land) was to be transformed into a productive greenhouse. The cultivation of exotic fruits and vegetables, such as tomatoes, paprika, asparagus and strawberries, had been planned. The sprinkling systems, constructed by agricultural experts and intended to ensure an optimum dispersion of water and fertilizer, failed under the management of the untrained *fellahs*. When the world market price for tomatoes plunged, the farmers eventually were forced into debt because there was no market or price guarantees from the government. Not even nature was willing to help. The Youssef-Ben-Tachfine dam built in 1972 stored less water than had been anticipated, unexpected night frost damaged the sensitive plants and sand storms buried the irrigation canals. In times past, native *Shluh* Berbers had grown barley only in rainy years, sometimes watering their plants with water drawn from wells; apart from this, they drove their goats up to the thorny Argan trees. The plunge into modernization, planned in theory by European engineers, was not a total failure, however. Alfalfa for the domestic market is now grown in the project area, rather than strawberries for export.

AT THE PILLARS
OF
HERCULES

TANGIER

RIF MOUNTAINS

TANGIER

Just in case you have heard of someone who knows someone else, whose beautiful blond wife simply disappeared without a trace whilst walking through the narrow winding streets in Tangier's *medina*, be aware that you should take the tale with a grain or two of salt. It appears that the oarsmen of the Carthaginian admiral Hanno's fleet already told such stories when they visited the Phoenician trading port of *Tingis* in A.D. 460. It is said that Odysseus was also here, and that even Hercules stopped by in *Tingis* on his way to meet Atlas, who helped him steal the golden apples of the Hesperides. Along the way Hercules found enough time to strangle the giant Antäus, create the Strait of Gibraltar and erect two pillars at the entrance to the straits. The Moroccans call the northern pillar *jebel el tarik* (Gibraltar), and the southern one, near Ceuta, *jebel moussa* (Monte Acho).

Tingis was seat of government for the Roman procurator of the ancient province of *Mauretania Tingitana* for some time. Silesian Vandals came in A.D. 429

Previous pages: Sand dunes in Erg Chebbi. Night life at the Jemaa el Fna in Marrakech. Left: Traditionally dressed Rifi woman in Chefchaouen.

and became the first long-term "tourists" to enjoy the city's mild Mediterranean climate. But what are 25,000 Germanic Vandals suffering from rheumatism, compared with the 300,000 international short-term vacationers who invade Tangier each year? The Vandals were finally driven out by troops led by Constantinople's Belisar in A.D. 533.

The Prophet's banner was hoisted over the city in 705, when Arab troops under the command of Moussa, conquered the city. After the Berber Tarik took over Catholic Spain in the name of Moussa in 711, the newly-converted Rif-Berbers demanded the same rights as the elite class Arabs. In the year of 740 they successfully drove out the Arab troops of the Ommiad caliph, who resided in the distant city of Damascus.

In 788 Moulay Idriss I, an Arab refugee and a descendant of the Prophet, formulated the first historical prejudice against Tangier's citizens: according to him they were a nagging, dissatisfied and truculent people. Some 400 years later Francis of Assisi added: "O dementa Tingis!" (Oh, crazy Tangier!).

Spanish Ommiads, Moroccan Berbers and Bagdad's Abbasid caliphs battled over the city, until the Sahara Berbers under Youssef ben Tashfin established Almoravid rule in 1083.

51

Ibn Battuta, one of the city's most illustrious sons, was born in 1304. He travelled some 100,000 km throughout Asia, Africa and Europe, and thus became the most famous explorer and travel chronicler of the Middle Ages.

The thriving seaport was first ruled by successive Berber dynasties until the Portuguese assumed power in the year of 1471. The Spanish took over in 1581, but in 1640 Tangier fell into the hands of the Portuguese once again. It was simply presented to England as a dowry when King Charles II married a Lusitanian Princess. In 1684 the English had to capitulate under a siege begun by Moulay Ismail and his Black horsemen in 1672, but before pulling out they almost completely destroyed the port and its facilities.

Painter Eugene Delacroix accompanied a French delegation to the city in 1832. Among the great number of paintings he made there was one titled "Religious Fanatics in Tangier". At that time the powerful Moslem brotherhood of Ouezzane had many followers. When, in 1844, Sultan Moulay Abd el Rahman supported Berber resistance fighter Abd el Kader in his effort to stop the advance of French troops on Algeria, the French cannonaded Tangier in reprisal.

The European struggle for power in a now militarily much weakened and almost bankrupt country began in earnest. The German Kaiser Wilhelm II, a staunch advocate of gunboat policy, arrived on board his ship "Hohenzollern" in 1905 in order to emphasize the German war industry's claim to Morocco's mineral resources. At the Conference of Algeciras in 1912 Europeans, Russians and Americans agreed to make Tangier an international zone, thus reducing the sultan's status to that of a puppet. A council consisting of Europeans, Moslems and Jews governed the city which now became a demilitarized, duty-free zone. The French and Spanish divided the rest of Morocco between themselves. Spain's Franco occupied the city during the Second World War, until the British and the French reestablished an international administration in 1945. Because of its special status as an open monetary market, Tangier became known as a bank center and a haven for speculators, spies and other denizens of the shady world. A large segment of the population turned to smuggling and the sale of drugs and weapons for a living. All forms of prostitution flourished. But Moroccan resistance fighters also found refuge here and conspired to drive out the Spanish and the French.

American writer Paul Bowles vividly describes this disreputable atmosphere in his novel *Let It Come Down*. Bowles has thus become something of a legendary figure in the city he has chosen to make his home, particularly since director Bertolucci filmed his novel *The Sheltering Sky*. He has also translated a muslim friend's autobiography recorded on a cassette. As his friend, Driss ben Hamed Charhadi, had never attended school, he was unable to write. This thrilling autobiography, set in the Franco era in Tangier, describes the environment of an underprivileged Moroccan, and has since been published.

Tangier was full of rich people in the forties. Woolworth heiress Barbara Hutton had the narrow winding streets in the *medina* widened to allow her Rolls Royce access to her palace in the *Amrah*-quarter. Authors like Gore Vidal, André Gide, William S. Burroughs and Truman Capote were part of the local literary circle. Tennessee Williams wrote his famous *A Cat on a Hot Tin Roof* here.

When Tangier was reunited with Morocco in 1960 – by that time the country was already independent – and its duty free status was abolished, it was really the beginning of its downfall. It has since lost much of its flair as a stylish Mediterranean resort and there is a slight air of decay attached to the city these days, especially obvious in the older hotels and

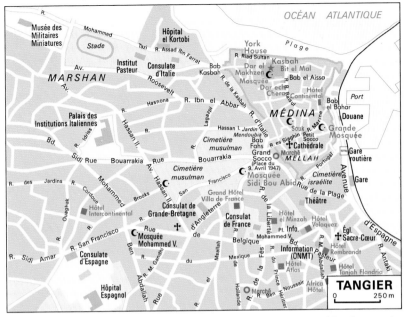

in the bar areas. In the meantime, however, industrialization and tourism have compensated somewhat for the economic slump that set in after 1960.

Grand Socco and Medina

Grand Socco means main market square, and it is the best place to start a tour of the city. It joins the new section, established after 1912, with the old *medina* situated on a hill above the harbor. Rif women dressed in colorful traditional costume sell vegetables and fresh mint at the Grand Socco (dervied from *souk* = market). Thursdays and Sundays are particularly busy days.

Flanking the Grand Socco, on the north side are the luxuriant **Mendoubia Gardens** containing an ancient dragon tree and the former residence of the *mendoub* (sultan's representative), which nowadays serves as the city court. Although these are not open to the public, one might just manage to persuade the caretaker to give one a short tour of the

building. On the west side, the mosaic-studded minaret of the **Sidi Bou Abid** mosque towers high over the Socco. The **covered market** is on the east side, right outside the old city wall.

Behind the horseshoe-shaped gate of **Bab Fahs** is where the walled-in old part of town begins, home of hashish dealers, pickpockets and all sorts of strange characters who give the place a somewhat decadent flair. If you go through the second gate to the immediate right, you will come to **Rue es Siaghin**, which used to be lined with Jewish goldsmith shops. To the south of this is the former Jewish quarter *(mellah)*. About 6,000 Jews lived here around 1900 - more than a third of the city's population in those days. The Star of David is still recognizable on the dilapidated synagogue. Since the Jewish exodus in the year of 1956, Moslems have taken over the textile and souvenir shops. The fact that the Spanish were able to erect a Catholic cathedral here in 1888 shows just how tolerant the Moslems were towards non-Moslems. On the other

hand, it assumably also emphasizes just how weak the sultan was.

The **Petit Socco**, known locally as *souk dakhel*, lies at the bottom end of the Rue es Siaghin. This is where the black-marketeers and smugglers used to conduct business. American writer W.S. Burroughs, author of *Junkie*, a novel about a drug addict in North Africa, partook of more than just a cup of peppermint tea here. Even today some illegal business deals take place on the café terraces. This is where the Rue des Chrètiens (renamed Rue des Almohades) red light district used to be. The wrought-iron balconies of the very traditional Hotels Mauretania, Becerra and Fuentes are reminiscent of Andalusian façades. Farther east, the **Rue de la Marine** leads directly to the *jemaa kebira* (Grand Mosque), constructed by Moulay Ismail to celebrate victory over the English in 1684. It was erected on the

Above: The casbah quarters of Tangier with ferry dock. Right: A stroll through the old part of the city begins at the "Grand Socco".

site of former Portuguese cathedral that had been destroyed by Moulay. Directly opposite is a *medersa* (Koran school) from the Merinid period. It is, however, still off limits to non-Moslems. There is nevertheless a very good view of the Bay of Tangier and the harbor from the terrace at the back of the mosque.

The Kasbah

To reach the **kasbah** one has to go back down the Rue de la Marine for some 100 m, turn right into Dar Baroud alley, a detour to No. 36, the nostalgic Hotel Continental built in 1850, is recommendable, and then left into **Avenue el Kaa**. Once in the *kasbah* proper, high above sea level, one will find covered arcades, winding alleys and hidden terraces. Passing the leather merchants on the **Rue Hadj Mohammed Torres**, cross the tiny **Place Oued Ahardan** and climb the **Rue Ben Raisul** steps leading up to **Bab el Aissa** (Gate of the Coast Guard). From here one has a splendid view of the *med-*

ina and the bay. One enters the 17th-century fortified Kasbah residential quarter through this gate. The **Kasbah mosque**, dwarfed by its octagonal minaret, stands in the *mechovar* (parade and meeting grounds), alongside the former court of **Dar ech Chera**, the **Bit el Mal** treasury and the **Dar el Makhzen** sultan's palace.

The ground floor of the palace now houses an **ethnological museum** with excellent exhibits of fine porcelain, beautiful jewellery of the kind worn by Berber women, weapons, hand-woven royal carpets from Rabat, brocade embroidery and much more. The **Musée des Antiquités** on the upper floors contains several mosaics from Volubilis, a statue of Juba II, who reigned over *Tingis* in 25 B.C., a Punic tomb, as well as a large number of outstanding paintings by Delacroix.

The **Sultan's Gardens** can be reached along **Rue Riad Sultan**, past the Terrace on the north side of the *mechovar*. Craftsmen can be observed here at their work. From the shady terrace of the folkloric Moorish café Le Détroit lookout where people come to watch and to be seen, there is a good view of **York House**, the 17th-century residence of the English governor, and – on a clear day – the Spanish city of Tarifa, some 30 km away.

Farther along the Rue Riad Sultan, via the **Place du Tabor** and Kasbah Gate, you leave the *medina*'s massive walls behind. It is a good 15 minute walk to the **Marshan** villa district. King Hassan II has his summer residence here. The former congressional palace on the **Rue Muhammed Tazi** houses the **Musée des Miniatures Militaires** belonging to U.S. media magnate Forbes. More than 80,000 brightly colored tin soldiers are on display in this military museum.

The New Town

Back again at the **Kasbah Gate** one proceeds across the **Zankat el Kasbah** and the **Rue d'Italie,** and down to the

Grand Socco, which is now officially referred to as *Place du 9. Avril 1947*. It was on this day that Mohammed V held his inflammatory speech adamantly condemning the Protectorate's colonial rulers. One of the pleasant, leisurely activities here consists in strolling with all the other shoppers between **Rue de la Liberté** (Zankat el Houria) and **Place Mohammed V** (formerly Place de France). The Delacroix Gallery exhibits works of modern Moroccan artists. Those venturing within the doors of the ultra-luxurious **Hotel El Minzah** should make an attempt to look respectable. Here one might choose to reflect on the social injustices prevalent in Moroccan society whilst relaxing with a cool drink at the egde of the pool on the hotel grounds.

The Café de Paris on Place Mohammed V, where *le tout Tanger* used to while away the hours during the 1940's, has undoubtedly seen better days. This is where the city's elegant main thoroughfare, the **Boulevard Pasteur** with its shops, banks, street cafés and the **Office**

du Tourisme, begins. The well-stocked bookshop *Des Colonnes* supplies the city's intellectuals with food for thought. At the eastern end of the boulevard is the popular Café La Colombe, an appropriate place to conclude a tour.

Ceuta

The beautiful coastal route S 704 leads one past **Cap Malabata** to the small fishing port and holiday resort of **Ksar es Seghir** and then continues on to the small Spanish enclave of **Ceuta**. A connecting ferry service operates between Algeciras and Ceuta. Approximately 70,000 Spaniards live on an area of slightly less than 20 sq.km. making up this peninsula. Situated at the mouth of the Straits of Gibraltar, Ceuta is, as a matter of course, of great strategic importance.

Ceuta was probably founded in the 5th century B.C. by Carthaginian seafarers.

Above: Since 1580 the Spanish flag has been flying continuously over Ceuta.

The natural harbor served them as a base for their trading routes to the Spanish "Land of Silver", and as well all along the Atlantic coast to the Gulf of Guinea. In A.D. 42 the Romans occupied the settlement and named it *septem fratres* after the seven hills surrounding the town, or **Sebta** for short.

The Vandals took over the city in the 5th century, but were eventually defeated by the Arabs in A.D. 710. Soon afterwards, a large Moslem army set out from here in 711 under the leadership of the Berber Tarik and conquered Spain.

When Sebta fell to the Portuguese in 1415, they pulled down the mosques and replaced them with Catholic churches. After Portugal and Spain were united by a royal marriage in 1580 Sebta, now already called Ceuta, finally became Spanish. Ever since then Morocco has been trying to regain the strategically important peninsula – so far without the least bit of success.

The approach from the mainland to Ceuta is guarded by the erstwhile Portuguese stronghold of **Candelero**. At the core of this modern Spanish city lies the **Plaza de Africa**. A late-baroque church, **Nuestra Señora de Africa**, dedicated to the patron saint of the town in 1726, is located at the north side of the shady plaza, right next to the old harbor, and a baroque **cathedral** on the south side of the plaza marks the spot on which a mosque stood until 1432. If one is prepared to walk the 5-km approach to **Monte Acho** (198m), the African counterpart to the Rock of Gibraltar, one will eventually be rewarded with a magnificent view of the entire city and of the Mediterranean Sea from the chapel of **San Antonio**.

Duty free shopping in Ceuta makes it extremely popular with both Moroccan and Spanish tourists, so that there are often long waiting lines at the border crossing at **Tarajal**, about 4 km south of the town center. Moroccan laborers returning from Europe during Id el Kebir

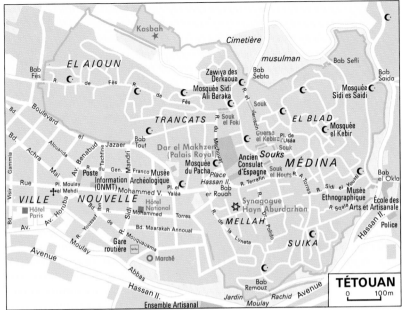

El Aioun — Kasbah — Cimetière — Bab Fès — de — Fès — Zawiya des Derkaoua — Bab Sebta — Bab Sefli — Bab Saida — Mosquée Sidi Ali Baraka — Mosquée Sidi es Saidi — Souk el Foki — Boulevard — Bd — Bd — Alouanda — el — TRANCATS — Souk du Machaef — Jarrazin — EL BLAD — Mosquée el Kebir — Achra — Jazaer — Bab Tout — Dar el Makhzen (Palais Royal) — Guersa el Kebira — Pl. de l'Usáa — Gammia — Mai — Av. Benabud — Tachfine — du Gen. Mandri — Mosquée du Pacha — Place Hassan II. — Souk el Houts — MÉDINA — Bab el Okla — Rue — Poste — Franco — Musée — Ancien Consulat d'Espagne — R. A. Torres — Pl. Moulay el Mehdi — Information (ONMT) — Archéologique — Pl. el Yaáa — Bab er Rouah — R. Terrafin — Sidi el Youssfi — Musée Ethnographique — École des Arts et Artisanale — VILLE — NOUVELLE — Hôtel National — Synagogue Hayn Aburdarhan — R. Sqala — Hassan II. — Hôtel Paris — Av. Horuba — Bd. Sidi Mohammed — Torres — MELLAH — Police — Av. — R. Youssef — de — Bd. Maarakah Annoual — Pl. Luneta — Polido — SUIKA — Moulay — Gare routière — Mouquauama — Avenue — Marché — Abbas — Hassan II. — Bab Remouz — Jardin Moulay — Rachid — Avenue — **TÉTOUAN** — 0 — 100m — Ensemble Artisanal

("Mutton Feastday") can also lead to kilometer-long waiting lines, as Moroccan border officials not without any reason tend to be particularly thorough then.

Once cleared, one is free to make one's way to the beautiful beaches of the Mediterranean. There are moderately priced hotels and bungalows situated all along the splendid sandy beaches of **Restinga-Smir, M'diq** and **Cabo Negro**. The large camping site at **Martil** is very popular among Moroccan vacationers in summer.

There is a turning along the P28, 14 km before Tétouan, leading uphill through a pine forest to the summit of **Jebel Kudia-Taifor**. The wonderful view from here of the Mediterranean coast makes the journey well worthwhile.

Tétouan

The provincial capital of **Tétouan** (pop. 150,000) lies in the **Jebel Mountains**, a western spur of the Rif Mountains, at the foot of Mt. Dersa. There used to be a river-port on the **Oued Martil**

which runs into the Mediteranean 11 km east of the city. The large and interesting *medina* of Tétouan is dominated by medieval Moorish-Andalusian architecture while the new part of town, which was constructed in 1913 as the administrative seat of the Spanish-owned Protectorate of Marruecos/Español, has more of a southern European flair.

The ancient Roman town of **Tamuda** was located 4 km to the south of present-day Tétouan, which itself dates back to the Merinid era in the 14th century. It was destroyed by the Spanish in 1399, and reconstruction by Moorish and Jewish refugees from Granada began in 1492. The Moslems took revenge on the Christians by capturing Spanish ships, which in turn instigated King Philipp II to destroy the port at Tétouan in 1565. It was, though, rebuilt once again in the 17th century under Sultan Moulay Ismail.

Following an attack on Ceuta by Rif Berbers, the Spanish occupied Tétouan in 1859. They were forced out by the English in 1862, but no sooner than after they had secured a unilateral trade agreement. Tétouan became capital of the Spanish Protectorate Zone in northern Morocco in 1913. It has served as the administrative capital of the province of the same name all the years since independence has been declared in 1956.

Driving through the new town along the **Rue Mohammed V**, one crosses the **Place Moulay el Mehdi** with its many sidewalk cafés to arrive at the **Archeological Museum**, located on the north side of the **Place al Yalaa**. It features exhibits such as stone-age tools, a model of the Cromlech (prehistoric cult site) in Msoura, interesting Carthaginian ceramics as well as Roman statues and mosaics.

Rue Mohammed V leads onto **Place Hassan II** on the outskirts of the *medina*. This is the busiest thoroughfare in the *ville nouvelle*, with its numerous cafés and restaurants, the former Spanish Consulate General and the 17th-century residence of the Alawi califs. Due south of here is the **Mellah**, which is best explored on foot, starting down the **Rue de la Luneta** and then coming back along the **Rue Docteur Polido** to the Place Hassan II. The quadrangular Jewish quarter was laid out in 1807 under the Alawi Sultan Moulay Slimane. Its wrought-iron balconies and window bars of the houses are Andalusian in character. The descendants of Jewish refugees from Spain lived here until recently. Oval-shaped arches, designed to prevent the houses from collapsing in the event of an earthquake, often span the lanes in the Jewish quarter. Visitors are allowed to enter the **Hayn Aburdarhan Synagogue** provided they are respectfully dressed and cover their heads for the time being there.

The usual approach to the *medina* is the one through **Bab el Rouah** (Gate of the Winds). To be on the safe side (re: pick-pockets) one should enlist the services of an offical guide. The old town itself, which is still surrounded by a wall with seven gates, today has more than 60 mosques, attractive plazas with ornate tiled fountains, colorful markets and busy lanes where craftsmen can be seen at work - among them carpenters, gold- and silversmiths, cobblers, tailors, dyers and lace makers. **Rue Terrafin** leads on to the fish and meat market - **Souk el Houts** – where pottery is also sold. Then one continues along **Rue Kzadriin**, the street of blacksmiths. **El Saffain** alley winds itself under a great number of archways and around countless corners until it finally reaches **Guersa El Kebira**, the bustling vegetable and second-hand market. The adjoining **Place Ousaa** in the **el Bled** quarter is essentially a textiles market where Rifi women wearing wide-brimmed hats and red and white striped *foutas*, the national costume worn in the Rif region, sell their wares.

A little farther north towards **Bab Sebta**, **Rue el Jarrazin** runs through the center of the artisan's quarter of the **souks**. Souk el Fouki, where bread, spices and various natural cosmetics are sold, is situated next to the burial mosque Sidi Ali Baraka. From here one can climb along the narrow alley to the *kasbah* of Tétouan for a bird's eye view of the erratic outlines of the old town. Returning down to Souk el Fouki, one can take **Rue du Mechouar** past the royal palace and back to Place Hassan II.

The **Musée Ethnographique** is located at the edge of the *medina*. It can be reached by way of the Rue Terrafin and then on down Rue Ahmed Torres and Rue Sidi el Yousti, the latter of which ends at **Bab el Okla**, near the museum. Directly opposite, just outside the *medina* walls, is the **arts and crafts school**.

The Rif coastline is not easily accessible, but for those who dare, it can be reached from Tétouan on the S 608 via Oued Laou and Bou Ahmed to El Jebha (merely partly tarred, 150 km). The piste

Right: Chefchaouen was the stronghold of Berber resistance in the Rif War.

CT 8509 going on from here to Torres de Alcala and the beach of Kalah Iris (an additional 60 km) is in relatively poor condition and requires a four-wheel-drive vehicle. Another 330 km along the narrow S 610 takes one to the bay of Al Hoceima.

Chefchaouen

In 1470, at the time, when the Portuguese began to move inland, after having conquered several important seaports along the Atlantic coast, Berbers from the Ghomara region under leadership of Sharif Moulay Ali Ben Rachid founded the town of **Chefchaouen** as a defensive bastion against the invading Europeans. After the Christian Reconquista had triumphed over Spanish Islam, a great number of refugees from Andalusia settled here. They lent the old town its surviving southern Spanish character: Winding alleys with white washed medieval houses, whose doors and windowsills have been lovingly decorated in a shade of pale blue.

The Berber rebel Abd el Krim ruled Chefchaouen from 1921 to 1926. He proclaimed an independent Islamic Rif republic in 1923 from where he organized the armed struggle against Spanish occupation. The city withstood several attacks and bombardments by the Spanish army, until it was finally conquered in 1927.

A walking tour of the charming *medina* is best begun in the eastern part of the new town, near the **Moulay Ali Ben Rachid mosque**, at the **Bab el Ain gate**. Many of the whitewashed gabled houses date back to the time when the city was first founded. Men and boys sit in their shops along the narrow alleys making *babouches*, sewing caftans or embroidering jellabahs. Continuing uphill through this charming part of the old town, one will eventually arrive at the very heart of the *medina*, the **Place Outa el Hamman**, which is towered over by an Alawi *kasbah* (17th century) and the octagonal minaret of the Great Mosque.

The picturesque square has several inviting small restaurants under the shade of mulberry trees at which one should at least enjoy a mint tea. A local speciality is *bsara*, a tasty broad bean soup served with fine olive oil.

A small museum was erected within the reddish brown walls of the *kasbah*'s battlements, which date back to the times of Moulay Ismail. Many artefacts on exhibit are mementos of Abd el Krim, the Riffian resistance hero.

There is a splendid view of nearby Jebel Tisouka (2,050 m) and Jebel Meggou (1,600 m), as well as the houses in the old town, from the battlements. **Place el Makhzen** and the quiet Hotel de Chaouen are just about 100 m east of here. The square is surrounded by several *souks* stocked with a great variety of carpets, textiles, clothes, leather goods, ceramics and copper ware.

Passing through the city gate on the eastern side of the older part of town, the **Bab Onsar**, one arrives at the fresh water spring of **Ras el Ma**, where locals often picnic. Fig trees shade the nearby tea terrace. On the opposite slope stands a solitary mosque, the **Jemaa Bouzafar**. It is perched above the road heading southward out of the city and thus provides an indeed beautiful view of the Mediterranean mountain region and of Chefchaouen clinging to the slopes.

Beyond Chefchaouen the road divides: P 39 branches off to the east, towards the town of Ketama, while Highway P 28 runs through oak groves, crosses the former borderline of the Spanish protectorate in the vicinity of Loukos Bridge, and then continues for 60 km before eventually reaching Ouezzane.

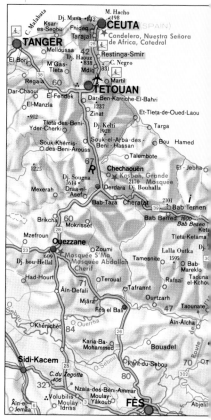

Ouezzane

Ouezzane is situated near Jebel Bou Hellal (609 m), on the southern edge of the Rif Mountains (pop. 40,000; market on Thursdays). For Moroccan Muslims, who have a predilection for mystical sufism, Ouezzane is the third most important place of pilgrimage, after Moulay Idriss and Fès. Focus of worship here is the *zawiya* (religious cult site) of Sharif Moulay Abdallah, a descendant of the Arab dynasty founder, Moulay Idriss. This Sufi sheikh established the headquarters of the Taibia Moslem Brotherhood in Ouezzane in 1727. Apart from practicing their religion, the members of the brotherhood were also involved in politics, inciting conflicts between the rebellious Berbers from the Atlas regions and the Arab Alawi sultans. However, when the eccentric Sheikh Sidi Mohammed collaborated with the French in the 19th century and even married an English woman, he did irreparable damage to the reputation of the religious order. His pen-

MEDITERRANEAN COAST

0   50 km

chant for worldly pleasures gave rise to the following folk saying: "Champagne turns to milk in his mouth".

The drive into the city leads through the tidy *ville nouvelle* lined with bitter-orange trees, and further on to the **Place de L'Indépendence** and to the *medina*, which is a pedestrian zone. Atypically, it is not walled in; as a religious center, the city was not likely to suffer attack. The steps of the **Rue Abdallah ben Lamlih** lead uphill, past the Grand Hotel, smack into the midst of the busy *souk* quarter. Ouezzane is noted for its olive oil and raisins, as well as the preparation of wool from the Rif region. Continuing across the **Place Bir Inzarane**, **Rue Haddadine** and **Rue de l'Adoul** one arrives at the

Moulay Abdallah Cherif mosque containing the mausoleum of the founder of the order. Pilgrims clothed in white robes frequently stand in the entrance to the elaborate tomb. By kissing the pillars they do hope to benefit from the saint's blessing energy (*baraka*). The seat of the Moslem brotherhood, the *zawiya*, is just beyond the *souks* of the carpenters and blacksmiths. The adjacent **S'Ma mosque** is characterized by its green tiles and octagonal minaret. **Rue Tawiya** leads downhill to **Bab Jemaa** and ends at **Place du Marché**, where numerous merchants erect their tents every Thursday. It pays to make the trip to 609-m high **Jebel Bou Hellal**. Orange, fig and olive trees cover its slopes, and there are magnificent views of the sparkling whitewashed houses in Ouezzane, the Ghezaoua foothills to the south and the Rif Mountains to the north (3-km drive and an additional half an hour on foot).

RIF MOUNTAINS

From Chefchaouen, eastward through the densely-wooded alpine landscape of the Rif Mountains, highway P 39 leads to **Ketama** (105 km). The road first winds its way up from Oued Lahou Valley to the village of **Bab Taza**. From now on the **Route du Rif**, built after the Spanish pulled out in the 1950s runs along the ridge of the Rif-Atlas, winding its way over 300 km from Tangier to the Algerian border. After 12 km, the thatched houses in the charming mountain village of **Cherefat** come into view. It is said that the village mosque is the oldest in the Rif region. High above the village, waterfalls and mountain streams splash and ripple down the side of the mountain. Visitors enjoy walking here, especially in spring, when the meadows are covered with flowers. Elms and various kinds of oak trees line the road. The mountain passes of **Bab Ternen** and **Bab Berret** (1,240 m) succeed each other on the spirraling road. The CT 8310 leading to the fishing village of **El Jebha** (43 km) branches off at the foot of **Bab Besen** (1,600 m). Four kilometers beyond the Besen Pass summit there is a beautiful view of the Mediterranean coast. At such altitudes in the Rif Mountains' alpine regions, with their ancient cedar forests, it can snow as late as April. There are often extreme drops in temperature in spring.

Farther east the road finally reaches **Ketama** (1,520 m). Cool summers and winter sports await one at the foot of Jebel Tidiquin (2,448 m), the highest of the Rif-Atlas mountains.

Right: Due to heavy winter rains, erosion is cutting into the Western Rif Mountains.

Say no: Hemp in the Rif

The obvious affluence of Rif farmers is certainly not based on the production of corn. All the roads leading to and from Ketama are notorious for the sale of hashish to tourists by the locals. Hemp *(cannabis sativa indica)* has been grown in the remote Rif valleys for hundreds of years. Originally, this uncultivated species of the hemp plant comes from the arid regions of the Middle East. The one-year old plant requires a lot of sun and produces both male and female shrubs which grow to a height of one and a half meters. Only the blossoms from the female plants produce resin. Dressed in leather aprons, the farmers walk through the hemp plantations when the shrubs are in bloom, collecting the resin on their aprons as they go. Afterwards they scrape the resin from their aprons and then press it through a muslin filter. It is either sold in brown cubes or plates as hashish or it is made into *majoun* jam and sold at the market. Kif, the dried blossoms and leaves of female plants, is easier to obtain and somewhat milder than hashish. It is smoked in a long pipe called *sebsi.*

Officially, cannabis plants are grown in the Rif for use in the pharmaceutical industry and it actually does help to relieve dysentery and psychosomatic ailments. It also helps those suffering from glaucoma, a condition painfully afflicting the eyeball. Throughout the Orient from Morocco to Kashmir its healing powers are well-known. Nepalese Shiva worshippers even consider it sacred.

Of course, most of the hashish is sold as a narcotic drug throughout Morocco. The "dope" is transported by boat from the small bays along the Rif coast to Spain and to some other European countries. There are rigorous laws against the possession of hashish in Morocco and visitors are warned not to be caught with drugs by the police. It would be far from pleasant to end up in a Moroccan prison.

Spanish ports serving Moroccan ferries are also patrolled by police with specially trained dogs – 24 hours per day!

The highest of the Rif mountains, **Jebel Tidiquin**, lies to the southeast of Ketama. This mountain is frequently covered with snow until the early weeks of spring. A bumpy track leads from Tleta Ketama (8 km south of Ketama, on the S 302 to Fès) up to the cedar forests close to the summit. It is well worth taking the turn off to the villages at the foot of Jebel Tidiquin. Here one can enjoy the magnificent mountain scenery and the picturesque villages where so many traditional crafts, especially leather work, are still carried out today. The craftsmen in these villages have such a good reputation all over the country that they make up the greater part of the workforce in the tanneries and leather factories in Fès. Tourists who are solely interested in sightseeing and not in purchasing drugs are not very welcome in the entire hemp-growing region, the historic center of which is the Asilah Valley.

Those travelling as far as Fès are advised to take the impressive zigzag scenic **Route de L'Unité** (S 302). Construction of the winding road was started in 1957 with a lot of volunteer labor from all over Morocco in order to unite the former Spanish and French zones. The Spanish had greatly neglected the infrastructure in their "protectorate". The trip along the gravel road 4304 from **Ain Acha** to **Qued Querrha Valley** is worth taking (90 km; 11 km after Taounate). The **Holy Spring of Fertility** is located in the village of **Bouadel**, just beyond the quaint weavers' village of **Oulad Azame**. Olives, figs and pomegranates grow well in the surrounding village gardens.

Pottery of the Beni Ouriaghel Women

Continuing east from Ketama, towards Al Hoceima, the P 39 makes its way to an upland plateau of cedar forests and across the 1,580 mountain pass (past the forks for the CT 8500 to El Jebha and CT 8501 to the beautiful beach in Kalah Iris) to

Targuist. This marks the beginning of **Beni Ouriaghel** territory, which stretches from the Oued Ghis Valley to Oued Nekor. The female members of this Berber tribe still make earthenware without the use of a potter's wheel: bowls, *Tajine* pots, water jars, butter dishes and jugs for olive oil are among the special items. After firing – this is usually done without glazing – the rich ochre colors shine through. The earthenware is then hand-decorated with ancient Berber geometric designs. The black color for the designs is won from the resin of the mastic tree. Although Ouriaghel earthenware is made without a potter's wheel, it is of very high quality and many of the products have become collectors' pieces.

The uprising in the twenties led by Abd el Krim in protest against Spanish rule took place in the heart of this tribal re-

Above: Rif Berber women with the traditional "fouta" participate actively in market life and activities. Right: Boats belonging to the Lamparo fishermen of Al Hoceima.

gion. Abd el Krim was born in the town of Ajdir, 10 km south of Al Hoceima. The Spanish General Silvestre suffered one crushing defeat in 1921 in the Anoual Gorge, about 20 km east of Al Hoceima. The Spanish lost 15,000 men and a great deal of sophisticated artillery. After this defeat the general committed suicide and, in 1922, the victorious Abd el Krim was proclaimed emir by the majority of the Kabyl tribe. He declared a *jihad* on the Spanish and French, and set up his head-quarters in Chefchaouen. Even today the people in this region look back in pride on the Rif uprising against the Spanish.

Al Hoceima Boat Trip – Kalah Iris

Apart from being a fishing port, the modern provincial capital of **Al Hoceima** has many beautiful beaches with a few moderately priced hotels and numerous small hotels. The town is situated on the crescent-shaped **Baie d'Al Hoceima**, and is surrounded by the steep Rif Mountains. It is probably one of the most scenic locations on the Mediterranean coast. Apart from the fishing industry and tourism, the sale of jewelry made from coral stones today is an important source of the town's economy, so much so that just recently a vocational school has even been set up to revive the manufacture of traditional Berber jewelry. The colored boats belonging to the Lamparo fishermen can be seen in Al Hoceima harbor and, with a bit of luck, one may be able to hire one of the boats for a trip along the rugged, romantic coast. The most beautiful part of the coastline lies to the west of Al Hoceima, the Spanish island of **Peñon de Velez de la Gomera**, towards Torres de Alcala. Along this part of the coast, at the foot of the **Bokkoyas Massif**, there are secluded bays with ideal diving conditions. They are only accessible from the sea, and sometimes dolphins follow the boats for miles on end. Divers can admire the red corals used to make Berber jewelry. The

island of Peñon de Velez de la Gomera served as a pirates' hideout in the 17th century; today it is only a Spanish penal colony. The picturesque fishing village of **Torres de Alcala** is situated on the Oued Bou Frah estuary. The ruins of a *kasbah* recall the historic port of Badis, formerly used by the city of Fès and left to the Spanish in the 16th century. There is an interesting graveyard dating back to this period. The tombs are arranged in neat rows and placed one upon the other, a form of burial that is unique to this region. The enticing white sandy beach at **Kalah Iris** lies some four km to the west of Torres. Its campsite is often crowded with Moroccan and Spanish tourists during the months of summer.

One can return to Al Hoceima on the small S 610 road. This route takes one through sheep-grazing pastures and past the abandoned village of Had Rouadi. There also is a turning six km outside the town to the black sand beach of **Sfiah**, and a campsite just short of one km outside Al Hoceima, at the **Plage el Jamil**.

Melilla

On its way from Al Hoceima to Melilla (170 km) the principal P 39 road passes the turnoff to **Plage Mouyahidin** (Club Mediterranée), continues through the fertile Oued Nekor Valley and then winds its long way up to the Toboggan Pass. Heading downhill again, one passes the small town of Kassita on the right, where the narrow S 312 mountain road to Taga branches off (100 km). Just beyond Midor and its crowded Tuesday market begins the sparse and arid high plateau of Gareb, which gradually slopes towards the bay of Nador.

Nador (pop. 50,000), a remarkably modern university and industrial town founded during the Spanish Protectorate, has nevertheless only very few sights to offer. Iron from the nearby mines of Segangane is reduced to steel here with coal from the province of Oujda. A plain small road branching off almost exactly on the Spanish-Moroccan border at **Beni Enzar** leads all the way through the rugged

65

Guelaia Peninsula to the lighthouse at **Cap des Trois Fourches**.

The small Spanish enclave of **Melilla** lies some 13 km north of Nador. No more than 12 sq. km in size, Melilla has continuously been a Spanish possession since 1497 and still has its administrative seat in Malaga. It is serviced regularly by ferries from Malaga and Almeria.

Melilla prospered greatly under the Spanish Protectorate. Its modern harbor was built in 1912 particularly to promote the export of zinc, lead and iron ore from the Rif region to Spain. Duty-free shopping, which enticed many visitors from neighboring Algeria until its independence in 1962, is still Melilla's main attraction today. Butter, alcohol and fuel are cheap here. However, with the end of the Spanish Protectorate Melilla declined rapidly. The current population of 60,000 is merely a little more than half of what it was in the year of 1955.

Above: The Moroccans would like to reclaim the Spanish enclave of Melilla.

Perched on top of a steep hill overlooking the port is the old town of Melilla, the **Medina Sidonia**, surrounded by thick 16th-century walls. There are various splendid views of the medieval *medina* from the ramparts of the **Baluarte de la Concepción**, which houses the **Museo Municipal** (municipal museum). The numerous alleys throughout the *medina* are frequently covered by archways. The beuatiful Baroque church of **Purísima Concepción** contains a revered statue of the town's patroness and a 15th-century figure of Christ of Socorro.

Beni Snassen Mountains

Continuing the journey on the P 27 towards Oujda, one eventually arrives at the **Moulouya Bridge** in Mechra Saf-Saf, which marked the border Spanish and French territory until 1956. Although the Moulouya is the longest Moroccan river flowing throughout the entire year, its water volume varies considerably between more than 200 cubic meters during the rainy season and 3 cubic meters a second at the end of the dry season. Its basin covers an area extending from the Middle Atlas to the High Atlas. On its way to the Mediterranean the river is used intensively for irrigation purposes.

A narrow mountain road, the S 404, branches off to the south about 10 km before Berkane and leads directly to the **Beni Snassen Massif** (1,500 m), a green oasis in the midst of the eastern Moroccan dry steppe. From **Taforalt** (market on Wednesdays) one can undertake a magnificent trip through the limestone mountains, which would finally bring one to Berkane (20 km). The tiny CT 5306 road begins one and a half km before Taforalt and runs through oak forests to the **Grotte des Pigeons** (early stone-age skeleton finds), before making its way to the **Grotte du Chameau**. One stalactite in this limestone cavern somewhat resembles a camel. Deep within the cavern are a number of subterranean streams and small lakes. After the detour to "camel cavern", one can proceed to cross the **Qued Zegzel**, which has cut a deep gorge into the limestone (**Gorges du Zegzel**). Continuing along the gorge towards Berkane, the road passes through irrigated orange groves and medlar fruit plantations. The latter is a tasty orange-colored fruit that is sold all over Morocco in spring. Vineyards cover the slopes of the Beni Snassen Mountains, where the famous **Vins des Beni Snassen** are produced. The vineyards were planted by French settlers in the twenties.

The route from the wine-producing town of **Berkane** on the S 402 passes through a fertile plain irrigated by the Triffa Canal and leads on to the seaside resort of **Saidia** (25 km) on the Algerian border. The official crossing is 20 km farther north on the P 27, in **Ahfir**. It is possible to go on from here to Tlemcen or Oran in the Algerian Kabylei region, given that political relations between Algeria and Morocco are cordial at the time.

Oujda

Oujda (pop. about 300,000) is the capital of the Oujda Province, which encompasses the greater part of the arid steppe region in eastern Morocco. The town is located in the fertile Angads Basin and was founded by *Zenata* Berbers in the 10th century. Its strategic location – the Algerian border is merely about 13 km away – always made Oujda potentially vulnerable to attack by invaders, and it has been the scene of many skirmishes over the centuries. So, no wonder it was given the byname of *medina el haira* (City of Fear). Romans, Vandals, Almovarids, Almohads, Merenids, Wattasids, Turks and, finally, the French succeeded one after the other in occupying the town. The legendary Casablanca-Oujda-Algier-Tunis railway line made it easy for the French to gain control in North Africa. Oujda's rapid economic growth in the 20th century was due primarily to railway linkage to the coal-mining operations in Jeruda and Béchar (now in Algerian territory) and the rich lead and zinc deposits in the area of Bou Beker.

Very little of historic interest remains in this remarkably prosperous industrial city. The lack of tourists, however, makes it very pleasant to stroll through the unspoilt *medina* and to explore the *kisseria* (textiles market) or the *souks* of carpet and leather goods dealers. The only monument truly worth visiting is **Bab Sidi Abd el Wahab** in the eastern sector, a relict of the ancient city wall. In days gone by the heads of those who had been executed were displayed before it.

Well worth a short visit, on the other hand, is the small, actually inconspicuous pilgrim's village of **Sidi Yahia**, which is situated in a fertile green oasis merely some 6 km east of here. It is a holy place for Christians, Jews and Moslems as well, the main object of veneration being the white-tiled *marabout* said to contain the tomb of noone other than John the

Baptist. The nearby cave of Ghar el Houriyat is said to be inhabited by *huris*, beautiful virgin maidens who await the faithful believers after death.

Highway 1, (Oujda- Rabat) heads west via El Aioun, Taourirt and Guercif on to Taza (173 km). From Taourirt one can also take the S 410 to the indeed beautiful Middle Atlas oasis of **Debdou**. This one is Jewish in character, surrounded by lush orchards and oak and Thuja forests.

The turning about 30 km before Taza soon takes one to **Oued Msoun**, a series of small waterfalls cascading down picturesque red sandstone slopes. The semi-nomadic *Haouwara* Berbers in this region keep granaries in the small town of **Msoun** and still construct reed and mud *noualas* (huts), which have yet become scarce elsewhere in Morocco. Heading south, the peaks of the Middle Atlas (Jebel Bou Iblane, 3,190 m) become visible, a sign that Taza is no longer far off.

Above: Tobacco is, by no means, the only thing smoked in Morocco's north.

Taza and the Jebel Tazzeka

The provincial capital of **Taza** (pop. 90,000) overlooks a narrow alpine valley separating the Rif Mountains from the Middle Atlas, the historically oft-contested Taza Corridor.

The Moroccan army still maintains a garrison here. This was the route used by Moulay Idriss on his way from Tangier, and both the Almohads and Merenids successfully launched their attacks on Fès from here. In 1135 the Almohad sultan Abd el Moumen set up a temporary residence in Taza. He had prior to moving to Marrakech a 3-km long wall built all around the settlement, which still partially surrounds the elevated *medina* (Taza haut). The monumental **Bab er Rih** (Gate of Winds) dates back to this doubtlessly grand Moorish era. A Merinid *medersa* (Koran school) dating back to 1325 now houses an ethnic arts and crafts museum. From the **Café du Pacha** at Bab Jemaa there is a splendid view of the nouvelle ville (new town) of Taza, about one km away.

Excursions to Jebel Tazzeka

For a scenic tour from Taza one can take the asphalt S 311 (137 km) through the nearly 2,000-m high limestone massif of Jebel Tazzeka, an area covered by oak and cedar forests, and providing summer pasture for semi-nomadic tribes. The absolute highlights of the tour are the **Cascades of Ras el Oued**, the beautifully situated **Dayet Chiker** and the kilometer-long subtaerranean limestone labyrinths of the **Grottes du Chiker** and **Gouffre du Friouato**. There is a narrow road leading up to the summit of **Jebel Tazzeka** (1,980 m). This little tour leads to the magnificent gorges of **Oued Zireg** to Sidi Abdallah des Rhiata and connects with highway 1 (104 km). From here one can either drive back to Taza (33 km) or continue farther west to Fès.

TANGIER
Accommodation
LUXURY: **El Minzah**, Rue de la Liberté 85, Tel: 35885. **Intercontinental**, Park Brooks, Tel: 36053. **Almohades**, Av des F.A.R., Tel: 40330. *MODERATE:* **Rembrandt**, Av. Mohammed V, Tel: 37870. **Africa**, Av. Moussa 17, Tel: 35511. **Atlas**, Rue Moussa Ibn Noussair 50, Tel: 36435. *BUDGET:* **Marco Polo**, Av. d'Espagne, Tel: 38213. **Continental**, Rue Dar el Baroud 36, Tel: 31024. **Ibn Batouta**, Rue Magellan 8, Tel: 37170. *HOLIDAY VILLAGES:* in the Bay of Tangier, on the coastal road towards Cape Malabata: **Tarik**, **Mar Bel**, **Club Mediterranée/Malabata**, Tel: 40588.

Restaurants
MOROCCAN: **Raihani**, Calle Murillo 10, Tel: 34866. **Le Detroit**, Rue Riad Sultan, Tel: 38080. **Hamadi**, Rue de la Kasabah 2, Tel: 34514. *FRENCH:* **La Gagarine**, Rue Victor Hugo 28, Tel: 34531. **La Grenouille**, Rue el Jahba el Outania 13. *ITALIAN:* **Florian**, **Nino**, **San Remo**, all in the Rue Murillo. *VIETNAMESE:* **La Pagode**, Rue Boussairi 3, Tel: 38086. *GERMAN:* **Le Coeur de Tanger**, Rue Annoual 1, Tel: 36456.

Nightlife
Deans Bar, Rue Amerique de Sud. **Churchill Club**, Rue el Moutanabi. **Morocco Palace**, Av. Moulay Abdallah 11. **Crudys Hiennese Bar**, Av. Prince Héritier 37, Tel: 37012.

Transportation
AIR: Royal Air Maroc, Pl. de France, Tel: 35502. **BUS: Gare Routière**, Pl. de la Marche Verte (at the harbor), Tel: 32415. **RAIL: Gare ONCF**, Allée de la Marche Verte, Tel: 39107/31201 (trains to Rabat, Casa, Meknes, Fes, Oujda). **RADIO TAXI:** Pl. du 9 Avril 1947, Tel: 35517. **FERRIES: Trasmediterranea** (Tanger – Algeciras), Av. de la Résistance 31, Tel: 41101. **Limadet Ferry** (Tanger – Algeciras), Rue Prince Moulay Abdallah 13, Tel: 32913. **Gibmar** (Tanger – Gibraltar), Bd. Mohammed V 22, Tel: 35872. **Comanav** (Tanger – Sète), Rue Abu El Inan 43, Tel: 32649.

Tourist Information / Post
ONMT, Bd. Pasteur 29, Tel: 32996. **Syndicat D'Initiative**, Rue Khalid Ibn Oualid 11, Tel: 35486. *POST:* **PTT**, Bd. Mohammed V 33.

Hospitals
Hôpital Al Kortobi, Rue Al Kortobi (Marshan), Tel: 34242 (Emergency call). **Hôpital Italien**, Rue Bouarrakia 104, Tel: 31288. **Hôpital Espagnol**, Rue Hôpital Espagnol, Tel: 31018.

Pharmacies
Pharmacie Centrale, Bd. Pasteur 48, Tel: 33741. **Pasteur**, Pl. de France, Tel: 32422.

RIF REGION
Accommodation
CEUTA: *LUXURY:* **La Muralla**, Plaza de Africa 15, Tel: 5149408. *MODERATE*: **Africa**, Muelle Canonero Dato, Tel: 514140. **Skol**, Av. Reyes Catolicos, Tel: 5141489.
BUDGET: **Malaga**, Isidoro Martinez 2. **Oriente**, Teniente Arabal 3.

SMIR-RESTINGA: (beach) *MODERATE:* **Carabo**, Tel: 8707. **Boustane**, Tel: 8707.

M'DIQ: *MODERATE:* **Golden Beach**, R. de Sebta, Tel: 6477. **Kabila**, R. de Sebta, Tel: 6855. *BUDGET:* **Playa**, Bd. Lalla Nozha, Tel: 7566.

TETOUAN: *MODERATE:* **Safir**, R. de Sebta, Tel: 7044. *BUDGET:* **Paris**, Rue Chakib Arsalane 11, Tel: 6750. **National**, Rue Med Torres 8, Tel: 3290.

CHEFCHAOUEN: *MODERATE:* **Hotel de Chaouen**, Outa el Hamam, Tel: 6324. **Asma** (panoramic view), Sidi Abdelhamid, Tel: 6002. *BUDGET:* **Magou**, Rue Moulay Idriss 23, Tel: 6257. **Ibza**, Rue Sidi el Mandri, Tel: 6323.

KETAMA: *MODERATE:* **Tidighine**, TEL: 16. *BUDGET:* **Saada**. **WARNING: possession of drugs is a criminal offence!**

HOCEIMA: *MODERATE:* **Mohammed V**, Pl. Marche Verte, Tel: 2233. **Quemado** (beach), Plage de Quemado, Tel: 2371. *BUDGET:* **National**, Rue de Tetouan, Tel: 3025. **Marrakech**, Rue Abdallah Hammou 2, Tel: 3025.

NADOR: *MODERATE:* **Rif**, Av. Ibn Tachfine, Tel: 3727. **Mansour Ed Dahab**, Rue de Marrakech 101, Tel: 2409. *BUDGET:* **Khalid**, Av. des F.A.R., Tel: 3720. **Anoual**, Tel: 3349.

MELILLA: *LUXURY:* **Don Pedro de Estopiñan**, Apartado Correos 312, Tel: 684994. *MODERATE*: **Rusadir San Miguel**, Calle del Teniente Aguilar de Mera, Tel: 681240. *BUDGET:* **Cazaza**, Calle Primo de Rivera 6, Tel: 684648. **España**, Calle del General Chacel 10, Tel: 684645.

OUJDA: *MODERATE:* **Terminus**, Pl. de l'Unité Africaine, Tel: 3211. **Al Massira**, Bd. Maghreb El Arabi, Tel: 5301. *BUDGET:* **Lutetia**, Bd. Hassan Loukili 44, Tel: 3365. **Simon**, Rue Tarik Ibn Ziad 1, Tel: 6303.

TAZA: *MODERATE:* **Friouato Salam**, Tel: 2593. **Du Dauphine**, Av. Prince Héritier Sidi Med, Tel: 3567.

THE ISLAM'S
WESTERN BORDER

NORTHERN ATLANTIC COAST
RABAT
CASABLANCA
SOUTHERN ATLANTIC COAST
AGADIR

NORTHERN ATLANTIC COAST

A zigzag road winds its way out of Tangier, first through the Marshan residential area and then through the hilly Montagne neighborhood, before heading west to the Cap Spartel lighthouse, which marks the northeasternmost endpoint of the North African continent. On a clear day the Spanish coastline is clearly visible from here. To the south of the cape, deep within a fossile cliff, are the legendary **Hercules Caverns**. The Romans used to quarry the cavern walls for great slabs of stone to use as millstones. Continuing south, always along the Atlantic coast, the route soon bypasses the rather simple, however not uninteresting archaeological site of Cotta before joining up with highway P 2, which connects Tangier with Rabat.

The small seaport of **Asilah**, which has an eventful history behind it, is another 54 km down the road. Both the Phoenicians and the Romans knew how to appreciate the benefits of this natural harbor. The fortified walls surrounding the town soon recall the long-gone days when Portuguese invaders occupied the place from

Previous pages: The plankton rich waters of the Canary Stream feeds countless sardines. Left: Andalusian colors in Larache.

1471 until 1578. The coat of arms of Portugal's king then Alfonso V still hangs above **Bab el Jebel** gate. In 1906 the notorious bandit, Ahmed el Raisuli, set up his headquarters in Asilah and even proclaimed himself the city's pasha. His notoriety increased after he kidnapped the British *Times* correspondent Walter Harris and collected the tidy sum of 14,000 pounds sterling for his ransom. During the Protectorate Raisuli collaborated with the Spanish while at the same time secretly receiving support from the German Kaiser Wilhelm II during World War I, who promised to make him sultan. Berber resistance fighters under Abd el Krim eventually took Abd el Raisuli prisoner in 1924. Each year in August internationally renown classical and folkloric concerts are performed in the **Palais Raisuli**, the former feudal residence of the self-proclaimed pasha. The city's modern yachting harbor also attracts many visitors during the summer. The colorful murals on the houses in the medina bear witness to the fact that many Moroccan artists have chosen to live in Asilah.

South of Asilah, near Souk Tnine de Sidi el-Yamani, a rather sandy track leads through groves of cork oak and eucalyptus to the **Cromlech of Msoura**, a prehistoric circle of stones around a tomb that is some 55 m in diameter (a model of this

73

neolithic cult site has been set up in the worthwhile archaelogical museum of Tétouan). Just before Larache one arrives at the **ruins of Lixus**, situated on the banks of the Oued Loukos. This ancient port was founded by Phoenicians in the 7th century B.C. In A.D. 42 the Romans integrated Lixus into their new province of Mauretania Tingitana. In Roman times the port facilities were situated next to the lower section of the city wall. Remnants of small factories for the preservation and storage of fish have been excavated. The remains of a theater, a thermal bath and an amphitheater are found in the eastern sector of the lower part of town. On the other hand, the upper town (Acropolis) is separated by its own wall, and includes a small basilica and a temple.

Larache, El Araish in Arabic, is a picturesque town on the Atlantic estuary of the Oued Loukos. The Spanish fortified the port in 1618, erecting a wall and a citadel, and thus left behind an ideal hideout for the pirates who came after they pulled out in the 17th century. The victimized Christian seafaring nations - by name France, Austria and Spain – retaliated and bombarded the town from sea on a number of occasions.

Larache came under Spanish influence during the Protectorate (1912-1956). Today, it has a number of interesting sights and features. The former Plaza de España, now called **Place de la Libération**, marks the transition from the Spanish new town to the Moslem old town. In the center of the plaza, a small garden has been laid out which is surrounded by a couple of sidewalk cafés and restaurants. Passing through the gate **Bab el Khemis**, one arrives at the interesting medina and the **Socco de la Alcaiceria** (former silk market), probably one of the country's most beautiful marketplaces.

About 35 km southeast of Larache lies **Ksar el Kebir**, a town of considerable historic importance in the fertile Loukos Valley. It was exactly here, in 1578, that the young Portuguese king, Sebastiao, fought the – for him – disastrous Battle of the Three Kings in which 25,000 soldiers lost their lives. The king's untimely death – he was drowned in the Loukos River whilst attempting to escape – caused a political crisis in Portugal, so weakening the country that it was easily annexed by Spain only two years later. The town of Ksar el Kebir, which surpassed Fès in importance during the 12th century, has an interesting medina with picturesque *fondouks* (merchants' inns).

There is a turnoff to the S 216 merely 12 km south of Ksar el Kebir, not very far from **Arbaoua**. It leads first along the coast to **Moulay Bou Selham**. The village, with its more than 10,000-year-old tomb of patron saint Moulay Bou Selham, is romantically situated on a lagoon called Merdja Lerga. Its beautiful sand beach, varied bird life, a few small hotels and a campsite make it an ideal place for a stopover. Heading farther south, highway 2 runs through bustling **Souk el Arba**, which is the central marketplace for the **Rharb**, Morocco's most productive agricultural region on the Oued Sebou. Many *colons*, French people who settled in the new colony, settled here during the era of the French Protectorate. They cultivated the vines that still produce grapes for Moroccan wine cellars.

Kenitra is essentially a young town, and consequently in a historical sense not as interesting perhaps as some of the older, more traditional towns on the coast. It was established in the year of 1913 by the French, who also constructed a port there that nowadays serves a wood- and food-processing industry.

It is well worthwhile to take the detour along the way to Rabat that leads to the small village of **Mehdia** on the estuary of the Sebou. There is a magnificent 17th-century kasbah there with a monumental portal. The Almohads had already established the port of El Mamora, at the same site in the 12th century, the name of

TANGER
C. Spartel ✈
Grottes d'Hercule
Cotta

Regaia

Manzla

Souk-el-Had-
el-Gharbia

Asilah
Bab El Jebel, ✈
Palais Raisuli

Souk-el-Arba-
Ayacha

•912

Cromlech
de Msoura
Souk-Khemis-
du-Sahel

Souk-Sebt-
les-Beni-Gorfat

Lixus ∴

Tleta-
Rissana

El-Arâich
(Larache) ✈

○ Makhazen

Socco de
la Alcaiceria

**Ksar-
el-Kehir**

Barga ○

73

Arbaoua

Mzefroun

ATLANTIC

Moulay-Bousselham

Basra ∴

Lalla-Rhano

23

Sidi-Mohammed-
el-Ahmér

Souk-el-Arba

OCEAN

Souk-Tleta-
du-Rharb

14

36

∴ Banasa

Mechra-
Bel-Ksiri

Allal-Tazi

42

38

Dar-Gueddari

El-Beggara

64

Sidi-Yahya-du-Rharb

KÉNITRA

62

Sidi-Slimane

**Sidi-
Kacem**

Mehdiya-Plage ✈

Dar-Bel-Amri

40

Forêt de

59

El-Kansera

Fondouk Askour, Bouknadel
Medersa Abu el Hassan

Jardins
Exotiques

la Mamora

Âin-el-
Jemâa

Bir-Chafii

80

Sidi-Allal-Bahraoui

**SALÉ
RABAT** ✈

82

Témara

Tiflèt

Sidi-Yahya-de-Zaër

Skhirate

Âin-el-Âouda

35

Khemissèt

Mohammedia

A86

92

Bouznika

DAR-EL-BEIDA
(CASABLANCA)

Nkheila

Had-
Brachoua

Mâaziz

Ouljet-es-Soltane

Louizia

82

37

Marabout ✈
Âin-Harrouda

Ben-Slimane

Âin-Sebaâ
Tit-Mellil

Sidi-Bettache

Djebel Mouchchene
1086

Sidi-Hajjaj

Souk-Jemaâ-
des-Feddalate

El-Harcha

Souk-Tleta-
des-Ziaida

Rommani

56

42

Medouina

Souk-El-Had-
de-Moualine-
El-Oued

Oulmès

46

Bouskoura

Souk-Jemaâ-
des-Melilla

Bir-Jdid

90

Bir-el-Kelb

Had-Rhoualem

El-Arba

Berrechid

Ez-Zhiliga

○ Marrout

El-Gara

Moulay-
Bouâzza

Rhmimiyne

Riah

El-Khatouat

845
Col-de-Khaloua

Taztot

Souk-Jemââ-
des-Oulad-Abbou

30

39

Benahmed

90

Aguelmouss

1604

Ras-el-Âin

49

Souk-Tnine-des-
Oulad-Bour-Hadi

Oulad-Saîd ○

Settat
(361)

Loulad

13

Bir-Mezoui

Kasba-de
Boulâouane ○

Sidi-Hajjaj

Plateau

68

Khouribga

**Oued-
Zem**

El-Khemissèt-
dés-Oulad-Bouziri

des Phosphates

Souk-
et-Tnine

```
NORTHERN
ATLANTIC COAST
0          50 km
```

which still survives in nearby **Mamora Forest**. Nearby, the popular beach resort of Mehdia Plage is situated directly on the Atlantic. Just 20 km south of here are the **Jardins Exotiques de Bouknadel**. This small, somewhat overgrown botanical garden was laid out by the French ecologist M. François in a by and large successful attempt to display the typical plant life of Africa and Asia.

Salé

Salé is a city situated on the north bank of the Bou Regreg estuary. Unlike Rabat over on the opposite side of the river, Salé has developed into a prosperous trading center over the past 1,000 years. The old town is surrounded by a huge 13th-century Merinid wall with eight impressive gates. An oriental bazaar-like atmosphere prevails within the walls and along all the

Above: The palace of Rabat has continuously been the main residence of the Alawi kings since the year of 1911.

narrow alleys of the old town. The entrance to the medina is through the opening of one-time gate, **Bab el Khebbaz**. The Rue Bab el Khebbaz leads to the *kisseria* (textil market) and then on to the busy **Souk el Kebir** pirates are said to have sold slaves here in the 17th century. Nowadays, the locals sell mainly earthenware, wrought iron wares, carpets, babouches, carpentry work and other handicrafts. Turning back down Rue Bab el Khebbaz for about 100 m and then heading west, one will come to **Souk el Ghezel**, the busy Salé **wool market**. Untreated wool is auctioned off on the shady square, while dyed wool is sold in the surrounding *hanouds* (shops). Goldsmiths and mat- and basket weavers are at work in the adjoining **Souk el Merzouk** as if the passage of time had never taken place. Passing by the ornate portal of **Foundouk Askour** and subsequently continuing along the **Rue de la Grande Mosquée**, where kaftan weavers have their shops, one will eventually arrive before the Moorish gates of the Abu el Hassan medersa. This nearly 700-year-old Koran school indeed is Salé's architectural jewel. A gallery with rounded pillars, which are decorated with colorful mosaics, surrounds the inner courtyard. The mihrab, or prayer alcove, is intricately framed with stucco work and the prayer room itself is covered by a carved cedar dome. There are wonderful views of Salé, Rabat, the Bou Regreg estuary and the Atlantic from the roof terrace.

RABAT

The capital city of Morocco has a long and variegated history, with prosperity mixing with instances of criminality and religious fanaticism. Phoenicians made use of the natural harbor on the Bou Regreg estuary as early as the 12th century B.C. In the 1st century A.D., the Romans expanded the harbor and established the town of Sala Colonia, which was abandoned during the 4th century.

In the 10th century, Moslem Zenata Berbers erected a *ribat* (crusader stronghold) on the steep **Oudaia Cliffs** overlooking the Atlantic in order to keep the sectarian Kharedjites at bay, who had broken away from the *Sunna* (an orthodox code of Islam).

The Almohads residing in Marrakech chose this town as a launching base for their campaigns against Spain in the 12th century. Their leader, Yacoub el Mansour (1184-1199) was a very ambitious man. He even renamed the town *Ribat el Fath* (Stronghold of Victory) and erected the mighty Oudaia Kasbah which proved unconquerable up until the 19th century. Al Mansour set out from here for *el Andalus* (Moorish Spain) and decisively defeated the army of the Christian king of Castille, Alfonso VIII, in A.D. 1195. With the rich spoils from this successful campaign he planned to expand Rabat into a principal city. At this endeavor he was not exactly modest: his **Hassan Mosque** was to become the second largest of the world.

Merely his untimely death in 1199 prevented its completion. The still extant, more than 5-km long **Almohad Wall** testifies to the grandeur of his plans. In the 13th century the pious sultans of the Beni Meri dynasty (Merinids) established a *zawiya* (seat of a Moslem-order) along with a Koran school and burial Mosque just outside the wall, next to the ruins of a Roman citadel, the **Chellah**. The City declined after this time. Moorish explorer El Wassan, who was christened by force Leo Africanus by Pope Leo X in 1520, visited the place in 1515 and found only 100 inhabited houses.

The Spanish Catholics had no idea just how much trouble they would create for themselves by banning the last remaining Moslems and Jews from the Iberian peninsula in 1609. Refugees from the town of Horgachos settled in the Almohad kasbah in Rabat. Shortly after this, Andalusian exiles occupied the depopulated Almohad town and reduced it to a quarter of its former size by erecting the **Andalusian Wall** around part of it. In its present-day state, the picturesque medina is still essentially the town created in the 17th century by the Andalusians.

The refugees earned their living by looting Spanish and Portuguese ships, an activity they liked to view as a kind of "holy war". The ransom money they collected for Christian prisoners ironically brought about a considerable boost in the economy. In 1627 the corsairs eventually declared their independence from the sultan and called out the pirate republic of Bou Regreg. The state council, consisting of 16 members, elected a new *kaid* each year. (To this day the French use the word *caïd* to describe an underworld leader, a mafia boss of sorts).

A notorious Dutch pirate, Jan Janssen, was elected as head of state in 1638 – a rather curious turn in Morocco's history. Daniel Defoe had his fictitious hero Robinson Crusoe spend two years in prison here after his boat had been seized.

The pirates saw to it that their offspring received the best possible training: they soon established a seaman's academy in the Oudaia Kasbah. Their ships posed a threat particularly for Christian shipping lines as far away as Newfoundland. However, European attempts to retaliate were unsuccessful. Due to the sand banks in the Bou Regreg estuary solely the flat-bottomed boats of the type used by the pirates could gain access to the harbor so that the kasbah practically remained inaccessible from the Atlantic.

After forcing an Alawi governor on the town in 1666, however, the Alawite sultans demanded a considerable share of the pirates' profits. Moulay Ismail forced captured Europeans to work on the walls of his new residence in Meknes, before demanding ransom money for them. Following Ismail's death in 1727, Rabat became the scene of continuous power struggles among his real an would-be

Above: Symbol of the city is the yet un-completed minaret of the Hassan mosque.

successors, and the might of the pirates began to wane slowly. Sultan Sidi Mohammed Ben Abdallah had a sumptuous palace erected on the south side of the Almohad wall in 1776, which served as a stopover for Alawi sultans on their way from Marrakech to their then seat of government in Fès. The detour via Rabat became necessary because hostile Berber tribes threatened the direct route through the Tadla Basin.

A New City Within Old Walls

Nevertheless, the Bou Regreg pirates were active until the year of 1829. A hapless Austrian freighter was the last ship ever they seized. In retaliation, technically by far superior European war ships attacked Moroccan ports on the Atlantic coast, thus putting an end to piracy.

It was merely after the French Protectorate Agreement, signed in 1912, that Rabat developed into the modern large city it has become today, with a population of 600,000. General Lyautey proclaimed Rabat capital and Sultan Moulay Youssouf left Fès to take up residence in Rabat. Due to the the rebellious Berber crusaders in and around Fès, life in the holy city had become too hazardous for the two rulers. Rabat, on the other hand, was safe. Furthermore, it had a pleasant climate as well as an efficient transport system. The sandbanks in the city's small harbor and its lack of modern facilities also may have influenced the General's decision in making Casablanca the nation's main seaport.

In 1913 Lyautey commissioned the architect Henri Prost to build a *ville nouvelle* (the new town) between the palace and medina, still within the 12th-century Almohad walls, which was to serve as an administrative sector. The very elegant **Avenue Mohammed V** is the new town's main thoroughfare. It starts off as an alley in the medina and then emerges as a modern shopping lane with exclusive bou-

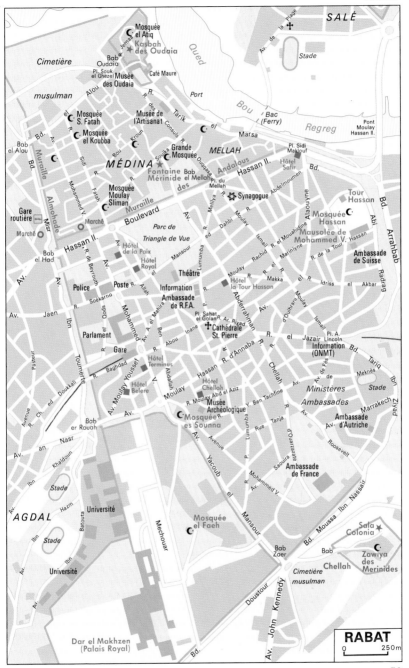

SALÉ

Av. de la Plage

Stade

Mosquée
el Atiq

Kasbah
des Oudaia

Bab
Oudaia

Café Maure

Oued

Cimetière

Pl. Souk
el Ghezel Musée
des Oudaia

musulman

Port

Bou Regreg

Bac
(Ferry)

Pont
Moulay
Hassan II.

Mosquée
S. Fatah

Musée de
l'Artisanat

Mosquée
el Koubba

el Marsa

Pl. Sidi
Maklouf

Grande
Mosquée Ouggass

MELLAH

Hôtel
Safir

Bd.

MÉDINA

Fontaine
Mérinide Bab
el Mellah

Hassan II.

Mosquée
Moulay
Sliman

Pl. du
Mellah

Synagogue

Tour
Hassan

Bd.

Gare
routière

Marché

Boulevard

Parc de
Triangle de Vue

Mosquée
Hassan

Mausolée de
Mohammed V.

Ambassade
de Suisse

Marché

Hassan II.

Hôtel
de la Paix

Hôtel
Royal

Théâtre

Bab
el Had

Police

Poste

Information
Ambassade
de R.F.A.

Hôtel
la Tour Hassan

Jaen

Parlament

Gare

Pl. Sahat
el Golan

Cathédrale
St. Pierre

Information
(ONMT)

Hôtel
Terminus

Hôtel
Chellah

Ministères

Hôtel
Belère

Musée
Archéologique

Mosquée
es Sounna

Stade

Ambassades

Ambassade
d'Autriche

Bab
er Rouah

Ambassade
de France

AGDAL

Stade

Université

Mosquée
el Faeh

Sala
Colonia

Stade

Université

Bab
Zaer

Bab
Chellah

Zawiya
des
Mérinides

*Cimetière
musulman*

Dar el Makhzen
(Palais Royal)

RABAT

0   250m

tiques just behind the Andalusian wall, where the marketplace is. International airlines and banks maintain offices here. When it reaches the neo-Moorish façade of the main postoffice, the avenue expands into a palm-lined boulevard, flanked by the modern buildings housing the government. Once past the railway station, it continues on to the 18th-century Jemaa el Sunna Mosquee.

The **Archaeological Museum** (Musée des Antiquités) is only one block farther eastwards just behind the mosque, on **Rue al Brihi**. It houses an indeed exceptional collection of early stone-age skeletal finds, bronzes, coins and Roman and early Christian sculptures.

Returning to the Sunna Mosque and then heading west along **Avenue Moulay Hassan**, one inevitably arrives before the 12th-century Almohad **Bab er Rouah** (Gate of Winds). This gate actually resembles a massive stone fort with its two protruding bastions. Four defensive compartments placed one after the other at different angles, practically made it impossible for attackers to get through. The former guards' quarters are now used for art exhibitions. The roof terrace affords splendid views of the new town, of the adjoining palace grounds and of the **university**, which has over 20,000 students. This is where political and intellectual leanings from the Orient and Occident fuse. On the one hand women's rights activist and sociologist Fatima Mernissi is opposed to the rigid dity of Islamic principles, while on the other devout Moslem students collectively reading the Koran discover that neither royalty nor nobility are proclaimed therein.

Seat of Power: The King's Palace

Heading back down the elegant Avenue Moulay Hassan, a monumental gate

Right: Gnaoua dancers at the gate to Chellah greet visitors of the Merenid tombs.

on the right hand side opens onto the palace grounds. In the forefront is a wide *Mechouar* (parade grounds) flanked on its eastern end by a grove of African tulip trees, the orange blossoms of which are shaped like tigers' claws. Before it stands the worthwhile mosque of **el Faeh**, where the royal family assembles on Fridays for noon prayers. When the king himself deigns to take part in the weekly procession to the mosque he almost always does so on horseback and returns to the **Dar el Makhzen** (King's Palace) in an elaborate horse-drawn carriage.

The palacial complex, which was built in the 18th century, was first expanded in the 19th and modernized in the 20th, not only contains the numerous royal chambers, but also the prime minister's administrative office, the *habous* (Ministry of Religious Affairs), law-courts, the barracks of the palace guards and as well the **imperial college** at which the princes are taught. About 2,000 palace officials live here, who wear a red *fez* as part of their oriental costume. The entrance to Morocco's seat of power is closely guarded by the king's Black Guard. In contrast to the monumental palace portal in Fès, the portal here surprisingly seems rather plain. It appears, though, that the nation's sovereign also rules over time: He didn't even shrink from keeping Her Majesty Queen Elizabeth II in person waiting here when she visited Rabat in October 1980.

Heading east from the palace gate, a wide street first passes the Ministry of Defence with its eye-catching pentagonal dome and continues out of the *makhzen* area towards the ministry district (site of the Ministry of Tourism, among others). Turning southwest, along the **Avenue Yacoub el Mansour**, it is not very far to the Almohad gate **Bab Zaer**. The Zaer tribe not only refused to pay taxes to the sultan in the dark past, it also had the unpleasant tendency of attacking royal cities – and Rabat was a mere 60 km away from their mountainous tribal domain!

Chellah: Merinid Necropolis

The Merinid dynasty was first established by the eager to fight Beni Meri Berber tribe, which was driven west in the 12th century by Arab nomads, to what is now eastern Algeria. In 1195 Beni Meri troops were shipped to Spain by the ruling Almohads in order to take part in what was eventually to become the great victory Battle of Alarco. The Merinids later drove the weakened Almohads out of Fès, and by 1269 the entire Maghreb region was under their rule. They were, however, unable to exert power over the enormous territory of their predecessors for long, and they soon lost the eastern regions we now know as Tunisia. The loss of Moorish Spain shortly after was even more devastating. Only Granada was able to defend itself against the very powerful Christian armies until 1492.

Under the influence of courtly life, the Merinid desert nomads quite soon gave up their coarse ways in favor of an urban lifestyle. This transition is clearly reflected in the richly ornamented portal of the Merinid necropolis, **Chellah**, which was originally laid out as a *zawiya*. This walled necropolis from the 13th and 14th centuries also encloses the ruins of an ancient Roman settlement, Sala Colonia, which is located about 500 m from the Almohad gate, Bab Zaer. Each of the gate's two protruding bastions is crowned by four turrets, which are supported by stalactite corbels. The obviously massive brick structure of the horseshoe-shaped gate is nevertheless optically effetctively aleviated by the means of artistic, skillfully designed ornamentation – a very specialty of Moorish master builders. The spandrel is covered with fine arabesques; two small half columns in the upper part, which have no supportive function, seem to lighten the wall considerably.

The high walls keep a serene garden secluded from the hectic city. The white blossoms falling from the angel's trumpet trees (*datura*) lining the path down to where the tombs are immediately catch the eye. Because of their toxicity, local

guides refer to them as "mother-in-law trees". On the way to the burial ground, from a top a terrace an the left, one can sometimes catch a glimpse of the Roman **Sala Colonia** excavation site. Unfortunately the site is not open to the public. The ancient city was by far the remotest advanced post in the southwestern part of the Roman Empire, and it had a good riverine harbor. A special rampart (the famous *limes*) erected only a few kilometers farther south primarily served to protect the residents from incursions by the Mauri and Numidi tribes. Going downhill one soon arrives at an olive grove with numerous tombs. In popular Islamic belief it is magically associated with the nearby **Spring of the Sacred Eels**. A flesh-and-blood marabout sells boiled eggs to women who sacrifice these eggs to the eels in the hopes of being blessed

Above: Honor guard at the mausoleum of former King Mohammed V. Right: Only the best was regarded good enough for the king's magnificent tomb.

with offspring. It is said that there once was a Roman thermal bath on the same site that was later replaced by a Moslem *hammam* (bath house).

The high sun-dried mud walls northeast of the spring protect the ruins of the Merinid burial mosque. An unobtrusive marble slab with Koranic inscriptions and arabesques mark the tomb of the "Black Sultan" Abu el Hassan. After reigning for two decades, he was forced to abdicate in 1351 by his own son Abu Inan. The sultan's favorite wife, an English woman who converted to Islam, is buried merely a few yards away. She was given the name of *chems ed duna*, twilight. The Merenid sultans, in particular Abu Inan, who is also buried here, demanded that Moroccans adhere to Sunnite teachings, and built Koran schools throughout Morocco in the hope of preventing Shiite sectarianism from spreading. A decaying *medersa* built during this time is situated right next to the burial mosque. The former cells of the *tolba* (students) surround a tiled courtyard with a purification fountain. The minaret, still in good condition, is a favored nesting place for storks.

Pride of the Almohad: Hassan Mosque

The **embassy quarter** is located in the southeastern part of the new town, right on the way from the Chellah to the Hassan Tower. As might be expected from the protectorate days, the former noble residence of General Lyautey and current French Embassy takes up the largest space in the park area between the Avenue Mohammed V and Avenue Roosevelt. The two historical figures thus honored not only had the French cornered between them in a geographical sense: in 1944 the President of the United States assured the Sultan of American support for Morocco's independence movement.

The Avenue de Fès leads directly to the **Hassan Mosque**. Begun in 1191, it was

to be the highlight of Yacoub el Mansour's new residence. It covers an area of 25,000 sq.m and holds 40,000 believers, so it might have been the greatest mosque of the Maghreb region. Due to Yacoub's untimely death in 1199, however, construction of the mosque was never completed. Its 19-nave ground plan covers a rectangular area 183 m in length and 139 m in width. No less than 16 portals were planned. A small proportion of the 312 columns and 112 pillars in the prayer hall has been restored, along with the *mihrab* (prayer niche) and the *kebla* (prayer wall). The **Hassan Tower**, Rabat's landmark, was to have attained a height of some 87 m-at 44 m the masons put down their trowels forever. Its aesthetic model was the Koutoubia Minaret im Marrakech. The **Mohammed V Mausoleum** is situated on the southern side of the mosque ruins. Designed by a Vietnamese architect, the tomb was decorated with marble, onyx and gold-leaf. The interlacing curved patterns on the outer wall of the pavilion also adorn the Almohad mi-

naret directly opposite. The remains of the sultan, who died as a result of an operation in 1961, were brought here in a white onyx sarcophagus on completion of the building in 1971. An *alim* recites Koranic verses at the tomb during the whole day. The green (Prophet's color) pyramidal ceiling is a reminder of Mohammed V's Arabic-sharifian descent.

The Oudaia Kasbah

The old harbor is situated beyond the Andalusian medina wall and can easily be reached via the Place Sidi Maklouf. Rowboats ferry visitors to and from the twin city of Salé. A bit farther along the Rue Tarik al Marga, on the left side, is the small **Musée de l'Artisanat** (Folk Art Museum). From here one can already see the mighty walls of the **Oudaia Kasbah**. The Almohad stronghold received its current name from the 17th-century Oudia mercenaries settled here involuntarily by Moulay Ismail as a means to control piracy. Crossing the **Place Souk el Ghezel** (former wool market), one arrives at the **Oudaia Museum** (National Museum of Moroccan Art), which is housed in a 17th-century vizierial palace. It houses a very impressive collection of Moroccan jewellery, hand-written Korans (until the 13th century), musical instruments and royal carpets. For a modest entrance fee one can stroll through the museum's Andalusian garden. The monumental 12th-century **Oudaia Gate** guards the kasbah's entrance. The **Rue Jemaa** just beyond the gate will take one through the still populous former corsair's town. Behind **El Atiq Mosque** (12th century), at the northern end of the stronghold, one will see a platform perched 60 m above the river. From here one has a panoramic view of the Atlantic, the estuary and the city of Salé. Heading back along the Rue Jemaa for a short stretch and then taking the **Rue Bazzo** downhill, one arrives at the **Moorish Café**. Here one can enjoy the view while savoring honey pastries and a tasty cup of mint tea.

CASABLANCA

Many Moroccan cities have had a very turbulent past. The prosperous metropolis of Casablanca, however, can almost be said to have no history at all. The royal cities of Rabat, Marrakech, Fès and Meknes cling to memories of their pious dynasties; but "Casa" embodies a new Morocco, pulsating with life and the energy of an up-and-coming new generation.

The oldest settlement in the area now occupied by Casablanca was the Berber Anfa, mentioned by Arab historians of the 8th century. During the 14th century the tiny port of Anfa became a pirate's nest and was consequently destroyed by the Portuguese in 1468, 1515 and 1575. Following the last assault, the Portuguese

Right: A relaxed chat at the edge of the small Medina in contrast to the big city hectic of the otherwise modern Casablanca.

erected the harbor stronghold Casa Branca, which they held against Berbers and Arabs until 1755. It wasn't until the end of the 18th century that Sultan Mohammed ben Abdallah re-established a Moslem town here, albeit one in which Europeans were still permitted to own factories and export wool and grain. The Portuguese word Casa Branca became the Arabic Dar El Beida (White House); in the Spanish translation it finally ended up as Casa Blanca.

When the French announced in 1912 that Casablanca thenceforth be considered Morocco's main port, the population increased dramatically: from 25,000 in 1912, to 1 million in 1960. Estimates for 1992 range from 3 to 5 million, as hundreds migrate daily from underdeveloped rural areas to crowd the *bidonvilles*, literally "tin-can towns", implying slums made up of shoddy huts.

Casa Tour

The harbor is as convenient a place as any to start a tour of Casablanca. A number of international hotels, the *gare du port* (main station for the Tangier line) and the modern **Centre 2000** shopping mall are situated near the harbor. Motorized visitors are well advised to leave their cars here, as parking can be a problem. In any case, the medina and colonial quarter are best explored on foot. The residential and beachfront area of **Ain Diab** is best reached by cab. They are not at all expensive and, since taximeters are required by law, no longer a financial risk. There is a 20 per cent surcharge on all taxi rides at night.

The elegant and beautifully palm-lined **Boulevard Félix Houphouet-Boigny** (formerly called Boulevard Mohammed el Hansali) leads from the harbor area directly to the city's center. This main thoroughfare has a large selection of Moroccan arts and crafts from all over the country on offer.

The **medina**, with its numerous winding alleys, is on the right. It has a *kisseria* where goldsmiths eagerly await customers. All along the Derb Omar delicious smells of fried fish, *kefta* (meatballs) and *kebab* arise from numerous restaurants. *Harira* soup and *chebakia* (honey pastries) are served during Ramadan. Water peddlers dressed in red robes and carying goat-skin water bags attract people's attention by ringing a bell as they go.

The Félix Houphouet-Boigny Boulevard ends at the very heart of the city, on the elegant **Place des Nations Unies,** where all the main roads leading to and from the city converge. The Avenue des Forces de l'Armee Royale, with a number of luxury hotels like the Sheraton, Mansour and Safir, branches off to the left. The countless sidewalk cafés, restaurants, cinemas, banks and travel agencies clustered around the Place des Nations Unies are dwarfed by the monumental Hyatt Regency Hotel. Hotel guests will find it particularly hard not to notice the life-size painting of Humphrey Bogart

that is adorning one of the walls in the hotel's attractive piano bar.

Heading south via Avenue Hassan II one arrives at the **Place Mohammed V,** formerly Place des Nations Unies. The large fountain in the middle of the square is lit up in the evenings from 8 p.m. until 10 p.m., and the cooing of numerous pigeons is frequently accompanied by the strains of European or of oriental music. The spacious square and the well-kept gardens that are surrounding it were laid out by General Lyautey's town-planner, Henry Prost, around the year 1920 in order to mark the heart of the administrative section in the European *ville nouvelle* (new town). There are a number of offical buildings in neo-Moorish style grouped around the square, among them the **préfecture** with its unmistakable clocktower, the monumental **Palace of Justice** with its massive pillars, the **main post office,** the **customs house,** the **national bank** and the **municipal theater**.

To get to the **Parc de la Ligue Arabe,** Casablanca's largest and perhaps most

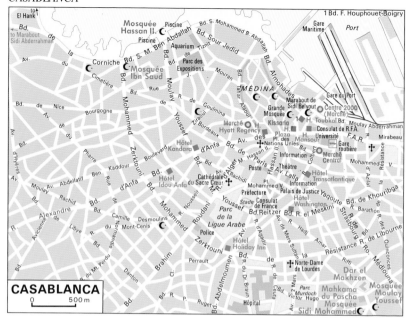

beautiful park, just cross the **Boulevard Rachidi** on the south side of the sqare. The cathedral of **Sacré Coeur** (built in 1930) at the far end of the park is now used as a place of learning by students from the university's law faculty.

The Parc de la Ligue Arabe is popular with all age groups. The well-kept flower beds, the palm trees and the secluded spots under the shady prichardiya trees make it a very pleasant place to relax and to escape the hustle and bustle of the city. Students often study their books as they stroll back and forth in the park. Here they can escape the noise and the crowded conditions they would otherwise be subjected to in their, usually, rather overcrowded homes. Refreshments can be had at the cafés, ice-cream parlors and restaurants. And children can vent their energy in the playgrounds.

If one feels like taking a stroll through the elegant pedestrian zone, one merely

Right: The port of "Casa" is the most important trade center for goods in the country.

needs to return to the Palace of Justice and head north along the **Rue du Prince Moulay Abdallah**. The pedestrian zone starts at the Boulevard de Paris. Fashionable Moroccan women buy their clothes at the boulevard's fancy boutiques, while the men sit back and chat in one of the numerous sidewalk cafés.

The short **Rue Aristide Briand** is a continuation of Casa's main thoroughfare, the Boulevard Mohammed V, which leads east from the Place des Nations to the **gare des voyageurs** (railway station of the Marrakech line). Shops, restaurants, cafés, bakeries, ice-cream parlors, book-shops and cinemas flank both sides of the busy boulevard. Here one can buy almost anything from raffle tickets to international newspapers, or casually have one's shoes polished.

The boulevard's main attraction, however, is the **Marché Central** (market) on the corner of Rue Colbert (open daily until 1 p.m.). The market has a large selection of meat (even including pork for its Christian customers), poultry, cheese,

fruit, vegetables and a great variety of fish. Everything looks clean and is appetizingly displayed. Even tortoises and canaries are to be had. The merchants are always friendly. Small fruit and vegetable and spice stalls are also found under the arcade by the outside wall of the covered market. The rich aroma of roasted coffee, mingled with sweet-smelling flowers and spices makes it diffcult for visitors to resist stopping at each one.

Every neighborhood here has its own market, of course. The one in the **Maarif** district where Spaniards and Italians used to live during the days of the Protectorate, for example, is especially interesting.

The audacious attempt to fuse Moroccan notions of a business quarter with European ones has proven quite successful in the **new medina**, which is also called *habous*. This **Neo-Moorish quarter** (in the southeast, to be reached via Route de Medouna) was laid out in 1923. Unlike the medinas of Fès and Marrakech, the old part of the city in Casablanca was way too small to cope with the rapid increase in population. According to the general aims of French policy, Arabs and Europeans were to be segregated in order to avoid possible clashes.

In the alleys south of the **Sidi Mohammed** and **Moulay Youssef mosques**, there are numerous rows of shops under shady arcades where merchants sell jellabahs, fossils, silver bracelets, daggers, copper kettles and plates, bowls made of thuya wood and numerous other Moroccan crafts. Fast-talking carpet dealers are only too pleased to show inquisitive tourists their hand-woven products. Beyond the Moulay Yussef mosque the alleys form a checkerboard pattern through the neighborhood where carpenters and tailors exhibit their goods, primarily for local customers. The Patisserie Bennis in the Rue Fkih el Gabbas is renowned for its *mechoui* (roast lamb) and *bastilla* (puff pastry filled with pigeon meat). Among the great number of sweet specialities, the *cornets des gazelles* (small cookies filled with marzipan) are particularly recommendable.

The **Mahkama du Pascha** court building located to the north of the Sidi Mohammed Mosque was erected between 1941 and 1956 and is well worth visiting. The interior shows a cross-section of traditional craftsmanship. Its rooms are decorated with cedar-wood carvings, stucco, colored fayence tiles and ornate wrought-iron gates. The **Royal Palace** built in 1912 under Sultan Moulay Youssef is not far away. It is situated in a park surrounded by high walls and is, unfortunately, not open to the public.

Back at the harbor, one might consider taking a trip along the picturesque coastal road, the **Corniche**. It is best to take a taxi and head west along the Boulevard des Almohades. The newly-constructed **Hassan II Mosque** stands on a rocky spit and its 175-m high minaret is raised at the sky like Allah's index finger. The Moroccans presented this house of prayer to their ruler on his 60th birthday. The donations,

Left: On 1920, the French architect Henri Prost spaciously planned the new city.

amounting to hundreds of millions of dollars, were indeed collected by officials throughout the country. The finished result of the tireless money-raising efforts on the part of the people is certainly something to be proud of. The mosque can accommodate 100,000 worshippers, thus making it the world's third largest after Mecca and Medina.

The **Parc des Expositions** (international exhibition center) is directly opposite the mosque, next to the **Sea Aquarium**. Heading west along the Corniche, past a number of large sea-water swimming pools, one comes to the **Ibn Saud Mosque**. Next to it is the palace of Saudi Arabia's King Fahd. Ever since the seemingly everlasting crisis in Lebanon, Morocco has become a popular alternative summer retreat for Gulf Arabs.

Beyond the **El Hank Lighthouse** the hilly residential area of **Anfa** comes into view above the coastal road. There are splendid views of the coastline and the Atlantic from here. With its elegant villas and luxuriant gardens, Anfa is the wealthiest neighborhood in town. Its residents can spend their time at the golf-club, the racecourse or at the greyhound track. The Mohammed V sports center with multifunctional facilities and soccer stadium seating 80,000 is also close at hand.

Continuing westward on the Corniche there will always be something to suit everyone's budget: seafood restaurants, outdoor cafés, elegant beach resorts (Sables d'Or, Le Lido Anfa Plage, Riad Salam, Kon Tiki), luxury hotels and fashionable nightclubs and discos. The long **Sidi Abderrahman Beach** marks the transition to the elegant **Ain Diab** neighborhood. Swimming in the Atlantic here is, by the way, not altogether without risk. Local youngsters play soccer on the beach; one can also jog or ride a horse along the water's edge. One may also choose to walk to the **Marabout Sidi Abderrahman** at low tide, which stands atop a cliff overlooking the sea.

ASILAH

Accommodation
MODERATE: **Al Khaima**, Rue de Tanger, Tel: 7230. *BUDGET:* **Oued Makhazine**, Rue Melilla, Tel: 7090. **L'Oasis**, Place des Nations Unies 8, Tel: 7186. **Sahara**, Rue Tarfaya 9, Tel: 7185. **Azilah**, Av. Hassan II.1, Tel: 7286.

LARACHE

Accommodation
BUDGET: **Riad**, Rue Moh. Ben Abdallah, Tel: 2626. **Espana**, Av. Hassan II., Tel: 3195.

RABAT

Accommodation
LUXURY: **Hyatt Regency**, Souissi, Tel: 21270. **La Tour Hassan**, Avenue du Chellah 26, Tel: 21401. *MODERATE:* **Belere**, Ave. M. Youssef, Tel: 69901. **Chellah**, Rue d'Ifni 2, Tel: 60209. **Safir**, Place Sidi Makhlouf, Tel: 31091. **Les Oudayas**, Rue Tobruk 4, Tel: 67820. **Terminus**, Ave. Mohammed V. 384, Tel: 60616. **La Felouque** (beach hotel).
BUDGET: **Bouregreg**, Rue Nador 1, Tel: 34002. **De La Paix**, Rue de Ghazzah 2, Tel: 34002. **Royal**, Rue Amman 1, Tel: 21171. **Central**, Rue al Basra 2, Tel: 67356. **Dakar**, Rue Dakar, Tel: 21671.

Restaurants
INTERNATIONAL: **Crépuscule** (good food), Zankat Laghouat 10, Tel: 32438. **Kanoun Grill**, in the Hotel Chellah. *MOROCCAN:* **Koutoubia** (good local dishes), Rue Pierre Parent 10, Tel. 60125. **El Mansour**, in the Hotel La Tour Hassan. **L'Oasis**, (inexpensive) Rue Al-es-Quofia 7. *CHINESE:* **La Pagode**, Rue de Baghdad 15. *PIZZA:* **La Mamma**, near the railway station. *FISH:* **La Felouqe**, Temara Plage. *STREET KITCHENS*: around the Bab el Had and Bab el Bouiba in the southwest corner of the Medina.

Shopping
Carpets, Leather and Crafts: Rue des Consuls and Rue Souika in the Medina.
Topographic Maps: Division de la Cartographie, Av. Moulay Hassan 31 (mornings only).

Tourist Information
ONMT, Av. d'Alger 22, Tel: 07-23272. **Syndicat d'Initiative**, Zankat Patrice Lumumba, Tel: 23272.

Hospital
Hôpital Avicenne, Souissi, Tel: 72871.

CASABLANCA

Accommodation
LUXURY: **Hyatt Regency**, Pl. des Nations Unies, Tel: 224167. **El Mansour**, Av. des F.A.R. 27, Tel: 313011. *MODERATE:* **Suisse**, Bd. de la Corniche, Tel: 360202. **Transatlantique**, Rue Colbert 79, Tel: 220764. **Bellerive**, Bd. de la Corniche 38, Tel: 367482. **Plaza**, Bd. Moh. el Hansali 18, Tel: 221262.
BUDGET: **Astrid**, Rue Ledru Rollin 12, Tel: 277803. **Georges V**, Rue Sidi Belyout 1, Tel: 312448. **Colbert**, Rue Colbert 30, Tel: 314241. **Lincoln**, Rue Ibn Batouta 1, Tel: 222408.

Restaurants
MOROCCAN: **Al Mounia**, Rue Prince M. Abdallah. **Imilchil**, Rue Vizir Tazi 25. **Sijilmassa**, Ain Diab (with belly-dancing). **Ouarzazate**, Rue Moh. el Qorri (inexpensive). *FRENCH:* **A ma Bretagne**, Ain Diab. **Le Cabestan**, Al Hank. **La Mer**, Al Hank. *ITALIAN:* **Don Camillo**, Rue de Verdun 13. *SPANISH:* **La Corrida**, Rue Gay Lussac 59. *LIBANESE:* **Le Beyrouth**, Rue Karatchi 7. *INDIAN:* **Le Tajmahal**, Rue Pierre Parent 95. *VIETNAMESE:* **Le Kim-Mon**, Av. Mers Sultan 160. *KOREAN:* **Le Marignan**, Rue Moh. Smiha 69. *FISH:* **Port de Pêche**, at the harbor entrance.

Shopping
Books: D.S.M. and **Feraire**, both on Bd. Mohammed V. **Stamps And Coins: Cotter Philatelie**, Av. Hassan II./Passage Slaoui. **Berber Jewellery: Aux Arts Islamiques**, Passage Slaoui.

Transportation
RAIL: Gare Casa-Port, at the harbor, trains to Fes, Rabat, Tanger, Paris. **Gare Casa-Voyageur**, at the east end of Bd. Moh.V., trains to Marrakech. **BUS: CTM-LN Gare Routière** (bus terminal), Rue Leon l'Africain 23 near the Marché Central, Tel: 312061, extensive services throughout the country, airport bus. **RADIO TAXI:** Tel: 25 50 30. **HORSERIDING: Ould Jamal** and **Le Ranch**, Plage Sidi Abderrahman.

Tourist Information
ONMT, Rue Omar Slaoui 55, Tel: 271177. **Syndicat d'Initiative**, Bd. Mohammed V, Tel: 221524.

SOUTHERN ATLANTIC COAST

Azemmour

The small city of **Azemmour** is located some 85 km southwest of Casablanca where the Oum er Rbia flows silently into the Atlantic. It is, still today, surrounded by its ancient medieval walls. The images of its whitewashed houses are reflected in the clear waters of the river. This remarkably picturesque scene best comes to view when approaching the Oum er Rbia bridge. The residents of Azemmour for the most part make a living from fishing and from selling agricultural products that grow in the fertile Oum er Rbia Valley, in the first place vegetables, different kinds of grain and citrus fruits. Weekly markets are held here traditionally on Tuesdays and Fri-

Above: For more than two-and-a-half centuries the Portuguese were able to hold on to their fortress, Mazagan. Right: The fishing seaport of Essaouira.

days. Azemmour, together with the more important seaports of El Jadida, Safi, Essaouira and Agadir, are former fortified trading stations of the Portuguese, where the ships were heavily loaded with goods, particularly with gold and cloth, destinated for trade in the Black African Ivory Coast slave market.

Azemmour has a well-preserved **medina**, which can be reached via **Rue Allal ben Abdullah**, **Place du Souk** and the market gate, **Bab el Souk**. The **kisseria** (textile market) is situated just beyond this gate. Proceeding north from here, one comes across the ruins of **Dar el Baroud**, the kasbah's former ammunition storehouse, built in 1513 by the Portuguese. This is the oldest part of the city; and after it was reconquered by the Saadians in 1541, it was designated as a **mellah** (Jewish quarter). The wall, erected by the Portuguese, with its numerous bastions and cannons, can easily be climbed by means of a stairway at its northeastern end. Please note, however, that a guide is required for this endeavor..

A road branching off the Place du Souk towards the north and following the kasbah wall to **Marabout Sidi Ouadoud** (1.5 km) offers a spectacular view of the mouth of the Oum er Rbia. Back again at the Place du Souk and proceeding farther northeast, one arrives at the sandy Atlantic beach of Haouzia (2 km). Quite a number of small seafood restaurants can be found there.

El Jadida

Located 16 km west of Azemmour is the town of **El Jadida**. In 1502 the Portuguese built a small fort on the site of the ancient Phoenician settlement Rusibis, which they expanded in the year of 1506 to a fortified city named Mazagao (in French: Mazagan). Mazagan successfully defended itself against the unremitting attacks launched by the Berber tribes and the Saadian army in 1541. The defenders of Magazan, however, were the only ones to be successful - all the other Portuguese bases on the Atlantic fell to the attackers.

It was not until 1769 that Lisbon was forced to surrender the city under siege from the Alawi army. When the Portuguese eventually withdrew from Magazan, they blew up large sections of the city; and despite it being renamed El Jadida (the New One), the city was still shunned by the Moslems. The *cité portugaise*, as it became known, soon was forced upon the Jews of neighboring Azemmour as their living quarters instead.

The entrance to the Portuguese city is via **Rue Mohammed el Hachmi Bahbah** (former Rua da Carreira). The best view of the medieval fortifications is to be had from atop its formidable battlements. The tour, for which one must hire a guide, begins at a stairway off of **Rue Mina** (to the right just beyond the city gate) and leads to the **Bastion of the Holy Spirit**. In accordance with crusader customs, the projecting corner bulwarks were given pious names. From above one can recognize that the wall was also protected by a moat, which is now dry. From the **Angels Bastion**, with its panoramic view of the fishing harbor and old town, it is just a few steps to **Porta do Mar**, the former Portuguese gateway to the sea. The walk may be continued along the battlements to the bastions **St. Sebastian** and **St. Anthony**, or one might choose instead to climb down to the picturesque narrow streets below.

In sharp contrast to the traditional windowless Moslem home in the Moroccan medinas, the former Jewish houses here have both balconies and windows. The abandoned synagogue to the northeast can still be identified by its Star of David. This Baroque building was originally a Catholic church built in the 16th century. From Rue Mohammed el Hachmi Bahbah it is a short walk down to the **Citerne Portugaise**, which was built in 1541, the year of the siege. For a time it functioned as an armory and bunker, as well as a cistern. Its late-Gothic ribbed vault supported by 25 pillars is beautifully reflected in the water at the bottom.

Leaving El Jadida on the route touristique 1301, one can travel along the magnificient coast towards Safi until reaching the worthwhile lighthouse at **Cap Blanc** (20 km southwest), which affords a nice panoramic view. A large industrial port was built in the 1980's near the village of **El Jorf Lasfar** mainly in order to facilitate the export of phosphate, which is mined in the area around Youssoufia, and today represents an indispensible source of foreign exchange.

Following route S121 from Cap Blanc to Oualidia, one drives for some time past a cultivated lagoon region. Various spring vegetables such as tomatoes, carrots, green peppers and potatoes are grown in plastic-covered greenhouses. Salt is extracted from sea water in several salinas. Fossilized shoreline terraces are evidence for the indeed extreme fluctuations of the sea level. The area behind this part of the coast is called **Doukkala**, a region inhabited by Arab tribes and traditionally used for the cultivation of grain.

The small fishing village of **Oualidia** is picturesquely nestled on a wide sandy bay surrounded by steep cliffs. Its residents make a living from oyster farming and domestic summer tourism. Besides a kasbah from the 17th century and a former royal summer palace, there are also a few rather modest hotels, a campsite at the beach and a good seafood restaurant to be found here. Located 35 km farther south, along a breathtakingly wild and romantic craggy coastline, is the worthwhile Cap Bedouza. Proceeding another 30 km along the steep shoreline, which boasts many viewpoints, one finally arrives at the provincial capital of **Safi**.

Safi

Safi was built in 1480 by the Portuguese to serve as a major fortified seaport. The Portuguese were driven out in the fateful year 1541, but the city retained its significance as a trading center. It still has one of the most important seaports in the country, second only to Casablanca. Sardines, caught in great numbers in the Atlantic's chilly, plankton-filled waters where the Canary Stream runs, are processed in Safi itself. The port then, as a matter-of-course, plays a major role in their export to the world. A harbor and a factory for the production of phosphoric acid were erected in 1965. They are connected by rail to the phosphate quarries in the central mesa area.

The remarkable craftsmanship of Safi potters is known all over the nation. The potters have settled in the northeastern edge of the city, next to **Zawinya Sidi Abderrhaman**. The colorful Safi ceramics are still fired the traditional way in old ovens with tamarisk wood.

The **medina** and the **mellah** are well worth seeing and are both located within the walls built by the Portuguese in the 16th century. **Rue du Souk**, a bustling shopping street, begins just behind the old city gate, **Bab Chaabah**, where spec-

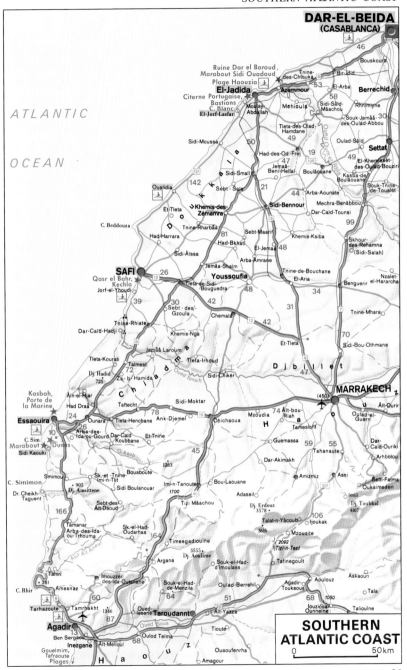

DAR-EL-BEIDA
(CASABLANCA)

46

Bouskoura

Ruine Dar el Baroud,
Marabout Sidi Ouadoud
Plage Haouzia   Tnine-
                    des-Chtouka   Bir-Jdid
El-Jadida   Azemmour   53   El-Arba   **Berrechid**
Citerne Portugaise,
Bastions   Moulay-   58
C. Blanc   Abdallah   Mehioula   Sidi-Saïd-
El-Jorf-Lasfar   Maachou   Rhnimiyne
                                                Souk-Jemâá- 30
                      Tleta-des-Olad-   des-Oulad-Abbou
Sidi-Moussa   Hamdane   **Settat**
                    50   49   Oulad-Saïd   49
                      Had-des-Od-Frej   19   El-Khemisat-
                            47   des-Oulad-Bouziri
              Sidi-Small   Jemâa-   105   Kasba-de-
                          Beni-Hellal Boulâouane   Boulâouane
Oualidia   142   Sebt-Saïd 21   Souk-Tnine-
                                      Arba-Aounate de-Toualet
Et-Tleta   44
Khemis-des-   **Sidi-Bennour** Mechra-Benâbbou
Zémamra   Dar-Caïd-Tounsi
C. Beddouza   99
         Tnine-Rharbâa   Skhour-
Had-Harrara   Sebt-Maârif   des-Rehamna
              81   (Sidi-Salah)
         Had-Bkhati   Khemis-Ksiba
Sidi-Aïssa   El-Jemâa 48
              Arba-Amrane   Nzalet-
         Jemâa-Shaïm   el-Hararcha
SAFI 26   Tnine-de-Bouchane
Qasr el Bahr, **Youssoufia**   El-Aria   Benguerir
Kechla   Tleta-de-Sidi-
Jorf-el-Yhoudi Bouguedra   48   Tnine-Mhara
      39   30 Sebt-des-   42   31
                Gzoula   70
      Tnine-Rhiate Chemaïa   12   42   Et-Tleta   Sidi-Bou-Othmane
Dar-Caïd-Hadji   Khemis-Nga
                Jemâa Laroum   Tleta-Irhoud
Tleta-Kourati Talmest   Sidi-Chiker   **Djibillet**
Dj. Hadid 72 Za-b-Hamida   47
     725
Kasbah, Aïn-el-Hjar   Sidi-Moktar   **MARRAKECH**
Porte de Had Draâ Taftecht 78   (459)   Aït-Ourir
la Marine 24 Ounara Tleta-Henchane Ank-Djemel Mzoudia 74 Aït-bou- Oulad-el-
Essaouira 26 Arba-des- Dar-Caïd   Chichaoua Riah Guern
C. Sim 10 Ida-ou-Gourd Koubbane Et-Tnine   Tameslont Dar-
Marabout Dunes   45   Guemassa   59 55 Caïd-Ouriki
Sidi Kaouki   Bouaboute 1263   Dar-Akimakh Tahanaute Arhbolou
C. Simimon Smimou   Imi-n-Tanoute   Bou-Laouane   Setti-Fatma
        905 Sidi Boulanouar 1700 40   Amizmiz Asni Oukaimeden
Dr. Cheikh- Dj. Amsittene   Adassil   Imlil
Taguent   Tizi Maachou   Dj. Erdouz   Dj. Toubkal
      166   Sebt-des-   3578   106   4167
          Aït-Daoud   Talat-n-Yácoub Ijoukak
Tamanar   3616   Mzouzite
Arba-des-Ida-   2092
ou-Trhouma Sk-el-Had-   Tizi-n-Test
      64   Oudarhas Timesgadiouine   Tafinegoult
              3555   Souk-el-Had-
           Argana Dj. Aoulime   d'Imoulass
C. Rhir 361 Imouzzer   Souk-el-Had-   Oulad-Berrehil   Agadir-   Aoulouz   Askaoun
   des-Ida-Outanane de-Menzila   Touksous 1050
Amesnaz   64   51   Aït-Yazza   Tala
Tamri 60   Iouzioua- Talioune
Tarhazoute Tamrhakht 1346 Oued- **Taroudannt**   Ounneïne
      8 87   Iessene   Tioute
Agadir   Ouled Telma
Ben Sergao   68   Ouaoufenrha
Inezgane Aït-Melloul   **H**
Gouelmim,   **a o u Z**
Tafraoute   Amagour
Plages

SOUTHERN
ATLANTIC COAST
0 _____ 50km

ATLANTIC

OCEAN

K l a

C h i a d m a

93

tators rally aound musicians and entertainers. Rue du Souk leads down to the **Boulevard du Front du Mer**. Unfortunately, the view of the ocean is obstructed by a railway line that passes over a pedestian underpass. Behind it lies the old seaport and the seaside castle of **Qasr el Bahr** – residence of the Portuguese governor in the first half of the 16th century. At the southeastern corner of the *medina,* the buildings of the old city are totally dwarfed by the ancient Portuguese stronghold of **Kechla**.

Traveling farther south, one soon crosses the **Oued Tensift** River just prior to reaching the market village of **Talmest**. The Oued Tensift originates in the Haouz Plateau near Marrakech. This region has been named **Chiadma** and is inhabited by Arab tribes. The Chiadma*, as* well as the Rehamma and Oulad Bou Sboa tribes, weave short-piled *gtifa* rugs, *kelims* and long-piled *chichaoua* rugs, which are decorated with ancient *wasm* symbols (brands).

Essaouira

Located some 55 km southwest of Talmest is the sightly seaport of **Essaouira** (formerly Mogador). It is said that already the Phoenicians operated manufactories for the production of purple (Tyrian) dye from sea snails on the neighboring Purple Isles. The Portuguese built the small seaport fortress of Mogador in 1506, but were driven out by 1541.

Essaouira, as it stands today, was built by the Alawi Sultan Sidi Mohammed in 1760. He had the city designed by one of his Christian prisoners, the French architect Theodore Cornut. It is partitioned by right-angled streets – an unusual feature for an oriental **medina**. Many buildings, of course, reflect European architectural styles, such as the harbor bastions.

Right: On the beach of Agadir, veils and jellabah are superfluous.

In 1765, Sultan Sidi Mohammed proclaimed Essaouira as Morocco's primary export harbor, which consequently attracted numerous Jewish merchants to the city – to this day its colloquial name is "Mellah". Particularly worth seeing is the idyllic **fishing harbor** and its town gate, **Porte de la Marine**, which was built in 1769. Improvised open-air restaurants serve the freshest sardines in the entire country. From the adjacent **Skala de la Kasbah**, the harbor fortress which is laden with Spanish bronze cannons, one has a formidable view of the medina, harbor and coastline.

It is enjoyable to stroll within the confines of the old city wall. Here one can stop off at the flea market, the jewelry bazaar, the spice and grain market and the alleys where the noted inlay artists of the city have their shops.

Inlay work from Essaouira is sold in souvenir shops throughout the country, but nowhere as reasonably priced as here. Silver threads and pieces of ebony or lemon wood are worked onto the surface of objects – from tea tables to tiny jewelry boxes – made of rose-, thuja- or cedar wood, to create intricate geometric and arabesque patterns.

The beaches in the dunes of **Diabat** and at **Cap Sim**, which are favored by surfers, are only accessible by somewhat rough roads; the pebble beach near **Sidi Kaouki Marabout** can be reached along the covered road numbered 6604.

South of Essaouira, in the arid foothills of the Western High Atlas Mountains, is where the thorny **argan tree** with its orange colored, olive-like fruit grows. This is the tree goatherds let their goats climb up into to "graze".

A somewhatt narrow road branches off highway P 8 just behind the Sunday marketplace of **Smimou** and eventually leads up to **Jebel Amsittene** (905 m, lookout tower), which is surrounded by a thuja forest and offers good hiking possibilities. The route CT 6664, which branches

off about 10 km after Smimou, takes one to a lonely beach at **Cap Smimou**, where many of the fishermen from the Berber *Hahah* tribe live in the summer.

Shortly before reaching **Tamri**, the road winds down to the valley of Assif Tinkert. Bananas are among the crops grown on a large scale in this valley due to its abundant groundwater and mild climate. Continuing along the steep coastline of **Cap Rhir**, the climate becomes increasingly dry; cactus-like euphorbia now line the road.

The beach at the fishing village of **Tarhazoute** is located 40 km south of Tamri. It is a popular destination for backpackers and RV-tourists (large campsite, seafood restaurant). Another 25 km farther south, past a sardine cannery and a cement factory, one arrives in Agadir, the tourist capital of Morocco.

AGADIR

The sea port of **Agadir** was completely rebuilt after a disasterous earthquake on February 20, 1960, and, consequently, the anticipated oriental flair is entirely missing. Only the ruins of the **Saadian kasbah** (dated 1541), perched 240 m above the city, are a reminder of old Agadir. Today sardines are processed and canned and various agricultural products from the Sous Valley (oranges, bananas and spring vegetables) are loaded onto big cargo ships in what is now one of Morocco's largest fishing harbors.

But the city's most important source of foreign exchange is definitely tourism. Basking a mild climate, and possessing a wide 8-km long magnificent sandy beach and a charter airport, "Sun City" can accommodate a great number of tourists throughout the year, and continuously takes a first place in the touristic statistics of the country (almost 4 million overnight stays per year). Numerous hotels of all categories have sprung up in the last 30 years, particularly in the vicinity of the beach (allegedly they are all earthquake-safe). Outside the peak season one can get very good deals at some of the large

95

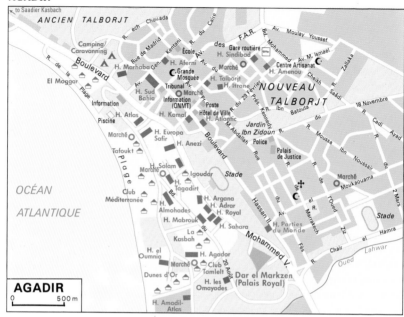

beachfront hotels. During high season, by way of contrast, it can be decidedly difficult to find accommodation anywhere at all along the overcrowded beachfront area. Boutiques, restaurants, bars and travel agencies line the three main streets running parallel to each other:**Boulevard du 20 Aout**, **Boulevard Mohammed V** and **Avenue Hassan II**.

Day Trips from Agadir

For those who would like to familiarize themselves with the southwestern corner of the country, cars can be rented without any difficulty in Agadir. Beaches to the south, especially the area around **Sidi Rbat**, **Sidi Ouassai** at the mouth of the Oued Massa, **Sidi Moussa d'Aglou** and **Tiznit** can all be reached within a day. A trip to **Taroudannt** in the Sous region can also be tackled in a day easily. Many travel agencies offer both interesting and inexpensive bus excursions to the royal city of Marrakech, to **Guelmim** particularly for the Sunday "camel mar-

ket" and to the town of **Tafraoute** in the Anti Atlas (Wednesday market).

Another very worthwhile outing is to the scenic waterfall at **Immouzzer des Ida Outanane**. On the way to the waterfall, one crosses the beautiful mountain valley of **Assif Tamrakht**, which is covered with red and white oleanders and has therefore been nicknamed "Paradise Valley". Immouzzer lies picturesquely at the foot of the impressive Western High Atlas, and is surrounded by very dense arghan forests. From spring to late autumn one can swim in the cool water of the falls, picnic under shady arghan and olive trees, or dine exquisitely in one of the numerous garden restaurants. The Honey Festival is celebrated here in May of each year. Far off the beaten track, one can enjoy peaceful hikes and leisurely walks at altitudes between 1,000 - 1,400 m. There are still many mountain trails here to be discovered by intrepid bikers who are properly equipped with a compass, an air pump, repair kit (argan trees have long thorns!) and water gourds.

SOUTHERN ATLANTIC COAST
Accommodation

EL JADIDA: *MODERATE:* **Doukkala**, Rue de la Ligue Arabe, Tel: 3737. **Palais Andalous**, Rue Curie, Tel: 3906. *BUDGET*: **Royal**, Av. Mohammed V, Tel: 2839. **Suisse**, Rue Zerktouni 145, Tel: 2816.

OUALIDIA: *BUDGET:* **Hippocampe**, Tel: 111. **Auberge de la Lagune**, Tel: 105.

SAFI: *MODERATE:* **Safir**, Av. Zerktouni, Tel: 4299. **Atalantique**, Rue Chaouki, Tel: 2160. *BUDGET:* **Anis**, Rue de Rabat, Tel: 3078. **Assif**, Av. de la Liberté, Tel: 2311.

ESSAOUIRA: *MODERATE:* **Des Iles**, Bd. Mohammed V, Tel: 2329. **Tafoukt**, Bd. Mohammed V, Tel: 2504. *BUDGET:* **Sahara**, Av. Okba Ibn Nafia, Tel: 2292. **Tafraout**, Rue de Marrakech 7, Tel: 2120.

Restaurants
ESSAOUIRA: **Chalet de la Plage**, Bd. Mohammed V, Tel: 2158

AGADIR
Accommodation

LUXURY: **Sahara**, Bd. Mohammed V, Tel: 840660. *MODERATE:* **Almohades**, Bd. du 20 Aout. Tel: 840233. **Europa Safir**, Bd. du 20 Aout, Tel: 821212. **Atlas**, Bd. Mohammed V, Tel: 823232. **Anezi**, Bd. Mohammed V, Tel: 840940. **Kamal**, Av. Hassan II, Tel: 823940. **El Oumnia**, Chemin Oued Souss, Tel: 840352. **Sud Bahia**, Rue des Administrations Publiques, Tel: 840741. **Adrar**, Bd. Mohammed V, Tel: 840737. **Salam**, Bd. Mohammed V, Tel: 840120. **Amadil**, Secteur Touristique, Tel: 840620. *BUDGET:* **Sindibad**, Pl. Lahcen Tamri, Tel: 823477. **Atlantic**, Av. Hassan II, Tel: 823662. **5 Parties du Monde**, Av. Hassan II, Tel: 822545. **Amenou**, Rue Yakoub el Mansour 1, Tel: 823026. **Itran**, Rue de l'Entraide, Tel: 821407.

Restaurants
FRENCH: **La Langouste**, Chemin Oued Souss, Tel: 823636. **La Mer**, Bd. du 20 Aout, Tel: 825341. *MOROCCAN:* **La Pampa**, Pl. Prince Sidi Mohammed, Tel: 822831. **Chez Mania**, Rue General Kettani. *FISH:* **La Piscine**, Rue de La Plage. **Du Port**, at the harbor. **Perla del Mare**, Residence Tafoukt. *GERMAN:* **Marine Heim bei Hilde**, Bd. Mohammed V, Tel: 822131. **Glacerie** (ice cream parlor), Residence Tafoukt. *ITALIAN:* **Mister Piccolo**, Residence Tafoukt. **Via Veneto**, Av. Hassan II. **Pizzeria Annoual**, Av. Prince Sidi Mohammed. **Miramar**, Bd. Mohammed V. *CHINESE:* **La Tonkinoise**, Av.

Prince Sidi Mohammed. **Kim Hoa**, Bv. du 20 Aout, Complexe l'Agador.

Nightlife
Biblos, Hotel Dunes d'Or. **Sherazad**, Bd. Mohammed V. **Tan-Tan Club**, Bd. des Dunes. **Jazz-Bar**, Bd. du 20 Aout.

Shopping
Weekly Market: (food, household utensils, simple jewellery) Saturday and Sunday in the walled-in *souk*-complex on the southeast fringe of town. **Souvenirs: Uniprix** (fixed prices), Bd. Hassan II. **Crafts: Ensemble Artisanal** (state shop, fixed prices), Rue du 29 Février.

Sport
WINDSURFING: Rental boards at the Hotel **Dunes d'Or**. *TENNIS:* **Royal Club de Tennis**, Av. Hassan II. Many hotels have their own tennis courts. *HORSERIDING:* For individual riders 500 m south of the Dunes d'Or. **Club Equestre**, 12 km southeast on the road to Ait Melloul. *GOLF:* **Royal Club de Golf**, 12 km on the road to Ait Melloul, Tel: 831278.

Transportation
AIR: Royal Air Maroc, Av. Général Kettani, Tel: 840808. **Aeroport Agadir – Inezgane** (8 km), Tel: 31418. **BUS: Gare Routière**, Rue Yacoub el Mansour, near the Hotel Sindibad (larger selection of overland buses in **Inezgane**, 12 km). **RENTAL CARS:** Avis, Av. Hassan II, Tel: 840345. **Europcar/Interrent**, at the airport and Bv. Mohammed V, Tel: 840337. **Hertz**, Av. Mohammed V, Tel: 840939. **Budget**, Av. Mohammed V, Tel: 823762. **MOTORCYCLES**: Bd. du 20 Aout/corner Hotel Atlas. **TAXI:** Place Es Salam. **Petit Taxi** (yellow roof, town service only), short distance rate 5-10 DH. **Grand Taxi** (blue, long distance), to the airport: 50 DH.

Hospitals
Hôpital Hassan II, Av. Al Moun, Tel: 822477. **Polyclinique**, Bd. Moulay Youssef, Tel: 824956.

Pharmacies
Grande Pharmacie d'Agadir, Av. Moulay Abdallah, Immeuble M 1, Tel: 20989. *NIGHT SERVICE:* **Municipalité d'Agadir**,Tel: 820349.

Tourist Information / Post
ONMT, Pl. Prince H. S. Mohammed, Tel: 822894. **Syndicat d'Initiative**, Bd. Mohammed V, Tel: 822695. *POST:* **PTT**, Av. Prince H. S. Mohammed.

MOORISH
MIDDLE AGES

**FÈS
MEKNES
VOLUBILIS
MOULAY IDRISS**

FÈS

"Huna fas!" – "There lies Fès!" Even from a distance the taxi driver from Rabat can't conceal his fascination with the city, which is also foreign to him. In his voice is that particular tone of enthusiasm that can also be read between the lines penned by Leo Africanus, one highly educated Moslem who was born in Granada and grew up in the former sultanate city of Fès. As a protégée of Renaissance Pope Leo X in 16th-century Rome, he wrote one of the earliest descriptions of Fès in a European language.

Today, at the close of the 20th century, the medina in Fès gives one the impression of being transported back to medieval times. All the people here, like the buildings, seem to come directly from another century: Forbidding walls keep the interiors of the old houses from view; veils or jellabah-hoods conceal the faces of passers-by; and the craftsmen's ateliers would better suit, for instance, the 16th than the 20th century.

In the course of time Fès has acquired a three-fold image: as "Holy City" and the intellectual-Islamic center of the Magh-

Previous pages: Fes el Bali is to be preserved with support from UNESCO. Left: Bab Boujeloud is a gate to the Middle Ages.

reb with its Kairawine University, which has produced significant *ulema* (religious scholars); as the capital of craftsmen and industrious merchants and as a city of contradictions – the difference between what the *fassi* (inhabitants of Fès) say and actually do is legendary. This character trait is aptly described by a Moroccan proverb that Paul Bowles cites in his Fès-based novel, *The Spider's House*:

"You say you're going to Fès. But when you say you're going to Fès, then it means that you're not going to Fès. However, I just happen to know that you are going to Fès. Why do you lie to me – you, my friend?"

From Idriss II to Hassan II

Once Sultan Idriss II had finally made up his mind to found a capital city for his dynasty, he made a lengthy search for a suitable place. The decision was finally made in favor of a valley to the south of the Jebel Zelagh. He purchased the region from two Berber tribes for 5,000 dirham. It is said that on February 3, 808, he personally determined the course of the walls and position of the city gates.

The newly established city of Fès attracted Berbers and Arabs, Christians and Jews alike. The Berbers settled on the right-hand bank of the Oued Fès, the

Arabs on the left bank. In the year 814 about 300 families who had fled from Cordoba in Andalusia, joined the Berbers; since then the eastern part of the city has always been referred to as the Andalusian Quarter. A similarly large number of refugees from Kairawine, a holy city in northeastern Tunesia, arrived in the city in 825. They settled in a quarter on the left bank of the river which was then named *Kairawine* after their place of origin. Years later, the grandson of Idriss II had mosques for Friday prayer constructed in both quarters – the Andalusian and Kairawine mosques.

The city's history was very turbulent during the first centuries of its existence. The two city districts were separated by a wall, due to the constant differences and never-ending rivalries between its inhabitants, both of whom then formed their own independent cities. Despite all of the internal unrest and a number of external threats, Fès developed very rapidly into a relatively prosperous and indeed affluent city. Mosques, baths and *fondouks* (merchant's inns) were built, as well as new and longer ramparts.

In the 11th century the Almoravids conquered the city and had the wall between its two main sectors immediately torn down. In addition, they enlarged the Kairawine Mosque. The obvious economic upswing, which had begun under the Almoravids in connection with the flourishing trade with Spain, also continued during the 12th century under the Almohad dynasty.

The Merinids captured Fès in 1248, and the city regained its former status of a capital which it had lost under the Almohads and Almoravids in favor of Marrakech. The era of the Merinids, which meant three centuries of peace and order, was a true blossoming period for Fès. The Merinid sultan Abu Youssef had a new

Right: A lot helps a lot – offertory box at the frequently visited mausoleum of Idriss II.

city, Fès el Jedid, erected next to the old city, Fès el Baliu. In the 14th and 15th centuries, with more than 100,000 inhabitants, Fès was not only a significant city for trading and craftsmanship, but also evolved into the intellectual and scholarly center of North Africa. As heir to the Spanish-Moorish culture following the Christian reconquest of Andalusia, Fès in the course of time simply became *the* metropolis of western Islam.

Around the middle of the 16th century the city began to decline with the advent of the Saadian dynasty. Only Ahmed el Mansour, the most famous of the Saadian sultans, showed any interest in Fès at all. Indeed, he had the already remarkable collection of the library at the Kairawine Mosque further expanded; on the other hand, though, he had two fortresses (Borj Sud and Borj Nord) constructed outside of the city walls – not for the defense of the city, but rather to maintain his control over its residents.

Under the Alawite ruler Moulay Rashid, Fès became capital city once again, albeit for six years only. He ordered the construction of the Cherarda kasbah, a barracks-like installation for his Berber troops. He also arranged for the restoration of the Medersa Cherratine, the largest of the city's Koran schools. During the brief period of Moulay Rashid's rule the tomb of Idriss I was also enlarged, the city walls considerably strengthened and a new bridge constructed over the Oued Sebou to ease access to the city for the caravans from Taza.

During the 18th and 19th centuries the city experienced riots, famines, epidemics, sieges, plundering and various other symptoms of bellicose times. The gates were demolished and then reconstructed. After the death of Sultan Moulay Hassan in 1894, the life of the royal court became increasingly decadent and European influence over Morocco grew ever stronger. Moulay Abd el Aziz, a mere spoiled child, acceded to the throne. Dubious ad-

Agglomerate Fès

visors of questionable loyalty caused the state ever greater debt, and let the sultan to distance himself from the city's religious leaders. These ultimately withdrew their support for him, and in 1908 named his elder brother Hafiz as the new sultan. This in turn displeased the Berber tribes in the vicinity, with the result that they laid siege to the city once again. The only thing left for the sultan to do at this point was to enlist the aid of French troops. In May, 1911, Christian troops entered Fès for the first time. The French Protectorate chose to move the capital to the more controllable Rabat and Fès, once the uncontested center of the country, has played little more than a bit part on the political stage since then.

Although Allal el Fassi, the leader of the Moroccan independence movement during the Protectorate, came from Fès, the majority of the city's residents could hardly be mobilized during the struggle for liberation. Nowadays, Hassan I pays a visit to the city of his ancestors once a year on his tour of Morocco.

The development of Fès was promoted by several interconnected factors. For one, the Sais Plain, its agrarian surroundings, is extroardinarily fertile. The cedar and oak forests of the Atlas Mountains, which supplied building materials for housing as well as working materials for many different businesses based on handicrafts, were once a mere 30 kilometers from the city. Numerous springs and as well the Oued Fès, which carries water throughout the year, insured ample supplies of drinking water for the city. Many of the buildings in the medina even had their own fountain.

Fès' position as a trading center for the caravans traveling between the Atlantic and Algeria and as a stopover in the trans-Saharan trading route between the Niger and the Mediterranean practically insured its rise as the undisputed commercial center of western Maghreb. The many fondouks in the old city are a reminder of this affluent medieval period.

Fès does not solely consist of the historical city quarters **Fès el Bali**, which is located in the valley, and **Fès el Jedid**, which was established on the plateau above the former. Considerably removed from the residential areas of the indigenous population is the spaciously proportioned *ville nouvelle*, established by the French overlords during the period of their mandate. In recent decades, modern residential satellites and makeshift slum lodgings (*bidonvilles*) were appended to the old city and the French new city. These provide sometimes decent, sometimes less so, housing for the city's over 600,000 residents.

Merely a small fraction of the people living in Fès today are *fassis* in the true sense of the word. The majority of the older traditional merchant families have already emigrated to the modern economic metropolis of Casablanca; rural emigrés have in turn taken over the existing housing and the former inhabitants' occupations in the Fès medina.

Medina Fès el Bali

In order to get a good overview of the old city, one should first set off on the posted "Tour de Fès" around the medina. Unforgettable panoramic views open up particularly to the north of the Merinid cemetery (*tombeaux mérinides*). Other great vistas open up from the **Borj Nord** fortress, currently housing an armament museum, as well as to the south from a *musalla* (place of prayer) at the **Borj Sud**, which can easily be reached on foot from the Bab Ftouh.

One might get the impression that all of **Fès el Bali** is one huge museum, but that would be far from the truth – the medina is very much alive! Over a quarter-million people live and work in the old city, which was elevated to the status of a cultural monument by the UNESCO in 1976. Since it is virtually impossible to find the way through the labyrinthine al-

leyways of the medina alone on one's first visit, it is advisable to take along a guide (settle the price beforehand!) in order to best enjoy Fès.

Of course, the way the alleys are paved make a rough orientation possible for the "insider", but that's not much help to a European (*rumi*) unfamiliar with the locality. The narrow streets and alleyways, the dense crowds supplemented by donkeys and mules – the only means of transport in this pedestrian zone – make getting one's bearing that much more difficult. A good rule of thumb: all paths leading downhill bring the visitor to the city's center, while those going uphill lead to the city's gates – or out, in other words. Whenever one hears the call *balek!*

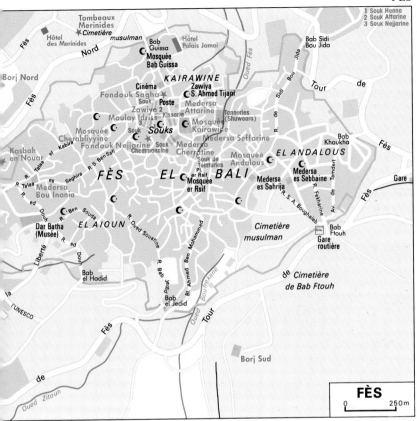

1 Souk Henna
2 Souk Attarine
3 Souk Nejjarine

balek! one should immediately clear the way as a heavily laden mule, maybe carrying dripping-wet hides from a tannery (and quite possibly taking up the entire width of the alley) is on the advance!

The city gates are the starting and at the same time the ending points of any visit to Fès. In order to make access to the medina easier, several additional openings have been cut into the city wall. One of the most important access-points for the general public is the main thoroughfare (built in 1974) from the former **Bab el Had** in the south to the **Plaza Er Rsif**, by way of which one can get to the heart of the medina with the taxi or the bus. The buildings that once stood along this route were wantonly demolished and, in

addition, the Oued Fès was canalized in order to create this approach.

The gates, which are still very traditional in structure and function, include the Bab Boujeloud, Bab Guissa and Bab Ftouh. **Bab Boujeloud** gives access to the medina from the west. Located in the neighborhood of this gate are a bus station, taxi-stand, inexpensive travelers' hotels, restaurants, street cafés and a cinema. Following the major lanes **Talaa el Kebira** and **Talaa el Seghira** one arrives directly at the **kisseria** and the **Kairawine mosque** in the center of the medina.

Bab Ftouh in the southeast is the entrance to the Andalusian Quarter. **Bab Guissa** in the north, once the traditional city gate for the farmers from the Rif re-

gion, is nowadays primarily used for the delivery of raw materials for craftsmen and retail businesses, including particularly wood, hides, olives and other agricultural products. For this reason many woodworking operations and oil presses are located in this area.

Mosques, Medersas and Zawiyas

The religious buildings constructed during the course of the Middle Ages are almost beyond count. Undoubtedly the most important facility of its kind is the **Kairawine mosque**, which was built in the year 862 and expanded during the first half of the 12th century under Ali ben Youssouf. It features 16 naves with 21 bays each, divided by 15 rows of columns, with a capacity of over 20,000 faithful. In the 14th century it was the center of a university, which was attended by as many as 8,000 students from

Above: Morocco's religious center is the old and venerable Kairaouine mosque.

every reach of the Islamic world during its heyday, and where they were instructed in Islamic theology and law. The Kairawine was and continues to be the religious center of Morocco, and its Koran scholars are the highest authority in questions of faith. Other mosques, also important though built later on, include the 9th century **Andalusian mosque** and the Merinid **Cherabliyyine mosque** on the Talaa el Kebira. Since setting foot in a mosque is forbidden to all non-Muslims without exception, it is merely possible to catch a quick glimpse of the temple courtyards when the gates are open.

The numerous Koran schools for preschool children, called *msid* in Fès, are easily overlooked even though they are quite audible. Almost all of them are still in use today. The Koran preschools in the medina can be distinguished by their large windows, equipped with elaborately lathed cedar latticework and a door in the same style. They are mostly located at lane intersections in the neighborhood of mosques (for example in the **Bou Touil** lane to the north of the Kairawine mosque). The children incessantly recite verses from the Koran in song under the strict supervision of their teachers.

Already under the Almohads, Fès had become known in the Maghreb as an intellectual and religious center. The first *medersa* wasn't founded, however, until the year 1323 – the **Medersa Seffarine.** The Merinids constructed the majority of medersas in Fès, some of which can also be characterized as independent schools, although others served merely as lodging for students of the Kairawine university. Curricula, organization and examinations of the sort we are familiar with today did not exist then. The most renowned Meridid medersas are the **Medersa Bou Inania**, established in 1351 in the Talaa el Kebira, and the **Medersa Attarine**, that was founded in 1330, situated next to the Kairawine mosque. Both of them are no longer in use and may therefore be visited. The students who lived in the Medersa Attarine came from the cities of the north – Tangiers, Larache and Kasr el Kebir. Residing in the **Medersa Cherratine**, the largest in Fès, were students from the Rif Mountains, eastern Morocco and from Algeria as well. Depending on their places of origin, the students preferred the medersas of their fellow countrymen, were they lived in spartan cells in almost monastic seclusion.

The **Medersa Bou Inania**, named after its founder, the Merinid sultan Abou Inan, is fascinating for its lucid architecture and profuse Moorish ornamentation consisting primarily of sculptured plaster arabesques, geometrically tiled mosaics and ornately carved cedar. A diversion of the Oued Fès separates the square interior courtyard, which is inlaid with white and rose-colored marble, from the prayer hall, which shelters the mihrab.

Somewhat smaller, but almost more impressive and even more playful in its ornamentation is the **Medersa Attarine**, a masterpiece of Merinid architecture from the early 14th century. One passes through a gateway with folding bronze doors with fine chase-work to get to the interior courtyard, in the midst of which stands a marble ablution chalice reminiscent of a floral calyx. Of further interest are the tiled mosaics in the courtyard walls displaying variations on a type of octagonal motif, referred to as Solomon's seal in Morocco. Also worthy of note are the arabesques composed of small pieces of chiseled tile in the passage (overarched by *muquarna* vaults) to the prayer hall, whose chief ornament is a very weighty bronze chandelier dating from 1329.

The most important zawiya of Fès is the **burial shrine** of Moulay Idriss II, the city's founder and patron saint. The structure, which was erected in the 13th century during the Merinid period and restored during the 15th century, is second only to the tomb of Idriss I in the city of Moulay Idriss as most important pilgrimage destination in Morocco. At this spiritually beneficial place, which is traditionally visited primarily by women, the pilgrims can beseech the saint for his *baraka* (blessings).

Crafts and Trade

Craftsmanship and various kinds of trade have always composed the economic backbone of Fès. Conscious of this fact, the city authorities – the pasha and his executive body – once kept all business activities under the strict supervision of market overseers, who had control over very nearly every aspect of the crafts and trades. The individual branches of these were organized into guilds (*hanta*) and were required to produce and/or sell their wares all concentrated in one place. Their combined efforts, however, were oriented solely towards preservation of the already-existant organization of production and marketing. As a result, a free market economy was unable to develop in Fès until the mid-20th century.

Among many of the crafts, the old traditional methods and technologies have been preserved to some extent, even though raw materials are often shipped in from Europe. Individual barterers, the horn comb-maker, the scissors-sharpener, the needle or awl maker, the slippers-maker, the lathe turner, the mosaic tile worker and many other practitioners of the traditional crafts are found scattered over the entire city. It is hardly possible to list them all; instead one will just have to discover them for oneself, step by step, in the medina of Fès.

When in Fès it is especially worthwhile visiting and observing the tanner, tinsmith, dyer and weaver at their common workplaces, where they have been producing their wares for centuries.

The **Dyers' Lane** (*souk des teinturiers*) runs along the western bank of the Oued Fès to the north of the Er Rsif square.

Above: The machine age has not yet reached Fès el Bali. Right: Plain pomegranite skins dye leather yellow.

Nowadays the craftsmen only dye wool and silk on occasion; they now work primarily with synthetic fibers. Instead of natural dyes, they now make do with chemicals. In the buildings along the street, men with soot-blackened faces prepare vats of dye for coloring skeins of yarn. The excess dye is wrung out of the bundles with short wooden sticks and it runs together into a dark black rivulet down the pavement stones of the lane.

Leaving the dyers and following the road two turns to the north, one eventually arrives at the **Place Seffarine**, were the coppersmiths are. Here the smiths hammer away at the large copper kettles which are either rented or sold to the rural population for use at their feasts. Especially important is that the kettles are lined with tin inside so they don't become toxic when heated.

Still further to the north, also on the left bank of the Oued Fès, one comes upon the largest of the three traditional tanneries, the **Shuwaara**, where cow, sheep and goat hides are processed. Laborers in

short pants balance on the edges of the vats with lime, pigeon droppings and clay, and frequently stand thigh-deep in the troughs of tanning-bark. Not only the repulsive filth, but also the intolerable stench make this work extremely hard for these men who practice one of the most scorned professions in Islamic society. Located in the midst of the city is the **Sidi Moussa** tannery (produces camel, cow and sheep leather); in the northeast is the **Ain Azliten** (only goatskin), the newest tannery, which was not established until the end of the 19th century.

In many of the medina's alleyways one can perceive a peculiar rhythmic noise – the clatter of the weavers' shuttle, which is flung back and forth from one catchrack to the other with the aid of a whiplike line. The weavers produce the fabrics for the full-lengths *jellabahs,* the traditional garment of the *fassis.* The buildings and chambers used exclusively by weavers are called *drez* in Fès. One of the most interesting and oldest *drez,* in which some 40 weavers ply their trade on three

stories, is located to the north of the Kairawine mosque.

The shops of the various types of merchants are situated in the center of the medina*,* as is true in all oriental cities. The *kisseria*, the central market place that can be closed off, is located exactly between the Kairawine mosque and the mausoleum of Moulay Idriss II. Within it the most sumptuous of wares are on sale, including scarves, silk, brocade, gold embroidery and also expensive slippers. The kisseria in Fès has burned down several times, most recently in the 1950's. The shops in the kisseria can – in contrast to all the other stores in the souks – be closed with metal shutters.

Those who choose to pass some time in the neighborhood of the slippers-shops between 4 and 7 P.M. will have a chance to admire a rather peculiar spectacle: Venerable men course through the lanes shouting out prices with an armfull of *babouches* (slippers), surrounded by many other men who are no less respectable. The latter are the *dallal*, the middlemen between the craftsmen and the bazaar merchants. Another similar dallal market exists for all kinds of clothing (mornings in the kisseria) and for leather (afternoons at the Bab Guissa).

In the vicinity of the kisseria there are a great variety of souks installed in the open squares and many alleyways. In the **Souk Attarine** (to the northwest of the kisseria), so-called "drug dealers" sell devotionals, candles and prayer-beads. The lane of the cabinetmakers (between Zawiya Moulay Idriss II and Talaa es seghira) opens into the **Souk Nejjarine**. The main eye-catcher of this plaza is the **Nejjarine Fountain**, which is sheathed in multicolored tile mosaics. At the **Souk Henna**, an idyllic plaza with a gigantic tree near the zawiya Moulay Idriss II, henna (as the name already indicates) is sold, plus articles for personal hygiene, pottery and ceramic wares. Fruits, figs, dates and sweets can best be sampled and purchased at the **Souk Chemmannine** to the south of the kisseria. Here one can also find gold embroidery work, such as proverbs from the Koran done on a dark velvet background.

Also located in the immediate vicinity are a number of fondouks, former trading houses that are utilized today primarily by wholesalers as warehouses. The **Fondouk Nejjarine** in the souk of the same name is one of the most beautiful of these; the oldest is the **Fondouk Sagha** in the Ashabine quarter, where mainly wool is stored. The **Fondouk Tétouan**, located near the Karawine mosque, is a former trading house and warehouse for merchants from the city of the same name.

Eating, Drinking and Relaxation

At **Sidi Mohammed's** in the Ashabine quarter (center of the medina) one can eat both well and inexpensively. His simple,

Right: Metalwork is a handicraft rich in tradition in the Medina.

clean restaurant is located near the cinemas. Recommended to those inclined to indulge in a rather more opulent Fès dining experience are the restaurants **Dar Tajine** in the south of the medina and **Al Firdaous** in the area of the Bab Guissa, both of which are installed in elaborately renovated traditional townhouses. The roof terrace of the restaurant **Palais de Fès** (next door to the Kairawine mosque) is the best place to sip a cup of *thé à la menthe*. From there one can take in the fantastic view over the old city, and peer into the courtyard of the mosque.

Sooner or later even the most fascinated traveler becomes tired, the white and blue mosaics suddenly start to dance before his eyes, and the mind, fatigued from the bewildering whirl of impressions gathered during the day, begins to clamor for relaxation and quiet. In order to extricate oneself from the confusing snarl of alleyways in the medina, one can either flee to "high society" or seek refuge in the "scene". The first plunges one into the midst of twittering birds and the intoxicating scent of an ocean of flowers at the garden of the **Palais Jamai**, a former viziers' palace, which, some time ago, has been remodelled into a hotel. It is located near the Bab Guissa, from which one can look down over the medina's maze of alleyways and buildings. The splendor of wealth is just as much a part of Fès as the dust of poverty. The second alternative, closer to the real life of Fès, is a visit to one of the kif cafés in the Ashabine quarter, which – it should explicitly be mentioned – are solely accessible to men. Should a woman, however, absolutely insist on intruding into this domain of the Moroccan male, then she should definitely be accompanied by a man. Caution is well advised in these establishments, where, among other things, the Fès underworld makes its dealings, and kif and hashish are smoked while idlers recline on reed mats, passing the hours with conversation, dice and card games.

The most satisfactory conclusion to a day in the medina is a visit to one of the Moorish baths (*hammam*), which are a part of everyday life for the Fès residents. The 700-year-old Merinid **Hammam Al Awiya Sidi Bel Abd** to the south of the kisseria offers an equal combination of pleasure and sightseeing. After a thorough cleansing in the hot and cold rooms and professional massage from the bath attendant one will have long forgotten the stresses and strains of the day while relaxing in the salon under a cubical cupola of old cedar wood.

Merinid Fès el Jedid

The Merinid city of **Fès el Jedid** was erected under sultan Abu Youssef in the year 1276, just beyond Fès el Bali. It was to house the administration, the army and the retinue of the ruler's court. As the Merinid governmental and administrative seat was laid out according to clearput clans, the visitor can get his or her bearings quite easily to this day.

The royal palace **Dar el Makzhen** is still used by Hassan II and his retinue when they pay their annual visit to Fès. Unfortunately, since the palace cannot be toured even during the ruler's absence, visitors must be satisfied with the view of the copiously ornamented entrance gate in classical Moorish style at the **Place des Alawites.** Doubtlessly, the brass smiths of Fès produced one of their veritable masterpieces here.

Situated south of the palace is the former Jewish quarter, the so-called **Mellah**. During the 14th century the Jews had to leave Fès el Bali and were forcibly settled here. As wards of the sultan (as were all Christians too) they had to pay a poll tax, which meant that the ruler always had direct access to his most important and secure source of income. The majority of the former inhabitants left their quarter in the 60s and headed in the direction of Israel. But it is still possible to discern the Jewish residential buildings by their numerous wooden balconies and wrought-iron latticework, a sure indication that

Jewish houses were more street oriented than that of the Moslems. It is worth paying a visit to the Jewish cemetery, which is located on the southern edge of the quarter, where several marble-sheathed tombs bear witness to the affluence of the former Mellah residents.

At the end of the bustling **Grande Rue du Mellah**, one finally comes upon the **Bab Semmarine**, which is adjacent to an impressive Merinid market hall. Here one has a chance to observe the housewives in their inexorable and steadfast haggling with the produce sellers, or the fish merchant confronting his assistant who, despite all his instructions, has failed to use enough water to keep the fish fresh.

The **Grande Rue de Fès el Jedid** starts behind the Bab Semmarine. It is the most important bazaar street in the Moslem district of Fès el Jedid, leading toward the north to the Bab es Seba.

Above: Moorish art is alive. In 1968 the new gate to the king's palace was built. Right: "Chebakia" – sweet, rich, delicious!

About halfway along this stretch, on the lefthand side, one will come across a Merinid building complex with a *hammam*, toilets and a baking oven. One should at least have a look at, if not make use of, the public toilet facilities, in which there is also a booth reserved solely for women – a rarity in the city's lavatory facilities.

Standing at the end of the souk street is the **Bab es Seba**, where casual laborers and craftsmen (who have brought their tools along) await potential clients. Past the gate, at the north entrance of the royal palace, is the old **Mechouar**, a square in which military drill exercises were carried out and was not actually constructed until the end of the 19th century. The west side of the plaza, which is delimited by high walls, is formed by the **Makina**, an armaments factory of the same age, built and managed by Italians. Nowadays it houses a carpet weavery.

Departing from here one can either head north through the **Bab Segma** and thus come upon the over three hundred-year-old **Cherarda Kasbah**, which

nowadays shelters a hospital and the university's theological department, or one can turn east from the Bab es Seba and so pass, en route to the Bab Boujeloud, the park grounds of the **Jardins Boujeloud**, which are located between Fès el Jedid and Fès el Bali. From the gardens it is not far to the **Dar Batha Museum of Handicrafts**, which has been installed in a former viziers'palace.

MEKNES

Meknes is situated in a fertile, amply watered plain right between the Zerhoun mountain range, which has just plentiful springs, and the Central Atlas. At first Meknes was merely an agglomeration of small villages, established in the 10th century by the Meknassa Berbers of the Zenata tribe of eastern Morocco. They named their settlement Meknassa es Sitoun – "Meknes of the Olive Trees". Under Roman rule, olive trees had already been cultivated in plantations as early as the first century A.D. The actual founding

year of the city was 1063, when the Almoravids erected a fortress here. Meknes then developed into a significant and frequently battled-over trading city due to its location, optimal for commerce since it was at the point of intersection for the major caravan routes. These connected the Islamic lands of the east with the Moroccan Atlantic plains and the Mediterranean seaport of Tangiers with the then affluent Sahel countries to the south. The Merinid sultan Abu El Hassan (1331-1351) began the construction of a medersa in Spanish-Moorish style, which was finally brought to completion by his son – and rival aspirant to the throne – Abu Inan (1348-1358).

Nonetheless, Meknes didn't achieve its rank as a royal city until the 17th century, when sultan Moulay Ismail (1672-1727), the most important ruler of the Arabic Alawite dynasty (still in power today), decided to establish his residence there.

During the 55 years of his rule he gave his insatiable passion for building free reign: about 25 kilometers of stamped

113

mud walls, 20 monumental gates, palaces, subterranean prisons, barracks, warehouses, stables and aqueducts were built in Meknes alone. Some 30,000 prisoners sentenced to forced labor, among them 2,000 Christian victims of the Salé pirates as well as countless black slaves, were forced to work for the sultan – and when their strength left them they were beheaded by the ruler personally and mixed right into the building materials. In order to make sure that he always had enough manpower at his disposal for his grandiose undertakings, he had his Black elite soldiers (who were also in bondage and even systematically bred) trained as masons. To this day the descendants of these soldiers are employed as King Hassan II's retinue of bodyguards.

Moulay Ismail's harem is said to have included more than 500 women with whom the sultan sired some 500 sons – at

Above: Bab Mansour is the entrance to the royal city of Moulay Ismail. Right: A jellabah gives protection from sun as well as rain.

best, his daughters weren't counted, at worst they were strangled at birth. He also had the ambition to marry Marie-Anne of Bourbon, later the Princess of Conti, an illegitimate daughter of Louis XIV, but the French court didn't take his appeals seriously at all.

Among the greatest challenges Moulay Ismail faced was the pacification of rebellious Berber tribes in the Atlas, who not only refused to pay tribute to the sultan, but also attacked his cities. For this reason he had Kasbahs laid out at strategically important points in his domain. These included particularly several garrisons for quartering horsemen, such as Chefchaouen and Kasbah Tadlah.

The English occupiers of Tangier were besieged by him for years, until they finally withdrew in 1684. He also was successful in stopping the Turkish Ottomans, who had already subjugated neighboring Algeria and constitued the prime hegemonial power in the eastern Mediteranean during the 17th century. Among the accomplishments of the sultan, this one was of inestimable value, since it allowed Morocco to preserve its own unique culture, a mixture of Arabic-Andalusian, Berber and Black African elements.

Following Moulay Ismail's death a war of succession flared up among his numerous sons and lasted some 30 years. In its course the sultan's residence was relocated to Fès once again, as well as to Marrakech for a time. The decay of Meknes, which subsequently set in, was accelerated by the great earthquake of 1755, which wrought havoc along the entire coast from Lisbon clear down to Dakar, destroying countless architectural monuments that had thus far weathered the storms of centuries.

Beginning in 1912, Meknes gained in importance again under French colonial rule, as the Protectorate administrators made the city into their main garrison. As French settlers also brought in capital and also modern agricultural practices, Meknes developed into a prospering agricultural center. On the southern banks of the Oued Boufekrane and the tract on which Moulay Ismail's grove of olive trees stood, the French laid out the **new city** *(ville nouvelle)* after 1912 as a purely European sector. The planner, Henri Prost, designed its broad avenues flanked by orange trees, as well as modern residential, commercial and adminstrative buildings. On the other hand, the medieval medina was neglected even though it had to accomodate an enormous influx of Moroccans in the course of the economic boom the city was experiencing.

The Moroccans consider Meknes to be one of the most beautiful cities in their country and praise its moderate climate, good air, ample rain and many-faceted employment opportunities in both industry and agriculture.

The trance practitioners (or mediums) of the traditional brotherhood of the **Aissaoua**, whose ancestral leader Sidi Mohammed Ben Aissa is considered as Meknes' patron saint, are renowned far be-

yond the country's borders. The holy man is extolled for his sweet temperedness and his ability to heal snake bites by the laying on of hands. Of his followers it is said that they are immune to snake venom and are even capable of consuming the reptiles raw. In their rituals on the occasion of the great *moussem* in the month of *mouloud* they act the parts of beasts. Various groups portray panthers, jackals, cats, lions, wild boars and camels. In addition to the animal incarnations, the Aissaoua also perform dances during which they step on sharpened swords and force iron needles through their cheeks, throats and shoulders – without shedding blood.

The Medina

The most beautiful panorama over the old city can be gotten from the terrace in front of the Hotel Transatlantique: The **medina** is situated on a hill above the northern banks of the **Oued Boufekrane** (Tortoise River), encircled by imposing earthen walls and monumental gates. Its

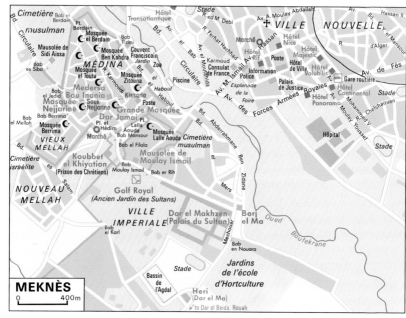

whitewashed and almost windowless buildings virtually overflow beyond the 300 year-old city walls. The Moslem old city has a maze-like tangle of narrow alleyways and lanes, as well as souks organized according to craft and type of wares. These are considerably smaller and less tourist-oriented than the bazaars of Fès. Whereas the Moslem buildings appear to be nearly completely lacking in windows, in the mellah, the former quarter of the Jews, tall windows open out onto the street. It is best to explore old Meknes in two separate tours. The first leads through the souks of the medina and requires a guide (with license in the Hotel Rif/New City); the second, and certainly easier as far as orientation is concerned, passes through Moulay Ismail's *Ville Impériale* (Royal City). The starting point for both routes is the central **Place El Hedim** at the Bab Mansour el Aleuj, the monumental gate which connects the me-

dina with the former imperial quarter. This "Plaza of Destruction" was utilized by Moulay Ismail in the 17th century as a collecting depot for construction material which he had brought in from throughout Morocco, including entire pillars of marble from Volubilis and Marrakech.

The **Dar Jamai Palace**, which now houses the local museum, is located on the northwest side of the Place El Hedim. The building was constructed around 1880 under the sultan-vizier Jamai, who also built the Palais Jamai in Fès (today a five-star hotel). Among the particularly charming aspects of the former viziers' palace is its beautifully planted and landscaped *riad* (patio); it typifies the aristocratic residence of the 19th century.

The rooms within it display the exhibits of the **Musée des Arts Marocains:** woodwork, ceramics from Meknes and Fès, carpets, textiles, embroidery work, Koran manuscripts, and wares of silver, copper and iron. Assumably most outstanding among these are the silver articles in Syrian style, a local specialty of

Right: Even non-Moslems may enter the sanctuary mosque of Moulay Ismail.

the smiths in Meknes, such as vessels and plates inlaid with silver thread (*damascene*). The rooms on the first floor provide very fine examples of Moroccan interior decoration with beautifully worked wooden friezes.

Behind the Dar Jamai a narrow alleyway leads into the **souks**, in which predominantly handcrafted products made in Meknes are on sale alongside produce from the surrounding countryside. Upon reaching the main bazaar lane, the **Rue Souk es Sebat** (Shoemakers' Street), a turn to the left takes one to the **Souk en-Nejjarine** (cabinetmakers' souk), after which the nearby **Nejjarine Mosque** was named. The latter comes from the Almohad period (12th/13th century) and was restored in 1757, at which point it was crowned with a new minaret.

Located behind the **Bab merrima** is the **Quartier Berrima** with a neighborhood mosque by the same name, and the **old mellah**. Several Jewish families have moved over to the new mellah, which begins further to the south at the **Bab el Khemis** (Thursday Gate), though the majority of Jews emigrated to Israel in 1956. The **Rue de Souk Bezzakin** leads from the Bab Berrima to the north. This is the street of basketweavers and textile merchants. It partly follows along the huge city wall and ends before the **Bab el Jedid** (New Gate), the place where the saddlers and blacksmiths ply their trade. From this point it is not much farther to the **Bab es Siba** (Gate of the Resistance). Beyond it is the entrance to the cemetery grounds with the **marabout** of the local saint Sidi Aissa.

At the Bab el Jedid it is best to follow the **Rue des Serairia**, that is the Armorers' Street, back toward the south to the Souk en Nejjarine and then continue past the teeming bazaar activity and countless **hanuds** (shops) lining the Rue Souk es Sebat toward the east. Shortly before coming to the **Great Mosque**, the visitor will happen upon Meknes' foremost art-

historical attraction: the **Medersa Bou Inania**, a Koran school from the 14th century, which was built under the Merinid sultan Abou Inan and resembles the medersa in Fès by the same name in both conception and execution. Its entrance is shadowed by an awning of green-glazed bricks; the gate of the tall edifice is overlaid with fine copper chase-work. In the middle of the Bou Inania's atrium, which is abundantly decorated with tiled mosaics, stands a round marble ablution basin that resembles an oversized seashell. Adjoining the east end of the *sahn* (interior courtyard) is a prayer chamber containing mihrabs, prayer-niches with beautiful stucco ornamentation. The structure is crowned by a cupola of cedar-wood pointing in the direction of Mecca. There are residential cells located on the first floor that continued to house students until 1964, since which time the medersa has had museum status. One shouldn't pass up the opportunity to climb up to the roof terrace, which provides a splendid view over the rooftops of the medina.

Continuing eastward, past the Souk Kebbabine, and then down along the Rue Sabab Socha, one comes to the **kisseria**, the market of textile merchants. This lane then connects with the **Rue Karmoudi**, which serves as the main axis of the medina, traversing it from the southeast to the northwest. This artery then proceeds as the **Rue Moussa** after the Place Souiqua, and leads to the former saddlemakers' quarter (*berdain* in Arabic), after which the local mosque, the plaza and the monumental Alaouite gate **Bab el Berdain** were named.

At this point one can stroll along the exterior of the city wall, following the Boufekrane River southeastward, to the **Bab Tizmi** (17th century), the gate of the potters' quarter. Alongside it stands the **Franciscan Cloister** in which orphans are taught embroidery and carpet-weaving. The **El Haboul Park**, extending between the river-valley and the city wall,

Above: Gigantic pounded mud walls support the vaulted ceiling of the Heri.

features a zoo which has seen better days, a Moorish café and a public swimming pool, which is predominantly frequented by men. By following the general flow of traffic one arrives to the Rue Dar Semen, the only street in the medina accessible to automobiles, and eventually reaches the Place el Hedim once again.

Ville Impériale

The commanding edifice **Bab Mansour el Aleuj**, the mightiest gate of Meknes and symbolic landmark of the city, forms the impressive entrance to Moulay Ismail's residential quarter. The sultan's master builder was a Christian who converted to the Islamic faith, hence the name el Aleuj (the Apostate). He was most probably a victim of the Bou Regreg corsairs. Although the wall is covered with a guilloche pattern accented with colorful tiles, its relatively ponderous forms still prevail. Passing through the weighty horseshoe-shaped arch (beneath which cap-vendors have their stands) one enters into the **Ville Impériale**, which covers an area altogether some five times larger than the medina.

The **Place Lalla Aouda**, located immediately behind the Bab Mansour, is defined to the north by a high wall and in the south by the Dar Kebira residential district. This was once the location of the **Dar Kebira** (Great House), Moulay Ismail's palace, which included 24 pavilions. Unfortunately, the merciless jaws of time haven't left much of its structures or grounds to posterity.

The **wool market** starts behind the **Bab el Filala**. Standing at its west corner is the **Koubbet el Khiyatin** pavilion, in which the sultan received foreign envoys. Directly beneath this building is the **Prison des Chrétiens**, a horrifying subterranean prison in which Christian forced laborers languished during the time of Moulay Ismail. If one enlists the services of the gate-keeper it is still possible to view the wrought-iron rings to which the miserable prisoners were chained.

Passing through the Bab Moulay one soon comes to the **mausoleum of Moulay Ismail**. After crossing through the mosaic-lined outer courtyard one has to take off one's shoes in accordance with Islamic norms before entering the prayer hall. The burial mosque of the absolutist ruler is – along with the mausoleum of Mohammed V in Rabat – one of the few mosques in Morocco which is open to non-Moslems. It is permitted to view the sarcophagus, which is flanked by two standing clocks – replicas of a gift presented by the "Sun King" Louis XIV. Grandfather clocks were highly fashionable at that time and have appeared in numerous mosques since then.

High walls flank the street which leads to the **Bab er Rih** (Gate of the Wind). To the right lies **Dar el Makhzen**, a section of the sultan's palace. The street finally ends at the **Borj el Ma** ("Water Fortress"; there is a gate by the river). Turning right one comes to the **mechouar** (audience plaza), from where one proceeds through the **Bab en Nouara** (Gate of the Waterwheel) to get to the **Dar el Ma** (Water House), which functioned as a *heri* (granary). The structure is comprised of 23 masonry arches that are twelve meters high. A portion of the roof collapsed during the great earthquake of the year 1755, resulting in some rather surprising perspectives. This is also the location the 40-meter-deep cisterns that insured the Ville Impériale's water supply. They are fed by the **Agdal** (water reservoir), which covers and area of 4 hectares and around which the students of the nearby agricultural college like to go for walks. There is a splendid view over the Ville Impériale from the roof of the *heri*.

If one turns to the left into the first street behind the granary one comes upon the **Dar el Beida** (White House), a fortress-like palace installation that was constructed in the mid-18th century by Sultan Mohammed Ben Abdallah. In 1919 the palace was transformed into a military academy. Today the elite students of the Sharifian army are schooled here.

About 500 meters to the southwest, by the el Djbabra sector, are the ruins of the **Rouah**, Moulay Ismail's horse stables. At one time 12,000 Arabian and Berber horses were bred and quartered here. Arabian horses were considered the best in the world and also thought of as superior war material. Therefore it was forbidden and punishable by death to export them.

VOLUBILIS

The charms of the ruins of **Volubilis** become evident at considerable distance to visitors approaching them from Fès or Tangier on the P 28 via the Col du Zeggota. The picturesque location of this former Roman city, surrounded by wheat fields on the gentle eastern slopes of the Oued Kroumane Valley, sort of reminds one of the Toscana. In antiquity the ancient groves of olive trees lining the road

supplied the city with the oil upon which its affluence was based. In those days, lions and panthers – the prime opponents (and "box-office" draws) of the gladiators in the arenas of Rome – were caught in the adjacent Jebel Zerhoun's (1,118 m) spring fed holm oak forests. Following the Roman victory over Carthage, the Berber kingdom of Mauretania also became obligated to pay tribute. Their king, Juba II (25 B.C.-A.D. 24) resided part-time in the city on the Zerhoun. However, after several rebellions by the Masmouda Berbers, Caesar Claudius placed the kingdom under direct Roman rule and divided it: from the eastern portion the province of Mauretania Caesariensis was established, the territory of which more-or-less corresponds to modern-day northern Algeria. The western half of Mauretania, corresponding approximately with the region of today's northern Morocco,

Above: Bacchus is Dionysius – the Romans fostered the Hellenistic culture. Right: The Corinthian columns of the basilica.

then became the new province of Mauretania Tingitana, whose chief administrator maintained residences both in Tingis (Tangier) and Volubilis. From that time on, the region was required to supply Rome with olive oil, grain, *garum* (fish-paste), *nigrum* (cork-oak tar), *thuja* (arborvitae) wood, ivory, horses and slaves. In addition, Volubilis was to be a garrison town for the defense of the limes to the south, protecting it from the Atlas Berbers by means of four advance military outposts. Roman roads lead to Tingis in the north, Sala Colonia (Rabat) in the west and, via the Taza Corridor, to the neighboring province in the east. With the founding of Constantinople in A.D. 330, the previously flourishing cosmopolitan city rapidly began to decline under East Roman rule. Nonetheless, Christian, Jewish and Moslem Berbers continued to live there until the advent of Moulay Idriss in A.D. 788.

The parking area at the entrance of the excavation sites greets the visitor with tall, shady mulberry trees, and sometimes unnerving souvenir hawkers. The café on the right-hand side is a pleasant place to relax in at the end of a tour, which, although it is marked out with red arrows, can be undertaken more comfortably with a guide. Some appealing photo motifs are created by the (to some degree at any rate) extraordinarily well-preserved mosaics amidst decayed old walls with their profusion of wildflowers.

The grounds are entered through the southeast gate, crossing over Fertassa Creek. One first comes upon the stone foundations of an **oil press**. One simply has to visualize the roughly two-meter high wooden screw that was once fitted to it, though precisely the same technology is still being used by olive farmers throughout the entire country. Looking out from here to the southwest one can see the holy city of Moulay Idriss, which is located only four kilometers away on a spur of the Jebel Zerhoun. Its founding in A.D. 789 once and for all sealed the fate of the old Roman city.

The sharp contrasts between the Roman and Arabic styles of urban planning are just plain to see: Here in Volubilis, the main and cross-streets are very clearly laid out, with right angles predominating. In contrast, the countless narrow dead-end streets of the Arabic city make the whitewashed cubical buildings appear as though they were indiscriminately piled on top of each other.

The paved path continues to the **House of Orpheus**, named after a mosaic which depicts the Greek singer playing a lyre and breaking out into lamentations over the disppearance into Hades of his beloved Eurydice, surrounded by animals of the forest in rapt attention. Archaeologists have brought to light an intricate system of water channels and heating shafts connected to the neighboring **Gallienus thermal baths**. Here the Romans indulged in sweatbaths, hot tubs, massage parlors and cold-water baths, after which they would retire to philosophize

in the *schola* (lobby). Following these intellectual exercises they gave their sexual desires free reign in the bordello just around the corner, already tititlated along the way by stone phalli.

The partially restored capital brace originates from the early 3rd century A.D. This classical tetrastylel site was dedicated jointly to Minerva, Jupiter and Juno. The five-naved **basilica** directly opposite it served as the courthouse. A pedestal on the west face of the adjacent **forum** once displayed busts of meritorious citizens. The subsequent **House of the Desultors** has only two remaining mosaics: A trick-rider sitting backwards on his horse turns a lap of honor while swinging his trophy; the image next to it shows a fisherman with hook and net.

The neighboring **triumphal arch** was constructed in A.D. 217 in honor of the emperor Caracalla, who granted Roman civic rights to all of the province's inhabitants as well as inventing price inflation by reducing the gold content of the realm's coinage by half. His father, the

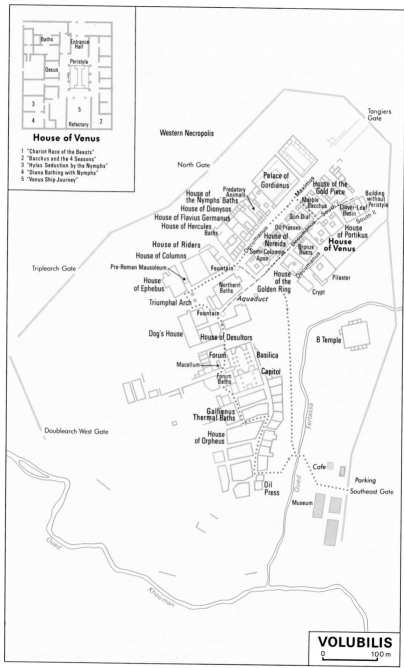

House of Venus

1 "Chariot Race of the Beasts"
2 "Bacchus and the 4 Seasons"
3 "Hylas Seduction by the Nymphs"
4 "Diana Bathing with Nymphs"
5 "Venus Ship Journey"

VOLUBILIS

0   100 m

soldier and emperor Septimius Severus, was a Berber; his mother, Julia Domna, is portrayed on a medallion on the upper right-hand side, beneath the architrave.

Following the *decumanus maximus* (main street) northward in the direction of the **Tangier Gate**, one will come upon the **House of the Ephebus** on the left-hand side, which was named after the one-and-a-half-meter high bronze statue of a young man found within it. The layout of this villa indicates that the Roman atrium (interior courtyard) was expanded here, following the Grecian example, into a sunny peristyle surrounded by columns.

After the **House of Columns**, featuring columns with spiral fluting, comes the **House of the Rider** with the mosaic motif of "Dionysus and the Sleeping Ariadne on the Beach of Naxos". A little cupid hovering over the scene is an indication that passion was soon to kindle between the daughter of the Cretan king and the god of wine. In the **House of Hercules** one can see depictions of the famous deeds of the demi-god, from the "Killing of the Lion of Nemea" to the "Clearing out of the Augean Stables" and the "Taming of Cerberus". In the **House of Dionysus** the four seasons of the year are depicted allegorically. Next, past the **Nymphs' Bath House** – its name is indication enough of the mosaic subject-matter – comes the residence of the provincial administrator, the **Palace of Gordianus**, with a horseshoe-shaped ornamental pool. At this point one crosses the main street, beneath whose arcades traders once displayed wares from the most remote provinces of the Roman Empire. Sea-nymphs, the pretty daughters of Nereus, god of the sea, are depicted in the **House of Nereids**.

The tour's crowning touch is a visit to the **House of Venus**, a former luxury villa. The mosaic "Chariot Race of the Beasts" is a persiflage of Circean doings with birds like peacocks and ducks as draft animals. Five medallions depict "Bacchus and the Four Seasons". In the adjoining room the argonaut Hylas, a companion of Hercules, is seduced by the nymphs of the spring as he is drawing water, opposite the Goddess of the Hunt cheerfully splashes about in "Diana Bathing with Nymphs".

MOULAY IDRISS

Moulay Idriss is Morocco's holiest city and most important pilgrimage destination. Some Moroccans make a pilgrimage to Moulay Idriss up to seven times in their lives in order to circumvent the expensive hadj to Mecca. It was established as the result of a familial dispute of historical proportions in distant Arabia. The Alids, descendants of Fatima, one of the Prophet's daughters, and her spouse Ali were mercilessly persecuted by the Abbasid caliphs ruling in Baghdad, who had only the Prophet's uncle Abbas in their pedigree. In A.D. 786, after suffering defeat in the Battle of Fakh near Mecca, the Alid Idriss fled to the western extremity of the Islamic world. In 788, the Moslem Auraba Berbers, who resided in the ruins of the Roman city of Volubilis and rebelled against the Arabic claims to dominion, chose – of all people – the Arab Idriss as leader of their tribe. After all, any enemy of their enemy, Harun al Rashid, was their friend. Endowed with a charismatic personality and venerable heritage, the sharif operated skillfully in political matters, in that he united the Auraba and Berghouata tribes and thus ruled over the northwestern section of Berber terrritory. In 790 he founded the city of Fès, which his son Idriss II developed into the first significant focal point of urban Arabic culture in Morocco. However, Harun al Rashid, the merciless caliph of Bagdad, was not idle. In 792 one of his henchmen succeeded in poisoning Idriss. The Berbers laid their leader Moulay (Commander) Idriss, the founder of the first Arabic dynasty on

Moroccan soil, to rest between two craggy hills on the western slopes of the Zerhoun Range, within sight of Volubilis.

An ascent to the **observation terrace** in the *khiba* (upper city) makes it possible to get a good view of the mausoleum of Idriss I, the religious heart of the city. Coming in from Volubilis, one turns to the left past the plaza where the *moussems* (pilgrimage festivals) are held, a bakery and a **hammam** (steam-bath) to the arrive at Persian-inspired round minaret of the **Sentissi Mosque**, which was donated by a pilgrim to Mecca in the year of 1939. The extensive calligraphic ornamentation displays vividly quite a number of variations of Mohammed's *baraka* (powers of benediction) in Cufic script. The continuing ascent leads first past the burial-shrine of Sidi Abdallah el Hajam and on up to the observation point.

The *horm* (sacred) areas dominate the *tasga* (lower city). Rising up majestically

Above: The most important pilgrimage in Morocco is to the mausoleum of Idriss I.

over the labyrinth of the dead-end streets is the massive rectangular structure of **Moulay Idriss I's mausoleum**, which dates from the 17th century. The bricks of the pyramid-shaped roof are finished with a green glaze (the Prophet's color). Directly to the right of the mausoleum is the huge Friday mosque with minaret; a zawiya (headquarters of a Moslem brotherhood), a Koran school and an expansive interior courtyard round out the complex. Until 1917, non-believers were not permitted to enter the city; nowadays the *nasrani* (Christians) can at least approach as far as the *horm* boundaries, which are also not supposed to be passed by mules. Restraint is well advised here – also when taking photographs!

Once a year the entire city becomes a hustling and bustling place when thousands of pilgrims flock to Moulay Idriss to attend the *moussem* festival, which lasts a week. Many stay in little tents that are set up outside of town. Among other events worth attending are the equestrian games known as *fantasias*.

FÈS

Accommodation

LUXURY: **Palais Jamai**, Bab Guissa (hotel with traditional flair in the Medina of Fes el Bali), Tel: 34331. **Hotel de Fès**, Av. des F.A.R. (in the modern part of Fes), Tel: 25002. **Les Merinides**, Borj Nord (high above the Medina, panoramic view), Tel: 45225.
MODERATE: **Volubilis**, Av. Allal ben Abdallah, Tel: 21125. **Sofia**, Rue de Pakistan 3, Tel: 24260. **Grand Hotel**, Bd. Chefchaouni, Tel: 25511. **Splendid**, Rue Abdelkrim 9, Tel: 22148.
BUDGET: **Olympic**, Bd. Mohammed V, Tel: 24529. **Amor**, Rue de Pakistan 31, Tel: 24529. **Kairouan**, Rue du Sudan 84, Tel: 23590. **CTM**, Bd. Mohammed V, Tel: 25602. **Excelsior**, Bv. Mohammed V. Tel: 25602. *BASIC:* Various hostels near the old town gates Bab Boujeloud (i.e. **Cascades**), Bab Ftouh and Bab Smarine (Grande Rue de Fes-Jedid).

Restaurants

MOROCCAN: **Dar Tajine**, Ross Rhi 15 (Medina, near the Place Rsif in the Andalus quarter), Tel: 34167. **Al Firdaous**, Rue Jenifour 10, (Bab Guissa, Medina). Tel. 34343. **Palais de Fès**, Rue Boutouil Karaouiyne 16 (Medina, at the back of the Karaouiyne Mosque). **Al Fassia** in the Palais Jamai. **Saadi**, Av. Mohammed es Slaoui (inexpensive). *FRENCH:* **La Djenina** in the Palais Jamai. **La Cheminée**, Av. Lalla Asma 6 (at the rail terminal), Tel: 24902.

Nightlife

Night club in the Hotel Volubilis.

Transportation

AIR: Royal Air Maroc, Av. Hassan II. **Aeroport Fès-Sais**, Tel: 24712. **RAIL: Gare du Tanger-Fès**, Av. des Almohades, Tel: 25001, trains to Tanger, Meknes, Rabat, Casa and Oujda. **BUS: Gare Routière CTM**, Av. Mohammed V, Tel: 22041. **RENTAL CARS: Avis**, Bv. de Chefchaouni 50, Tel: 26746. **Hertz**, in the Hotel de Fes. **Interrent**, Av. Hassan II, Tel: 26545. **TAXI:** Av. Mohammed es Slaoui, Tel: 25297. **HORSERIDING: Club Equestre Moulay Idriss**, Hippodrome Moulay Kamel.

Shopping

International Press/Books: Librairie, Bv. Mohammed V. **Market: Marché Municipal**, Bv. Mohammed V. **Crafts:** countless shops in the Medina – bargaining is essential. Fixed prices at the Ensemble Artisanal, Av. Allal ben Abdallah.

Hospitals

Hôpital Omar Drissi, Place de l'Istiqulal, Tel: 34551.

Tourist Information

ONMT, Pl. de la Resistance, Tel: 23460. **Syndicat d'Initiative**, Pl. Mohammed V (near Grand Hotel), Tel: 24769.

MEKNES

Accommodation

LUXURY: **Transatlantique**, Rue el Meriniyine, Tel: 20002.*MODERATE:* **Zaki**, Bd. Al Massira, Tel: 22591. **Rif**, Zankat Accra, Tel: 22591. **Bab Mansour**, Rue Emir Abdelkader 38, Tel: 25239. **Volubilis**, Av. des F.A.R. 45, Tel: 20102.
BUDGET: **Majestic**, Av. Mohammed V 14, Tel: 22033. **Continental**, Av. des F.A.R., Tel: 20200. **Panorama**, Av. des F.A.R., Tel: 22737.

Restaurants

MOROCCAN: **Annexe Restaurant Metropole**, Zankat Cherif Idrissi, Tel: 22576. **Al Ismaili**, in the Hotel Transatlantique. **Novelity**, Av. de Paris 5, Tel: 22156.
ITALIAN: **Pizzeria Le Four**, Zankat Atlas/ Av. Mohammed V, Tel: 20857.

Shopping

Crafts: Meknes specialities are embroidery and silverthread inlay-work on decorative iron objects – from bracelets to animal figures. **Ensemble Artisanal**, Bd. Zine el Abidine (Quartier Riad). **Kissariat de Bijoux** (jewellery), Kissariat de Tissus (embroidery, textiles), both in the Medina.

Sport

TENNIS: **Club de Tennis**, Lahboul. *GOLF:* **El Mancha**, Tel: 30753.
SWIMMING: **Le Club Petanque**, Carrefour Amir Abdelkader.
FISHING: **Fishing Club de Moyen Atlas**, Av. Hassan II (fishing permits for the region).
HORSERIDING: **Hippodrome Zitoune**.

Hospital

Hôpital Moulay Ismail, Av. des F.A.R., Tel: 22805.

Tourist Information

Office National Marocaine du Tourisme (ONMT), Place Administrative, Tel: 24426. **Syndicat d'Initiative et de Tourisme**, Esplanade de la Foire, Tel: 20191.

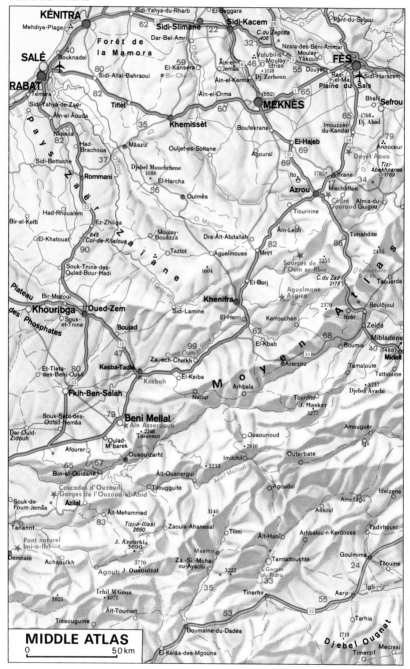

MIDDLE ATLAS

0   50 km

NOMADS, CEDARS AND SECLUDED SEAS

MIDDLE ATLAS

MIDDLE ATLAS

The mountain range of the Middle Atlas, which consists of Jura limestone, is called *el atlas el mutawassit* by the Moroccans. They extend northeast from Tamelelt over 400 kilometers to Guercif. In the west, the range begins on the edge of the *meseta* as the rainy (1,200 mm annual precipitation) Atlas Plateau, reaching altitudes of up to 2,400 meters. Its highest peak, the **Jebel Bou Naceur** (3,340 m), is located in the folded zone of the Middle Atlas, far to the east on the border of the arid steppes. Forests of holm (or evergreen) oak grow on the north and west sides of the thinly populated range, while in altitudes over 1,800 meters there are also the mighty Atlas cedars. The choice of work for the locals is quite restricted. Some emgage in limited and primitive agriculture. Charcoal and lime are also produced in small quantities.

Numerous small lakes surrounded by chunks of basalt, called *dayets* or *aguelmane* by the Berbers, conspicuously bear witness to the enormous gas explosions that occured here during the volcanically very active Tertiary Period. The extended high-altitude karst areas above 1,600 me-

Previous pages: The Ouzoud water-falls – refreshment in the Middle Atlas.

ters, which are sometimes still snow-covered in March, are annually sought out in springtime by semi-nomadic herdsmen – mostly Berbers – along with their flocks of sheep and goats.

Life in a Tent

Resembling broad camels' backs, the *khaimas*, dark brown tents of the nomads, fit into the landscape so well that one frequently has to look twice to see them. The size of these tents can vary from 15 to 60 square miles. In general, the true nomads have larger tents than the semi-nomadic *transhumants*, who spend the frigid winter period in villages. A *khaima* consists of a roughly two meter long roof pole (the *akammar*), which is adorned on its underside with magical symbols to protect against the evil eye. This roof pole is placed on two center poles over which the approximately seven-meter long main span (the *triga*) is placed. This structure supports the tent and lends it its curvilinear form. The tent covers (*aflij*) consist of several strips about 70 cm wide. They are woven of black goat's wool by the women, who also occasionally work palm-fibers into them, allowing the air through during dry weather, but swelling up when it rains and thus rendering the tent watertight. The number of

aflij determines the width of the tent. The individual strips are meticulously sewn together and then fastened over a wooden angle-bracket and an unbreakable guy line (usually made of hemp) onto pegs (frequently olive-wood). The free ends of the *aflij* are fringed, which allows rainwater to drip off. The sides of the tents, which are often copiously embroidered with ornamentation to stimulate fertility, are raised up in the summer, while in winter additional strips are put on. In earlier times the transhumants and nomads gathered together in regular tent villages, mainly in order to better defend themselves against surprise attacks.

In the more remote areas, foreigners are sometimes invited into the tents of hospitable nomads, a good opportunity to become familiar with the nature-bound lifestyle of these people. Their most im-

Above left: Oak trees and blossoming poppies in a barley field. Above right: Weatherbeaten semi-nomad. Far right: A "khaima" near the Oum Er Rbia springs.

portant sources of income are their goats and sheep; dogs guard both the herds and the tents. Mules are particularly kept for hauling water and transporting the entire load of household effects including the tent. The nomads also frequently keep chickens in a pen made of thorny brush. Standing in the area of the tent entrance is the indispensable clay oven, in which flat bread (khobza) made of freshly milled barley is baked.

In essence, the *khaima* is actually laid out exactly like any normal Moroccan home: there are certain areas for receiving guests, separated sleeping quarters for women and children and a compartment for men. The warm carpets are woven and knotted by the women during the day, while the men keep an eye on the livestock in the pastures. The nomads frequently store water in *guerbas* (goatskin bladders). Butter is also churned in such leather containers or in homemade earthenware vessels.

It goes without saying that a part of any invitation includes the obligatory tea ce-

remony. The indispensable sugar-loaves are stored in beautifully ornamented containers, which are quite often made of silver. Solely the head of the household has a key for it, evidence that, at least in the past, sugar was a precious commodity. The correct preparation of the green tea is the still today business of the patriarchs. Fresh bread and homemade butter are frequently served as a snack; the meal is traditionally initiated with the words *bismillah* (in God's name). Naturally, the large families, particularly the (usually numerous) children, are delighted to receive gifts from their guests.

From Meknes to Marrakech

En route to **Marrakech**, the "Pearl of the South", one departs **Meknes** (elevation: 550 m.) on route P 21, which soon ascends the western edge of the Middle Atlas range once it passes **El Hajeb** (1,050 m). At this point the traditional pasture regions of the Berber nomads of the Beni M'Guild tribe begin. The view is splendid looking out from **Ito-Balcony** (1,430 m) over the old volcanic cone and lava flows of the Tigriga Valley. Afterwards one drives a 67-kilometer stretch through **Azrou** (1,250 m), which is for the most part populated by vacationers from Meknes and Fès during hot weather. There is also the opportunity (17 km further on toward Marrakech) to take a rewarding sidetrack to Khenifra (80 km), via the alpine resort of **Ain Leuh** on the S303 to the **Oum er Rbia Springs**. Passing through expansive cedar forests – which are home to the *magot* (Barbary ape) – and through sparsely populated highlands (altitude around 2,000 m), one eventually arrives at the Oued Oum er Rbia. This river, boasting the largest flow of water in Morocco, runs through a deep gorge, which can be explored with the aid of native guides. However, the blue springs one encounters here are nowise the actual source of the Oum er Rbia, which is still a two day's hike away; instead, these are salt springs, which empty into the river's upper course.

131

Located about 20 km further to the south is the deep blue lake **Aguelmane Azigza** (elevation 1,600 m), surrounded by stalwart Atlas cedars and precipitous rock faces in which kites make their nests. At the east end of the lake is a picnic spot under the shade of evergreen oaks. Through an adjoining arid valley, which also happens to be a place where the nomads commonly pitch their camps, one can walk along the cedar forest and then hike up to a height with an excellent view. The path is lined by archaic lime kilns. From Lake Azigza the traveler can proceed for some 25 km by way of the somewhat narrow, but asphalted CT 3485 to the provincial capital of **Khenifra** (Sunday market) and route P 24, which leads further to the southwest.

About 20 kilometers before Kasbah-Tadla, route CT 1909 turns off toward El Ksiba; this is the road taken every year in September by curious onlookers to the unique "marriage market" of the Ait Haddidou in the **Imilchil** region. On this trail, though, one can also explore the Central High Atlas and, by way of the more than 2,800 m high passes, reach the Todhra or Dades gorges to the south.

In **Kasbah Tadlah**, one should indeed take a look at the old adobe bridge which spans the Oued Oum er Rbia, built in the days of Moulay Ismail, as well as the 300-year-old kasbah established for its protection. To date it has been spared the invasion of tourist busses on the busy Fès-Marrakech "racetrack".

The city of **Beni Mellal**, 30 km to the south of Kasbah Tadlah, is the agricultural center of a fertile plain on which oranges, sugar cane and vegetables are cultivated on large landed estates, all made possible by intensive canal irrigation. The nearby **Ain Asserdoun** spring is popular among the indigenous population as a weekend picnic spot.

Right: Horses, sheep and goats enjoy the green pastureland on Aguelmane Azigza.

Since the main highway to Marrakech hasn't got much to offer in the way of landscape, it is more interesting to turn off onto route 508 (18 km west of Beni Mellal) in the direction of Afourer. It winds its way up to the **Bin el Ouidane** reservoir, offering splendid views en route of the orange plantations down in the plains. The reservoir's dam, 130 m in height, was constructed by French engineers in the fifties (photography is unfortunately prohibited!). Afterwards, the S 508 continues to gain in altitude, and 27 km past the dam it arrives at the Tuesday market of **Asilal**. From there a bumpy mountain trail (the CT 1809) forges off into the Middle Atlas. Starting out from Tabant in the Bou Guemes Valley, one can undertake a fine trekking tour to altitudes of over 4,000 meters.

On the continuing journey to Marrakech one should definitely pay a visit to the **waterfalls of Ouzoud**, unique in the Maghreb. Here the Oued Ouzoud plunges into a 110 meter deep valley basin in which several small lakes have formed, connected to each other cascades. A shady hiking trail leads from the edge of the rock face through groves of fig and olive trees and downwards to these natural "swimming pools". When the water level of the Oued Ouzoud permits, it is possible to cross the river and proceed along the slopes of the valley to the gorges of the **Oued el Abid**. The return route passes through the olive tree plantations of the northern high plateau and back to the parking area at the unassuming *auberge*. Located behind it, near to the waterfall, are small grain mills in which farmers from the village of Souk Tleta grind barley and wheat. There is a mule-powered oil press in the village proper. Its traditional design is quite obviously reminiscent of the Roman period.

Back on the S 508 it is possible to take a sidetrack to **Demnate** and further on to the rock bridge of **Imi n'Ifri**. The **Oued Ifri**, as a tributary of the Oued Lakhdar,

traverses the Jura limestone of the High Atlas through a deeply incised karstic grotto. Swifts, crows and bats make their nests in the countless caves and nooks of the reddish-brown oxidized rock slopes. From Imi n'Ifri, a washed-out trail leads to an interesting bit of natural history: Fossilized dinosaur tracks, which were made by the hind legs of species that once hunted its prey in the (former) mud-banks. Furthermore, large dinosaur eggs have been discovered here. The several spots where the finds have been made are scattered over a relatively small area and can all be viewed on foot (guides are available at the bridge or in Demnate). From Demnate the way to Marrakech is either by driving via **Tamelelt** (large market on Sundays), or on the rather small route 6206 along the northern edge of the High Atlas through Sidi Rahhal.

From Fès to Midelt

Highway P 24 begins in Fès. It first cuts across the irrigated and therefore very fertile Sais Plain, and then ascends to the summer resort of **Imouzer du Kandar** (38 km), which is situated at an altitude of 1,350 m on the escarpment of the Kandar Massif, already part of the Middle Atlas range. In the hot season it is an ideal refuge for heat-plagued urbanites from the plain. The village's small market hall has a considerable selection of fruits and vegetables. A few kilometers past Immouzer, a smaller road, the CT 4630, branches off to **Dayet Aoua**. On this route one can set off on a rather rough lake tour to the *dayets* (lakes) **Iffrah**, **Iffer**, **Hachlaf** and **Jerane**. Due to the lack of signs and poor condition of the road surface, this excursion should be left to those with both a 4WD vehicle and a very good sense of orientation.

The gabled-roof brick vacation houses of **Ifrane** (1,650 m), which was established during the French protectorate period, are somewhat reminiscent of Alsace. The royal palace, a former luxury hotel, also looks more like a medieval castle than the residence of an Arab sul-

133

tan. Munching on a piece of strawberry cake in the one and only patisserie, one can participate in the idle affluence of the indigenous upper class. On the continuing journey to Midelt, an interesting sidetrack passes over the 1,934-m Tizi-n-Tretten to **Mishliffen**, the up-and-coming skiing village with several lifts on the slopes of Jebel Hebri (2,104 m).

If one decides in favor of the route through Azrou on the way south, it is possible to include a visit to the **Gouraud Cedar**, which at a height of 40 m and a trunk circumference of 9 m is the largest Atlas cedar in the central range. Access, however, is on a 4-kilometer dead-end road. **Azrou** (1,250 m) the main town of the Beni M'Guild Berbers, is known for its exceptional deep-napped sheepswool carpets, which can be purchased at reasonable prices in the cooperative of the carpet-makers' school. Past Azrou highway P 21 climbs through beautiful cedar

Above: The cedars at Col du Zad are skirted with snow sometimes even as late as April.

forests to a 1,945 meter high pass connecting to the treeless Tighza Plateau, which slants down to the valley of the Oued Guigou. Storks nest in the dizzying heights of a basalt face before the village of **Timahdite** (1,800 m). Continuing uphill along the basalt riverbed of the meandering Guigou, one arrives at obviously volcanically-formed highlands, the traditional pastures of the semi-nomadic Beni M'Guild. The largest lake in the area, the **Aguelmane Sidi Ali** (abundant fish) is named after the Berber holy man Sidi Ali ou Mohand. His *marabout* (grave) is located on the lake's southern shore. Migratory birds stop off temporarily in the surrounding marshes during spring.

Afterwards the route P 21 gains even more altitude and crosses the **Col du Zad**, the main ridge of the Middle Atlas, which is also the watershed between the Atlantic Ocean and the Mediterranean Sea. The extensive cedar forests in this area are mostly inhabited by magots, tailless Barbary apes, which belong to the macague family. Unfortunately, these animals, which can grow up to a half meter in size and live up to 30 years, have become an endangered species due to the vigorous deforestation.

Continuing from the col one descends to the **Moulouya Valley** through extensive forests of cedar and evergreen oak along a gorge that still conveys some feeling of the old caravan routes. In Zeida (1,450 m) the road crosses the Moulouya River, which flows through a desolate, arid plateau on the southeast edge of the Middle Atlas range and empties into the Mediterranean near the Algerian border. On the horizon, towering up from the dry steppe of the **Plaine des Arid,** are the impressive ridges of the Central High Atlas with their 3,000-meter peaks, often covered with snow into May.

There is only one tourist-class hotel far and wide, which is located in **Midelt** (1,500 m), a small town at the foot of the Jebel Ayachi. The town itself hasn't much to offer besides a rather modest market, but it is well suited as the starting point for excursions into the mountains (Jaffar, Tattiouine, Ayachi, the Aouli Gorge; see the following chapter).

In the surrounding area there are a number of mines where manganese, copper, tin, zinc and other ores are produced. Also found in the mineshafts of the region around **Mibladene** are a variety of sparkling minerals, which are offered for sale in Midelt and along the main tourist routes. Among the most beautiful is vanadinite, a compound of lead, vanadium and anglesite (lead sulphate). Cuprous minerals are noted for their greenish-blue hues. They include copper pyrite, azurite, malachite and the particularly attractive brochantite, which features magnificient emerald-green crystals. Lead glance, or galena, is called *khol* in Morocco, where it is used by women as eyeshadow. The darkly gleaming crystals of the mineral are finely pulverized and marketed as Berber eyeshadow in small cosmetic bottles sealed with wooden pegs.

MIDDLE ATLAS

Accommodation

SIDI HARAZEM: *MODERATE:* **Sidi Harazem**, Tel: 06- 45522.

IMMOUZER DU KANDAR: *MODERATE:* **Royal**, Av. Mohammed V, Tel: 06-63080. *BUDGET:* **Des Truites**, Tel: 06- 63002.

IFRANE: *LUXURY:* **Mishliffen**, Tel: 056-6416. *BUDGET:* **Grand Hotel**, Av. de la Marche Verte, Tel: 056-6407. **Perce-Neige**, Rue des Asphodeles, Tel: 056- 6402.

AZROU: *MODERATE:* **Panorama**, Tel: 056-2010. *BUDGET:* **Azrou Hotel**, Route de Khenifra, Tel: 056-2116. **Des Cedres**, Place Mohammed V, Tel: 056-2326. **Royal Amal**, near the bus terminal.

SEFROU: *BUDGET:* Sidi Lahcen Lyoussi, Tel: 60497.

KHENIFRA: *MODERATE:* **Hamou Azzayani Salam**, Tel: 058-6020. *BUDGET:* **Hotel France**, Route de Khenifra.

KASBAH TADLA: *BUDGET:* **Hotel des Alliés**, Marché Central.

BENI MELLAL: *MODERATE:* **Chems**, Route de Marrakech at km 2, Tel: 048-3460. **Ouzoud**, Route de Marrakech at km 2,5, Tel: 048-3752. *BUDGET:* **Gharnata**, Bd. Mohammed V, Tel: 3482. **Hotel de Paris**, Nouvelle Medina, Tel: 2245. **Vieux Moulin**, Route de Kasba Tadla, Tel: 2788. **Ain Asserdoune**, 4 km to the east at the Ain Asserdoune spring.

BIN EL OUIDANE: *BUDGET:* **Hotel du Lac**, at the western lakeshore.
CASCADES D'OUZOUD: *BUDGET:* **Auberge** (very basic), at the car park. **Camping**.

DEMNATE: *BUDGET:* **Hotel-Restaurant Fetouka**, at the market.

MIDELT: *MODERATE:* **Hotel Ayachi**, Rue d'Agadir, Tel: 2161.

Shopping

CRAFTS: **AZROU**: **Ensemble Artisanal**, Tel: 056-2056. **KHENIFRA**: **Ensemble Artisanal**, at the Oum er Rbia bridge.

AROUND
JEBEL M'GOUN

CENTRAL HIGH ATLAS
IMILCHIL
M'GOUN TREK

CENTRAL HIGH ATLAS

When seen from the viewpoint of the multitude of modern-day motorists, the Central High Atlas – which has flouted them up to now – represents an immense traffic obstruction. From the Tizi n'Tichka Pass in the southwest it extends 300 km to the Talrhemt (Tagalm) Pass in the northeast. The African continent rammed against the European plate several times in the last 350 million years. As a result, the six chains of the Atlas range, running parallel toward the northeast, came slowly into being in the Moroccan impact zone. The Jurassic limestone of the range has been folded upward to altitudes as high as about 4,000 meters, covering a 100-kilometer wide region between the Middle Atlas in the north and the Jebel Saghro in the south.

Among the most prominent peaks of the Atlas range are, in the west, the **Jebel Anrhomer** (3,607 m), in the middle the **Rat** (3,190 m), **Tignousti** (3,820 m), **Irhil M'Goun** (4,068 m), **Ouaoulzat** (3,770 m) and the **Jebel Azourki** (3,390 m). Located further to the northeast in the transition zone to the Central Atlas are

Previous pages: Camel nomads at the Cirque de Taffar. Left: The "Kadi" marries an Ait-Haddidou couple (Moussem of Imilchil).

the **Jebel Masker** (3,277 m) and as well the Jebel **Ayachi** (3,737 m).

On the southern edge of the range the rivers M'Goun, Dades, Todhra, and Ziz have all created spectacular gorges. Their waters feed the river oases of the South. Hikers and climbers are particularly attracted to the gorges of the **Tessaout** (Wandras), **Tiflout**, **Arous** and the upper **M'Goun** in the heart of the massif. The agriculture of the Haouz and Tadla Plains would be impossible without the irrigation waters of the Atlas rivers Tessa-out, Lakhdar and Assif Melloul. The Central High Atlas is Morocco's rain-catcher and primary water storage. Of course, the precipitation – and the vegetation along with it – decrease drastically from north to south, as well as toward the east as the distance from the Atlantic Ocean increases. While in March the northern routes may often still be blocked by snowfall at altitudes as low as 1,000 meters, on the range's southern edge the first hot sandstorms may already be raging. In the course of a single day temperatures can range as much as 30° C – "a cold land in which it gets very hot" as was quite fittingly remarked by the first French resident general in Morocco, Lyautey. During the summer, convectional storms are a consistent part of the afternoon agenda. The forests which were still dense 1,000

139

years ago are now severely depleted; to the east of the Irhil M'Goun they have disappeared almost completely. At altitudes of up to 3,000 meters there are still isolated ancient black juniper trees with trunks a meter thick. Their resin supplies the pleasant-smelling Arabic incense. The holm or evergreen oak is found up to 2,500 meters. The Atlas cedar, once broadly distributed at this altitude, now grows in the High Atlas only at the foot of the Ayachi Massif in the northeast. The prickly cedar and cypress flourish up to 2,000 meters, the Aleppo pine up to 1,800 meters. The thuya (arborvitae) grows only at lower elevations in the northwest. Heavily overgrazed and degraded thorny brush, which grows around villages, consists mostly of kermes oak, boxwood, mastic trees, brooms and dwarf palm or palmettos. Oleander and willows grow along the river courses. The former's glorious rose-hued blossoms can be admired

Above: Wednesday market at Ait Oumrar near Midelt with view of Jebel Ayachi.

at altitudes reaching some 2,500 meters. The farmers of the mountain's river oases are increasingly planting fruit trees: apples, apricots and peaches as well as small almonds in warmer locations. The silver poplar is a fast-growing wood producer in the south. Barley, rye, potatoes, turnips and carrots are cultivated here on cleverly irrigated terraces, as is maize in warmer areas in autumn. In high valleys to the north of the main ridge nut trees flourish between 1,800 and 2,400 meters. At the head of such valleys there are lush high pastures, named *almus* by the Berbers. They extend east as far as the upper valley of the Dades. Here, quite unique at this latitude in Africa, even hay is made! On the mountain slopes, however, the vegetation is mostly rather sparse and almost always reduced to thorny scrub, being spiny or even poisonous in order to fend off the greedy maws of sheep, goats and other vegetarians.

The steep faces of the mountain gorges are an eldorado for a multifarious community of birds ranging from the ring-

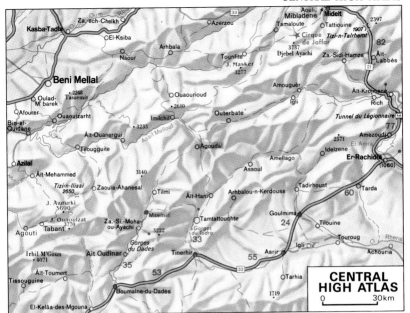

dove to the golden eagle and griffon vulture. The spines of the numerous porcupines are used in cosmetics by Berber women. Foxes, jackal wildcats, lynxes and even leopards make up the predatory animal population of the region. Magots (Barbary apes) romp about in the dense forests of the northwest. On the warmer southern slopes one may encounter tortoises and various lizards, including the thorn-tail, as well as vipers and scorpions. The latter are rare, but dangerous! In the clear mountain streams one can fish for trout and barbel. Gazelles and moufflons, however, even though immortalized in Neolithic rock carvings, are no longer found. The hiker will most frequently encounter domesticated sheep and goats, donkeys and mules, the latter astonishingly nimble in rough terrain. In the arid heights of the east there are also the dromedaries of the nomads.

The western half of the High Atlas, as far as the Dades Gorges, is the traditional settlement region of the Shluh Berbers, who do speak a tongue called *tashelhite*.

These hardy, tenacious mountain farmers cultivate the river oases, but they also keep herds of sheep that are lead up to the high pastures by the village shepherds in the summer. There, the Shluh herdsmen usually spend their nights in an *azib* (simple hut). In contrast, the *Beraber* tribes further east, distinguished by their *Tamazirt* dialect, are confirmed *khaima* (tent) dwellers, though today mostly only in the summer. After the spring planting these semi-nomadic tribes leave their oasis villages such as those of the Ait Haddidou between Imilchil and Rich. Entire families then make for the high-altitude pastures between Jebel Azourki and Jebel Ayachi with their herds, tents and carpet looms.

Midelt, Jaffar and Ayachi

The former mining town of **Midelt** (1,490 m) is situated at the base of the Jebel Ayachi (3,737 m), which is covered with snow until April. This is where the arid steppes of the eastern high plateaux begin. Extending to the Algerian border, this is until today the habitat of the nomads, still little-touched by the modern age. Until the sixties, Midelt lived by mining argentiferous lead ores in **Mibladene** (10 km) and **Aouli** (25 km) in the **Moulouya Gorge**. Production is no longer profitable, and the dilapidated mining facilities look like some sort of surreal film scenery. Former miners occasionally venture into the shafts in search of minerals coveted by collectors. But beware: What the pushy street peddlers in Midelt sell is mostly worthless!

The efficiently run Hotel Ayachi is an ideal base for excursions to the **Cirque de Jaffar** and **Jebel Ayachi**. Landrovers and pickups can be arranged from here. You leave Midelt to the west on route number 3424, passing by the *kasbah miriam* (Franciscans once attempted to establish a mission here). After 6 km of tarred road, a road turns off to the left, presenting the option of a little side-trip to a small river oasis with the villages of **Flilou** and **Tattiouine** (from Tattiouine one can ascend Ayachi in 2 days). Further west (starting at the Miktane ranger station) a throughly weathered piste hemmed by holm oaks makes the lengthy ascent to the Jaffar Pass (2,250 m, the piste is 25 km long). At the top of the pass there is a splendid view over the Ayachi Massif to the southwest and the **Jaffar** cirque with its ancient cedars. Semi-nomadic peoples make their winter homes here in permanent earthen dwellings. The very friendly family in the uppermost farmstead offers lodging to hikers and can assist in organizing ascents of Ayachi. Early risers in good physical condition can climb up to the top of the ridgeback (3,737 m) in a two day's hike. The narrow Jaffar Gorge, some 4 km in length, begins at the lower outlet of the basin. When the water level is low one

Right: Strongholds of the semi-nomadic Ait Haddidou in the Assif Melloul Valley.

can hike through it. On the return journey to Midelt you can easi-ly avoid the bumpy road 3424 by following a track to the north, 500 m beyond the head of the Jaffar Pass, to the Wednesday market of Ait Oumrhar, where a paved road begins.

IMILCHIL

Route 3424 (for four-wheel drive or vehicles with good clearance only!) continues west from Jaffar, passing groves of pines, then via the P 3425 through the high valleys (dry starting in May) to the Saturday market of **Imilchil** (2,000 m, about 165 km from Midelt; 110 km from El Ksiba). The nearby Plateau des Lacs is swathed in a romantic legend. The two factions of the **Ait Haddidou** tribe, the Ait Brahim from the upper course of the Assif Melloul and the Ait Yazza from the lower course of the same river were once enemies. A young man of the Ait Brahim fell in love with a girl from the Ait Yazza tribe. However, their parents were against the marriage. The lovers then cried until their tears created Lac Tislit (lake of the bride) and Lac Isli (lake of the groom). Every year in September, the semi-nomadic Ait Haddidou – the descendants of the Sanhadja who once were much-feared caravan robbers – celebrate a huge *moussem* at the grave of their patron saint, Sidi Ahmed Oulmghani in **Agoudal** (30 km south of Imilchil). Perceived by Koran scholars as a questionable pre-Islamic custom, this is a harvest festival with the chance to choose a new partner: Divorced or widowed Berber women – recognizable by their pointed bonnets – seek out their intended themselves.

Continuing south from Agoudal, we have the bone-shaking route P 6905, which soon passes through some impressive scenery and over the **Tizi n'Ouanu** (2,800 m) before, reaching the breathtaking **Dades Gorges** just beyond **Msemrir**. Passing **Ait Oudinar** (1,800 m), a total 125 km brings us to Boumalne (1,600 m)

and the veritable realm of the date palm. Track 3445 is hardly any less appealing, guiding the traveller over the Tirherhouzine Pass (2,700 m) into the spectacular **Todhra Gorge**s and further on to **Tinerhir** (1,350 m, 88 km).

Bou Guemes Valley and Irhil M'Goun

Mountain route 1809 begins right in the Middle Atlas village of **Azilal**, opening the way (via Ait Mehammed) to the **Bou Guemes Valley**. After rain or snowfall, four-wheel drive is by all means necessary. A more direct, paved all-season road over the Tizi n'Oughbar is under construction (CT 1808). It is intended to provide access to the planned winter sport center between **Jebel Ouaoulzat** (3,770 m) and **Jebel Azourki** (3,690 m).

Tabant (1,850 m) is the venue for the Sunday market of the broad, fertile valley of the Ait Bou Guemes Berbers. Very recently the **CFAMM** vocational training center was established here. Indigenous mountain guides receive training and traditional crafts are promoted. The center is always helpful with the preparation of a trek or skiing tour and also provides visitors with lodging.

Set up with guide, pack-mule and tent, in the course of a nine-day tour you can explore one of the most beautiful areas in the Central High Atlas and ascend the highest mountain in the region, the **Irhil M'Goun** (4,068 m), which is covered with snow from November to May.

M'GOUN TREK

On the **first day** (Tabant-Talat Rirhan, 7 hours) one leaves **Tabant** heading east, hiking up the broad Guemes Valley to the nearby village of **Ait Imi** (1,900 m), which is surrounded by walnut trees. At the end of the village is a row of grain mills which are driven by the water of a *seguia* (canal). Here, the ascent to the Ait Imi Pass begins, following a broad mule path, which leads south. Once, before the French Protectorate authorities constructed the road over the Tichka Pass, this was

143

a significant caravan route which connected the rose-oasis of Kelaa M'Gouna and the lower Dades Valley with the sultan's capital, Fès. The Shluh Berber tribe of Ait Imi profited from the lively traffic of goods through the territory they commanded. At 2,100 m altitude you pass by the Arhbalou n'Ait Imi Springs, and arrive at the top of the **Tizi n'Ait Imi Pass** (2,910 m), after four hours' ascent altogether, with a splendid view of the more than 4,000 meter-high main ridge of the M'Goun Massif. The path now continues downhill into the **Assif M'Goun Valley** and after 2 1/2 hours arrives at the remote village of **Talat Rirhan** (2,250 m; overnight lodging or tenting possible).

If you set your sights on crossing the Atlas Range instead of making a roundtrip, then a hike of three days right along the old caravan route from Mrabtin over the Tizi n' Ait Hamed (3,000 m) passing Ameskar and Alemdoun will bring you to

Above: Nut trees and barley fields nourish the mountain farmers on Assif Tessaout.

Bou Thrarar in the south. An attractive alternative is to set off east through the Assif M'Goun Valley with its numerous small gorges, then head south following the Valley of the Roses up to Bou Thrarar. Heat resistent enthusiasts might also follow the waters of the M'Goun through the Dades and Dra Oases on out to Zagora. Count on two weeks.

On the **second day** of a roundtrip (Talat Rirhan – Arhbalou n'Laasif is a 6 hour hike) one treks up the M'Goun Valley, passing the dilapidated **Tighremi n'Ait Ahmed** and then following the valley of the Assif Oulliliymt to the west. It is possible either to climb through the Tarhia n'Ait Allel Gorge (20 m of rope needed) or to pass around it to the north. Later, the river bed broadens out; after six hours of solid hiking, one arrives at the **Arhbalou n'Laasif Spring** (2,650 m) at a suitable spot for pitching tents beneath the east ridge of the M'Goun with a view of the north face of the main peak.

On the third day (Arhbalou n'Laasif-Tilibit n'Tarkedit, nine hours) the route continues upriver to a path-crossing at 2,800 m altitude. Do not take the path, which continues straight ahead to the Tizi n'Oumsoud and on further into the Arous or Tessaout Valley; rather, head south, ascending to the east summit (3,993 m) of the M'Goun Massif. This mountain peak is sacred to the Berbers: Pilgrims come here to make entreaties for the fertility of their fields. Follow the ridgeback to the west until reaching the trigonometric point marking the **Irhil M'Goun's** main summit (4,068 m). When the weather is good the view from here is indeed magnificent: Over the Dades Oasis and the Jebel Saghro south to the stony desert of the Sahara's northern edge as well as of Jebel Ayachi (3,737 m) to the east, which is frequently snow-covered into May.

Hiking further west along the ridgeback the descent is via the Tizi n'Igwantoula (3,650 m) and then south, arriving after nine hours in all at the **Tilibit**

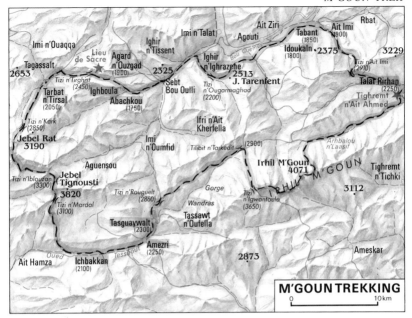

Imi n'Ouaqqa
Tagassalt
2653
Lieu de Sacre
Agard n'Ouzgad (1900)
Ighir n'Tissent
Imi n'Talat
Ait Ziri
Agouti
Tabant (1850)
Ait Imi (1900)
Rbat
Idoukaln (1800) · 2375
3229
Tizi n'Ait Imi (2910)
Tizi n'Tirghist (2450)
Ighboula
2325
Ighir n'Ighrazene
·2513
Tizi J. Tarenfent
Talat Rirhan (2250)
Tarbat n'Tirsal (2050)
Abachkou (1750)
Sebt Bou Oulli
Tizi n'Ougarmaghad (2200)
Tighremt n'Ait Ahmed
Tizi n'Kark (2850)
Ifri n'Ait Kherfella
Jebel Rat 3190
Imi n'Oumfid
Tilibit n'Tarkedit (2900)
Arhbalou n'Laasif
Aguensou
Irhil M'Goun 4071
GOUN
Tighremt n'Tichki
Tizi n'Iblouzan (3300)
Jebel Tignousti 3820
Tizi n'Rouguelt (2860)
Gorge
Tizi n'Igwantoula (3650)
RHIL M'GOUN
3112
Tizi n'Mardal (3100)
Wandras
Tasguaywalt (2300)
Tassawt n'Oufella
Ait Hamza
Oued Tessaout
Ichbakkan (2100)
Amezri (2250)
2873
Ameskar

M'GOUN TREKKING
0   10km

n'Tarkedit, a plateau with lush pastures (by Moroccan standards) at the end of the **Oued Tessaout** valley (tenting is possible at abput 2,900 m).

On the fourth day (Tilibit n'Tarkedit-Amezri, five hours), the hike starts out to the southwest along the Tessaout River until the valley narrows into a gorge. The passage through the about 15-kilometer long **Wandras Gorge** can merely be recommended to practiced climbers (armed with at least 60 m of rope, pitons and harnesses) when the water level is down; in addition, any attempt should start from below (from Amezri), since a number of waterfalls have to be negociated. Hikers and mules circumvent the gorge to the north, ascending to 3,200 meters in the process. On the way they have the option of a short detour to the south to catch a glimpse of the spectacular canyon-like Tessaout Valley. The river has scoured its way to a depth of more than 700 meters through the dolomite rock. Then the path descends gently to the **Tizi n'Rouguelt** (2,860 m), a broad mule-path, which has since days of old been passage through the mountains between Abachkou and the Bou Guemes Valley in the north and Skoura and the Dades Valley in the south.

One follows this path downwards, southwest to the village of **Tasguaywalt** (2,300 m) on the Tessaout River and then continues to the neighboring village of **Amezri** (2,250 m), where the valley floor broadens out. Barley is cultivated on the terraced fields; nut trees flourish (simple guesthouse, tenting on the river).

Then, on the fifth day (Amezri-Ichbakan, four hours) the hike takes you gently downstream along the Tessaout River. The steep valley walls move closer and closer together until they form an imposing gorge. The valley floor broadens out again after a walk of about four hours', at which point the **Ichbakan** villages come into view at 2,100 m. The upper village is constructed high above the river, protectively situated on a spur of rock. The rough-stone walls of the houses literally appear to grow out of the rock itself and convey the impression of an archaic

fortress. A spring rises under some nut trees about half-way to the lower village (tenting or indoor lodging).

On the sixth day of the trek (Ichbakan-Tizi n'Iblouzan, seven hours) you leave the Tessaout Gorge by way a path above the village which climbs the steep north face (700 m change in altitude) and thereby brings you to a sweeping hollow (abundant water in spring). This is crossed heading in a northerly direction towards **Jebel Tignousti** (3,820 m). A mule path leads up to the **Tizi n'Mardal Pass** (3,100 m). Once on the west side of Tignousti, the path continues to the **Tizi n'Iblouzan** (3,300 m) located opposite it. From the head of the pass one can make an excursion to the summit of Tignousti (three hours). Camping at a spring below the pass to the southwest.

On the seventh day (Tizi n'Iblouzan-Tarbat n'Tirsal, some five hours) the hiker ascends from the spring to the top of

Above: Mules are an indispensible means of transportation in the M'Goun region.

the Iblouzan Pass once again. From that point descend northwestward, then, heading west along the southern edge of the **Jebel Rat** (3,190 m), go around the massif, following the path which leads north to the pass of **Tizi n'Kark** (2,850 m). A gully begins here, widening into a valley as it proceeds downhill; the village of Tarbat n'Tirsal is located in it. (2,050 m; guesthouse, camping at the stream bed).

On the eighth day (Tarbat n'Tirsal-Abachkou, five hours) you follow a channel east up to the **Tizi n'Tirghist** (2,450 m). A site of Neolithic rituals is located east of the head of the pass. Chiseled into flat slabs of rock are images of horsemen with lances, warriors, hunters, cattle and panthers, all worked over 4,000 years ago. Since the end of the most recent Ice Age (roughly 10,000 years ago), which in the lower altitudes of North Africa was primarily a rainy period, the Central High Atlas range has served as a retreat for inhabitants of the Sahara. Hunter-gatherers followed the herds which shrank away from the once-fertile savannah, migrating along the river courses up towards their higher-altitude sources. There, the rival tribes battled over the hunting grounds of the high pastures. The rock engravings obviously were part of their hunting and fertility magic and implorations for good fortune in conflicts.

From the pass the route descends continuously following the notch-valley of the Assif n'Tirghist southeast to the small village of **Agard n'Ouzgad** at an altitude of about 1,900 m. Further downhill one soon comes upon the dilapidated Ighrem n'Oumlil fortified granary (*tighermt*), after which you pass by the houses of **Ighboula**. At this point the hike continues through the tribal region of the Ait Bou Oulli, along the Assif Bou Oulli as far as the village of **Abachkou** (1,750 m) Overnight lodgings are available, and there are tenting places on the river.

On the ninth day (Abachkou-Tabant, seven hours) the route along the bed of the Assif Bou Oulli is lined with walnut trees and heads downriver to the Saturday market of **Sebt Bou Oulli** and on to **Assaka**. At this point the mule path turns into a broad trail leading northeast to **Ighir n'Ighrazene**. Beyond this village one leaves the valley, ascending southeast on small paths, through a pine reforestation area and up to the **Tizi n'Ougarmaghad** (2,200 m). Then you hike along the northern flank of **Jebel Tarenfent** (2,513 m) high above the Jorro Gorge with a view over the wide Bou Guemes Valley. Continuing northeast, going downhill and passing the hamlet of Asuikine, you come to the valley carved out by the Arous River. After crossing the allurial fan of the Arous, one arrives at the village of **Idoukaln** (1,800 m) and the bank of the Bou Guemes. The fertile floodplain soil of the astonishingly broad valley bottom was deposited thousands of years ago when a landslide dammed up the river at the valley's western end. Now, following the river bed eastward you return, via **Agard n'Ouzrou**, to **Tabant**.

CENTRAL HIGH ATLAS
Accommodation

MODERATE: Accommodation in this category can be found only in the mountain foreland, in **Azilal** and **Midelt** (see chapter on Middle Atlas), **Errachidia**, **Tinerhir**, **Boumalne**, **El Kelaa** and **Ouarzazate** (see chapter on River Oases). *BUDGET:* In **Demnate**, **Imilchil**, **Todhra Gorges**, **Ait Oudinar** (in the upper Dades Valley). In the trekking region **Bou Guemes/M'Goun/Azourki** there are *BASIC HOSTELS (gîtes d'étape)* in the following villages: Agouti, Ait Imi, Amezri, Arouss, El Mrabtin, Ikhf n'Ighir, Imelghas, Iskattafene, Oulmzi, Tajgagalt, Taghia, Tabant (CFAMM), Tarbat n'Tirsal and Zawyat Oulmzi.

Weekly Markets (souks)
Abachkou (Saturdays), **Ait Tamlil** (Tuesdays), **Azilal** (Thursdays), **Imilchil** (Saturdays), **Tabant** (Sundays), **Zawyat Ahansal** (Sundays), **Boumalne** (Wednesdays), **Msemrir** (Saturdays), **El Kelaa** (Wednesdays), **Tilmi** (Wednesdays).

Transportation
TRUCKS on their way to the markets are the cheapest (and often the only) public transport in the Central Atlas region; trucks usually depart the evening before market day or in the early morning hours, return jouney (late) afternoon. **TAXI WITH FOUR-WHEEL-DRIVE:** In Azilal, Ouaouizarht, Demnate, Ait M'hamed, Midelt. **TAXI:** In Skoura, El Kelaa, Boumalne, Tinerhir

Equipment
Pannier or pack-sack for pack-mule, backpack, sneakers for crossing streams, mountain boots, sleeping bag, tent. Your (well-stocked) first aid box should include: Lip salve, broad-spectrum antibiotics, gastro-enteric medication, antihistamines, cortisone, electrolytes, water purifier, analgesic, elastic bandages, elastoplast.

Trekking Information
ONMT, Azilal, Tel: 488334. **ONMT**, Ouarzazate, Tel: 882485. **Club Alpin Francais** (CAF), Casablanca, Rue Général Henrys 1, BP 6178, Tel: 270090. **Centre d'Information sur la Montagne (CIM),** Ministère du Tourisme, Rabat, Rue d'Oujda 1, Tel: 722643. **Centre de Formation aux Métiers de la Montagne (CFAMM)**, Tabant (guides, mules). *MAPS:* **Division de la Cartographie**, Rabat, Av. Moulay Hassan 31, Tel: 7-65311 (mornings only).

THE RIVER OASES
OF
THE SOUTH

FROM MIDELT TO ERFOUD
TAFILALET AND ERG CHEBBI
FROM ERFOUD TO
OUARZAZANE
DRA VALLEY

When crossing the main ridge of the High Atlas on the way south, the approach of the desert becomes unmistakeable. The vegetation becomes ever sparser, and the pines and evergreen oaks, still present as dense forests on the slopes facing north, where precipitation is relatively plentiful, are almost completely absent. The High Atlas is a classic climatic divide. It protects the Moroccan heartland, the *meseta*, from the hot Saharan winds of the *chergui*, and causes moist Atlantic air masses to rain out. In its rainshadow, the average annual rainfall hardly reaches 100 millimeters. Agriculture without some form of irrigation is no longer possible. Nonetheless, the ample rain and snow which fall in the High Atlas (more than 1000 mm per year) benefit the arid south as well: Hundreds of thousands of oasis-farmers live off small irrigated parcels along the river-oases of the Ziz, Todhra, Dades and Dra. These southern Moroccan life-giving arteries originate in the Central High Atlas and flow from the massif in spectacular, deep gorges. On the edge of the predominantly arid mountains of the Jebel Saghro they wind like green ribbons through a rubble-strewn landscape and end as *wadis* (dry except in the rainy season) in the *hammada* (rocky desert), the *serir* (stony desert) or the *erg* (sandy desert).

The culture of Arab and Berber nomads once played a dominant role in the social structure of the Sahara and helped camel-breeding tribes like the Tuareg, who controlled the caravan routes, to power and wealth. It has been in decline in Morocco's south – as in all neighboring desert states – since the middle of the 20th century. This is due in part to the arbitrary colonial borders drawn by the French, which were carried over to the modern nation-states and have been jealously guarded ever since. Ancestral nomadic routes between distant pastures, to which the tribes migrated, living under dark *khaima* tents, as well as the old caravan routes of the Sahara are now impassable as a result. At the same time, the camel had to give way to motorized vehicles as primary means of transport, resulting in the nomads' losing their trade monopoly as well as prestige and in the camels they bred decreasing in value. The increasing desertification of the Sahara is accelerating the once-proud camel riders' slide into poverty; the oasis farmers – who were once subjugated and frequently plundered by them – do not exactly regret this new state of affairs.

Previous pages: Children on the threshold of a mud house. Left: Ait Benhaddou's residential strongholds are falling to ruins.

151

The Shluh Berbers are sedentary farmers, descendants of the legendary Masmouda Berbers who founded the Almohad Dynasty in the 12th century. Their villages are located in the mountain valleys of the High Atlas and in the southern foothills from the Atlantic to the sources of the Oued Dades and the Oued Todhra. The Negroid *haratin*, descendants of former slaves, are especially numerous in the river oases. The *mrabtin* villages are inhabited by the descendants of holy men, frequently Berbers with some Arabic elements in their genealogy. When the name of a village begins with *oulad* (Arabic for children) then most probably the forefathers of its inhabitants came from Arabia. The land-owning Arabs of the oases are partly descendants of erstwhile warrior-nomads (Doui Menia on the lower Ziz; Oulad Yahis and Roha in the Dra region), partly the offspring of Arabic merchant families. Many of them lay claim to the honorary title *chorfa*, which is supposed to indicate their distinguished lineage going all the way back to the Prophet himself. This membership in the Islamic nobility helped clear the way for the rise of the Saadis from the Dra Valley in the 16th century and, in the 17th century, for the seizure of power by the Alawis from the Tafilalet. They still govern the country today.

In contrast to the houses of rough stone in the mountains, in the oases a tamped mud construction method is used. In a wooden form, a mixture of wet clay or mud, chopped straw and small stones, giving the mixture some lightness and malleability, is pounded with a tamper until it becomes firm. The form is pushed along horizontally from section to section, thus lining up one block after the other. Since clay is water-soluble, the coping of the wall must be protected from rain by slabs of slate and palm fronds. In the upper portions of multi-storied structures, adobe bricks are worked in in such a manner that they form magical defen-

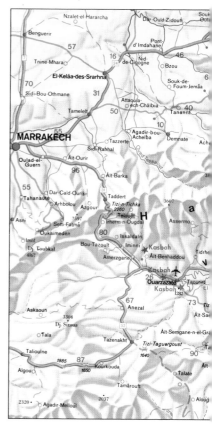

sive symbols in rhombic forms, triangles and zig-zag patterns. Phallic battlements on the walls protect the residents from the threat of infertility, which the evil eye could visit upon them. The ceilings of the rooms consist of plaited reeds, which rest on white poplar or palm trunks.

The houses and villages of southern Morocco's river oases along the "Route des Kasbahs" in the Dades Valley are architecturally indeed unique. A *ksar* (plural *ksour*) is a walled village of adobe buildings. Particularly beautiful, still-inhabited examples of such villages are to be found in the Tafilalelt and the Dra Valley. *Tighremt* (plural *tighermatine*) are fortified village communities consisting of dwellings, granary and stables on sev-

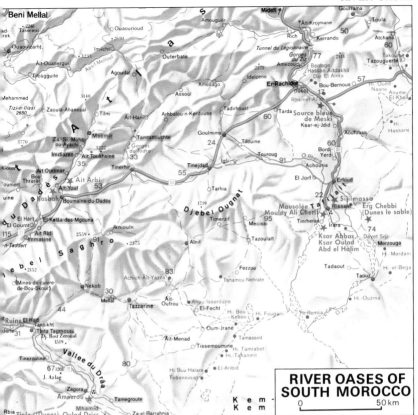

**RIVER OASES OF
SOUTH MOROCCO**

0   50 km

eral levels. Well-preserved *tighermatine* stand, for instance, along the route P 32 between Tinerhir Ouarzazate. The fortress-like community granary of a village is called *agadir* (pl. *agadirt*) or *ighrem*. A *kasbah* (pl. *ksabi*) describes a feudal ruler's citadel. Usually *ksabi* are situated at strategic points in the territory formerly ruled by the Glaoua Berbers, as, for example, in Tinerhir and Taourirt. Many of these traditional fortified villages have now been left to decay gradually: Nomadic attacks on sedentary farmers ceased in the 1930's following the Foreign Legion's pacification of the region, with the upshot that many oasis farmers no longer feel it necessary to maintain their once-essential traditional defenses.

FROM MIDELT TO ERFOUD

To the south of Midelt the road climbs from the desolate Plaine des Arid in the High Atlas to 1,907 m and the **Tizi n' Talrhemt** (Camel-mare Pass). Vegetation is sparse on the slopes: twisted old thuja trees (arborvitae), juniper bushes and esparto-grass defy the erosion which has been accelerated by overgrazing. Beyond the market-town of Rich one arrives at the upper course of the Oued Ziz, which has its source in the tribal regions of the Ait Haddidou in the Central High Atlas. These semi-nomads were once feared caravan robbers – the name of a spring 20 km from Rich was appropriately named *Ain khrob ou hrob* – "Drink and Flee".

153

On its course southward, the Ziz River has carved out the deep **Gorges du Ziz**. In 1930 the Foreign Legion constructed the **Tunnel du Légionnaire** at this bottleneck, which was of strategic importance for the sending of reinforcements to the south. The P 21 runs through the gorge half-way up and further downstream repeatedly opens up beautiful vistas over the green of oasis fields lined with date-palms and the ochre hues of adobe villages in the valley. It's a refreshing sight after the barren plateau of the eastern Atlas.

Shortly before reaching Er Rachidia, the Ziz is dammed by the **Barrage Hassan Addakhil**. The dam protects the villages along the river's lower course from inundations and renders possible the controlled irrigation of the date-palm groves of the Tafilalelt – if the winter rains in the mountains have been sufficient. Situated at the southern limits of the High Atlas is

Above: Palm trees shade the fields in the river oases. Right: Water and baraka are determining factors in the date harvest.

the provincial capital **Er Rachidia** (1,060 m; 20,000 inhabitants), which was built up into a garrison town for the Foreign Legion in the thirties under the name Ksar es Souk. Today the Moroccan army is the city's most important employer; Er Rachidia is also the educational center of the province. Street cafés beckon passers-by for a bit of relaxation; provisions can be re-stocked in the small market hall.

20 kilometers further south, located in a grove of palms on the edge of the Ziz Oasis, is the **Source bleue de Meski**, a refreshing spring which feeds a swimming pool constructed by the légionnaires in the fifties. The neighboring campsite is besieged by bazaar hawkers and village children. Meski is a good starting-point for a hike in the Ziz Valley. There, well away from the beaten "tourist track", one can become acquainted with the traditional agricultural techniques of the *fellahin* amid the idyllic surroundings of their remote villages' earthen architecture. Crossing the river, one comes upon the village ruins of **old Meski** (western

154

bank). Then you can hike downstream on either side of the irrigation canals (*souagi*) through paradisiacal gardens with an abundance of bird life, passing by picturesque *ksour* and *marabouts*. After a good four hours you arrive, by the village of Oulad Aissa, at the main route P 21, which leads to **Erfoud**.

Oasis Agriculture

The farmers maintain a three-tier style of cultivation in the river oases. Barley, wheat, broad beans, vegetables and forage plants are grown on the ground. The second story is made up of fruit trees including apricots, quinces, pomegranates and plums. The third level is formed by the fronds of the numerous date palms. Since only the female palms bear fruit, the oasis farmers plant between 30 and 50 females around one male tree. In order to maintain this ratio, the trees are reproduced with cuttings. Humans also assist in pollination. The male inflorescences are hung for a certain period in the

crowns of the female trees that are to be pollinated, or used immediately for hand-pollination. In springtime male inflorescences of especially fertile varieties are frequently seen for sale in the *souks* (weekly markets) of southern Morocco. The trees produce their first harvests after between three and seven years. From its 40th to 80th year the date palm reaches its optimum yield of up to 150 kilograms per tree. After this age most of the palms are cut down and used as building material. The kind of date sold at Christmas in Europe is not particularly important in Morocco. Moroccans mostly place a higher value on the starchier, mealier types. Due to their high sugar content, dates virtually preserve themselves and can therefore be stored for months at a time. After the harvest, which takes place in October, the fruits are given a second drying on the threshing floors, this allows remaining moisture to evaporate. The date palm takes well to the quite saline soils of southern Morocco, although they do require a lot of water – 6,000-8,000 cubic

155

meters annually per hectare. The palms also require an average annual temperature of roughly 21°C and are very susceptible to frosts. Over the last few years, such oasis idylls have been tainted by ailing date palms. This is due in part to the shortage of water during the drought years, which recur periodically as well as to the over-use of the ground water (partly at the consequence of the drought); on the other hand, *bayoud*, a fungal disease that causes the death of the palms within two years, has been spreading through North Africa. This has meant that Morocco, once a net exporter of dates, now has to import them to meet domestic demand, which is especially high during the festival month of Ramadan.

TAFILALET AND ERG CHEBBI

Route number P 21 runs south from Meski along the Oued Ziz, passing by the

Above: Only the children are pleased about a sandstorm in Erg Chebbi.

picturesque *ksour* El Jedid and Ait Amira. After 56 kilometers it reaches **Erfoud** and the major oasis region of **Tafilalt**, where over 700,000 date palms flourish. The harvest in October is celebrated with a pleasant, colorful festival. Besides its small market, Erfoud has virtually no interesting sights to attract visitors, though it is a convenient starting point for excursions to the sand dunes of the **Erg Chebbi** because of its hotels and Land-Rover rental agencies.

It's best to head out in the early morning or late afternoon to avoid the heat, past the **east gate** (Borj Est) on the route CT 3461 (asphalted at first) heading south, passing a **fossil site** in the *hammada* (rocky desert) left of the road. In the Palaeozoic there was a warm sea with coral reefs at the site of this inhospitable desert. Approximately 400 million years ago it was the habitat of the elongated *orthoceras* and the spiral-shaped goniatite – forerunners of the modern squid. The most frequently discovered species of trilobite are the up to 15-cm long specimens of the genus *phacops*. The fossils are polished and commonly offered for sale individually, although they are also available in whole slabs suitable for use as table-tops. Work and opportunities to earn money are rare in Tafilalet, therefore the fossil merchants follow tourists' vehicles for kilometers on rickety bicycles, their indigo turbans fluttering in the wind, trying to sell their wares at any cost, including limb!

Even from a distance the brilliant glowing red *barchane* (sand dunes) of the **Erg Chebbi** are easily recognizable. At the foot of these sand mountains, which are over 100 m high and steep enough to go "sand-skiing" on, there are a few modest cafés (37 km from Erfoud), on the roofs of which you can spend a romantic desert evening. The local waiters and dune-guides frequently perform a drum concert on their *darbukkas* until the hush of the desert and the glowing stars of night have arrived.

On a walk through this almost uncannily noiseless ocean of sand, you might also spot a few animals. The black tiger-beetles leave minute tracks behind them on the gently undulating surface. Among children of the desert, the common skink is a popular toy, which they quite aptly call the "sand-fish". These lizards have a streamlined body and smooth, shiny skin. If the reptile is released on loose sand it wriggles under the surface quick as a flash and moves along beneath the surface. The skink can close both its aural and nasal orifices. Its eyelids are transparent – it has honest-to-goodness sandglasses. The sand-fish reaches a length of up to 30 cm, is ovoviviparous, producing eggs that hatch within the body of the mother. There are, of course, other creatures here whose credentials are not quite as good. The individual who gets a glimpse of the highly venomous horned viper and lives to tell the tale should go to the next *marabout*, light a candle and thank his or her creator.

Some 15 kilometers further south is the desert village of **Merzouga.** Its oasis gardens – something one would hardly expect to find in this area – receive water through a canal from the Er Rachidia reservoir 150 kilometers away. To the west of the village lies **Dayet Srji**, a lake in the middle of the desert, which forms in the spring if there has been enough rain. No, what is sometimes seen here is not at all a mirage, it is indeed visited by whole throngs of pink flamingos. The black desert, the reddish sand dunes, blue water and the sparse green of the lakeshore with the rose hue of the birds certainly constitute one of the most beautiful impressions of the Moroccan Sahara.

Departing the lake, you must keep on a northwesterly course over sandy trails (sometimes difficult for cars, guide necessary), arriving after about 30 kilometers at **Rissani**, the main town of the Tafilalet. Located on its edge is the **Moulay Ali Sherif Mausoleum**. Besides a huge mosque built in the fifties, the facility contains the tomb of the founder of the Alawi Dynasty, which has ruled Morocco since the 17th century. Only Muslims are granted entrance. Palaces of Alawi viziers dating from the last century are located in the vicinity – both the **Ksar Abbas** and the **Ksar Oulad Abd el Halim** are worth a visit.

Rissani has a remarkably well-attended market (Sundays, Tuesdays and Thursdays). Near the **souk** there is a walled **ksar**, which is still inhabited. Passing through a single large gateway in the defensive wall you come to a small square with a fountain, *hammam* and a mosque. Turning off from it, the traveller can make an interesting tour of the medieval district – through covered alleyways which provide much-appreciated cool and shade during the heat of summer – enjoying an architecture found otherwise only in the villages of the Sahara itself.

Even in the early 20th century, Rissani was the beginning and end of a caravan

route via the Tanezrouft through the Sahara to the Niger. Until the 19th century, the legendary town of **Sijilmassa**, whose ruins can be viewed somewhat to the north of Rissani, was a trading center for jewels, precious woods, slaves, gold and ivory. Since the city was built of mud, little remained after its destruction at the hands of hostile nomads. Accounts by travellers of medieval times, such as those of El Wassan (later converted and known as Leo Africanus), report of the enormous wealth of this caravan city, a wealth due primarily to the indefatigable pack animal of the desert, the camel. A brief, essential description of this extraordinary beast follows.

Ships of the Desert

The body of the camel (or one-humped dromedary) is perfectly adapted to the desert climate. Its air filter is perched on a

Above: In the Todhra Oasis. Right: "The stroke of a sabre" in the Dades Gorge.

long neck, keeping the nasal membranes about two meters above the desert surface, which can easily reach temperatures in excess of 70°C. Camel hooves are so wide that one could almost think of them as special sand-tires and, with its full-time four-leg drive, the dromedary can leave even the most up-to-date rally jeep in the dust on the steep slopes of the dunes. A glimpse at the condition of the hump permits a quick appraisal of the camel's travel-readiness – almost like a gasoline gauge. If the hump is full and firm, the beast is 100% ready to roll. On the other hand, if it is sagging and limp, then it's high time for the food and water troughs. The camel hump consists of fat which is metabolically transformed into water when needed. One kilogram of fat yields roughly one liter of water. The water balance is essential for life: the camel can recapture about 30% of the moisture in its exhaled breath thanks to specialized membranes and make it through two weeks without water if need be (humans last a maximum three days). Then, however, the beast can swill up to 135 liters of water in a very short time. The largest portion of the water is stored in the red blood cells, which then expand to as much as 240 times their minimal volume. There are certain bacteria in the camels' intestines capable of absorbing the nitrogen products that other mammals excrete through the urinary system. In this manner as well, the desert-ship can save water since it doesn't need to eliminate as much urine. While the two-legged members of a caravan are already quite close to the paradise of the *huris* with an increase of 3,5° C in their body temperature, the camel can handle up to 9° without much problem, thus sweating less and saving coolant water. Their insensitive palates enable them to munch on the thorny desert brush without injury. They allow themselves to be ridden, carry loads of up to 200 kilogramms and supply milk, meat and wool. The Arabs explain the arrogant expression of the camel with the fact that this animal alone knows Allah's hundredth name.

FROM ERFOUD TO OUARZAZATE

In order to get from the Tafilalt back to the classic "Route des Kasbahs" one drives from Erfoud on the asphalted route number 3451 through El Jorf in the direction of Tinjedad. Several well-preserved fortified villages lie on this stretch. Long rows of mounds up to three meters in height appear on the desert steppe along the way. These belong to the subterranean *khettara* systems, now in disuse, which formerly provided the oases with water from the nearby peaks of the Jebel Ougnat. These clay mounds are found at the entrance and excavation shafts of the canals, which run horizontally under the surface. The road runs only a small distance from the mostly dry course of the Oued Rheris, which has its source in the Central High Atlas. The nomads put their camels to pasture in this area. The herds can frequently be seen at their watering places right along the road. However, the great days of the camel caravans are over for good, so most of the beasts wind up in the army's stewpots.

In **Tinjedad** you encounter the national highway P 32, which runs along the southern edge of the High Atlas. It connects Agadir with the oasis of **Figuig** (worth a visit) located far to the east on the Algerian border. The ruins of the **Tinerhir kasbah** appearabout 55 kilometers to the west of Tinjedad. It was established at the beginning of the 20th century by the powerful Glaoua clan where the Oued Todhra leaves the High Atlas, for the purpose of subjugating the farmers of the river oases and controlling the important caravan routes to Fès.

North of the town, the spectacular **Todhra Gorges** are reached by way of an asphalt road which has some splendid vistas into the deeply incised Todhra Valley with its oasis gardens. The gorges' almost vertical rock faces are nearly 300 meters high and within 10 meters of each other at the narrowest point – a field day for free climbers. Rare birds make their nests in the walls; these are counted by British birdwatchers with almost inconceivable passion. In the very midst of the gorges are two nice restaurants awaiting guests. They are situated directly under an overhang – only Allah knows when it will come down.

Coaches have to return to Tinerhir on the asphalt road in order to continue to Boumalne. On the other hand, fans of rough and dusty mountain trails, who travel according to the maxim "the path is the goal" will find their heart's delight on the continuing journey north through the Todhra Gorges. The CT 6902 forks in **Tamtattouche**; whereas the CT 3483 leads straight on via Ait Hani to Imilchil; to the left the CT 3444 turns off to the west over a 2,800-m pass to **Msemrir** in the **Dades Valley**. At that point, one of the most breathtaking gravel roads that Morocco can boast of starts – the trail **CT 6901** to **Boumalne** (65 km). It accompanies the Dades River on its course to the south and, beyond the archaic stone village of **Zawija Sidi Moha ou Ayachi**, ascends to over 2,000 m altitude at the beginning of the kilometer-long, deeply incised **Dades Gorges**. The vistas on the way are overwhelming: Far below, the blue ribbon of the river snakes along between precipitous rock faces, whose horizontally layered geological structure can be clearly discerned. In the background, the mountains of the High Atlas often wear gleaming white snowcaps on into early summer. After a winding descent, the river is crossed via a ford. On the narrow terraces along the riverbanks, lined by white poplars, the Berbers cultivate barley and vegetables. The repair work necessary on the field walls after the high

water of springtime is a fatiguing task. Passing by the picturesque villages of **Ait Toukhsine** and **Imdiazen,** one arrives at the **Sabre Cut –** the most critical section on this stretch. The trail through this imposing bottleneck runs along only just above the water level and is therefore frequently flooded or damaged after the rather frequent thunderstorms of summer. Beyond it, the gravel road ascends to a 1,950-m pass with abundant impressive views. Its steep serpentine descent southward has already been the doom of some trucks with overheated brakes and burned-up clutches. Better not forget to recite the words *bismillah* (in God's name) and *inshallah* (with Allah's help) – *before* entering the first hairpin turn! With this precaution and a relieved sigh of *hamdulilah* (Allah be praised) in the valley, nothing can go wrong. A peppermint tea in the cosy *auberge* (lodge) of **Ait Oudinar** is one of the best panaceas for overheated nerves. Haij Youssef, the helpful and efficient host, has experience with the organization of trekking tours to Jebel Azourki and Irhil M'Goun.

Down the valley, the paved road begins a short way past Ait Oudinar. Among the most beautiful photographic subjects in southern Morocco are the *tighermatine* (fortified villages) of **Ait Arbi**, which are situated on the left bank of the Dades in front of a wall of eroded basalt which, due to its rounded forms, is named quite fittingly the "Brain of the Atlas". Several kilometers further south, the **Kasbah Ait Youl** lords over a bend in the river. This well-preserved former citadel, crowned by four corner towerlets, can be viewed from the inside in exchange for the appropriate *bakshish*.

On the edge of the High Atlas at **Boumalne** (1,600 m), the Dades arrives at a broad rubble-strewn plain, bordered in the south by the arid **Jebel Saghro** mountain chain, which is crossed by the trail CT 6907 in the direction of Nekob – quite a suspect stretch for breakdowns.

Right: The tighermatine (residential stronghold) of Ait Arbi in front of the "brain of the Atlas".

Situated high above the souk grounds (Wednesday market) of Boumalne is a four-star hotel, a rather strikingly individual piece of architecture, which boasts the coldest swimming-pool in the Saharan forelands.

The P 32, or "Route des Kasbahs", continues west, passing the still-occupied earthen fortresses of relatively well-to-do oasis farmers in El Hart and El Goumt, continuing along the Dades to **El Kelaa M'Gouna**. In the oasis gardens of this area women farmers are seen wearing magnificent brocade garments as they pluck the rose blossoms from long hedges – later processed into rosewater and rose oil. Dried flower petals are sent from here to spice merchants throughout the country. The Moroccans offer rosewater to their guests as refreshment; the flavor of baked goods is also refined with it. Each year in May, the Berber tribes of the region (the Ait M'Gouna and the Ait Atta among others) come together on the *souk* grounds of El Kelaa to celebrate their colorful **Rose Festival** with traditional

folk dances. From Kelaa one can either follow the Assif M'Goun to the north, over trails to Bou Thrarar, then on foot to the Irhil M'Goun (4,068 m), or else hike westward along the lower Dades Valley, passing by archaic Berber villages well away from the stream of tourists.

Further towards Ouarzazate, the P 32 accompanies the lower course of the Assif M'Goun, whose tamped-mud *tighermatine* before the background of a High Atlas cloaked in snow well into May provide seductive subjects for the camera. Profusely decorated fortified houses stand in the villages of **Ait Ridi** and **Immasine** as well as in the little town of **Skoura** (Monday market). The reservoir of the **Barrage** (dam) **El Mansour Eddahbi** appears roughly 20 km past Skoura. The water of the Dades is stored here to supply the irrigation needs of the extensive palm groves in the adjoining Dra Valley to the south.

On the edge of **Ouarzazate** (1,160 m, Sunday market) stands the feudal **Kasbah of Taourirt**, owned by the Pasha of

161

Marrakech until 1956. This former citadel of the Glaoua tribe is now a museum and can be toured. The entrance through a horseshoe arch leads to the interior courtyard, the prime ornament of which is an 1884 German cannon with a rifled barrel. Its accuracy once made it a feared wonder-weapon far away, to which the heads of defeated enemies were brought as offerings! In the fortress courtyard, one can experience (on request) the *ahouach*, a really fascinating step-dance of Shluh Berber women accompanied by tambourines, the *darbukka* and large drums. In the first and second floors of the restored adobe citadel, the prayer hall, harem chamber and dining room can be viewed. From a garrison-town for the Foreign Legionnaires, Ouarzazate has risen to become Morocco's Hollywood, with the **kasbah** of Taourirt its most popular film backdrop. The ci-

Above left: The Dra Valley near Agdz. Above right: Up higher to the date harvest! Right: The well-fortified Ksar Tissergate.

ty's youth play out their scenes on **Avenue Mohammed V**, where, in addition to a number of souvenir shops, there is the "sinful" supermaket of Greek Moroccan-by-choice Dimitri (his selection of wine, ham of pork, chocolates, cured meats and provisions is indeed unrivalled).

12 kilometers to the west is the well-preserved kasbah of **Tiffoultoute**, in which a evening meal spiced up with a bit of folklore can be arranged. The ultimate tourist magnet of the province is the fortified tamped-clay village of **Ait Ben-haddou** (32 km to the northwest of Ouarzazate), which rose to fame thanks to Orson Welles' film *Sodom and Gomorrha*. The village of dilapidated fort-residences, which is almost deserted now, is picturesquely situated in the valley of the Assif Mellah on a former caravan route, over which gold and slaves were transported from Timbuktu to Marrakech. The rather challenging mountain trail number CT 6803 follows the old trade route, passing the stork-guarded kasbah of **Tamdaght**, north through the Ounila Val-

ley up to the "Mother of all kasbahs" – the feudal castle of **Telouet** (1,800 m), which is quite imposing even in its current state of dilapidation. It was the historical ancestral seat of the Glaoua tribe (56 km from Ait Benhaddou, tours possible). A small asphalt road from the **Tichka Pass** (about 2,260 m) connects to the well-developed route P 31 leading to Marrakech.

DRA VALLEY

The P 31 runs from Ouarzazate to the southeast in the direction of Zagora (164 km). Beyond the spartan oasis of Ait Saoun it leaves the *hammada* and climbs up to the **Tizi n'Tinififft Pass**, which crosses the Jebel Saghro at an altitude of 1,660 m and has some fantastic views of the almost unvegetated range's geological strata covered with a dark veneer of "desert polish". Soon the Jebel Kissane (1,531 m) appears to the south like some kind of terraced pyramid towering over the **Oued Dra**. Located in the valley is

the small town of **Agdz** (Thursday market), whose bazaar structures are quite photogenic, behung with colorful carpets and *kelims* from the Tazenakht region.

At this point the road continues along the extensive date-palm groves of the agricultural Dra Valley. Opposite the *ksar* ruins of **Tamenougalt**, which was formerly the central town for oases along the section of the Mezguita beginning here, a kasbah rises up over the left bank of the Dra which was once the residence of well-to-do Jewish caravan traders. The weekly market of **El Had** takes place on Sundays; Tuesdays in **Tleta Tagmoute**. At these you can haggle over the price of a *burnus*, the traditional Berber hooded cape. Some extraordinarily well-preserved walled villages of adobe construction line the river oasis on both sides. The *ksar* **Tinsouline** is particularly enchanting before its background of Jebel Bou Zeroual's geological strata. Along the way there are a number of *marabouts* (graves of holy men) in the midst of modest cemeteries; some of the former have

picturesque whitewashed domes, some conical clay fixtures. They are most frequently shaded by ancient umbrella acacias or stalwart tamarisks.

In **Zagora**, a very dusty wind whistles through the Avenue Mohammed V. Only on market days – Wednesday and Sunday – is this provincial capital on the edge of the *hammada* shaken from its lethargy. Then, urban Arab women in their garb of blue and the country women of the Arab Oulad Yahia and Roha tribes cloaked in their black *haiks* come streaming into the souk grounds, which are bedecked with the white tents of merchants from throughout the country. At the end of the town a hand-painted camel signpost of charming naiveté indicates that Timbuktu is a mere 52 days away by caravan. In the former days the salt caravans from Taoudenni actually formed the basis of this trading center wealth. Here, in the 16th century, the Arabic Saadis emerged

Above: The acacia on the Marabout of El Had has defied many duststorm.

as Morocco's new ruling dynasty. Nowadays, two air-conditioned oases with several swimming pools are open to heat-refugees in Zagora: the tradition-steeped Hotel Tinzouline at the town entrance and the super-modern Club Reda on the banks of the Dra. No bathing in the Dra! Danger of bilharziasis!

For well-equipped *hammada* enthusiasts, the trail CT 6953 heads west out of Zagora to the spring-oases of the Jebel Bani – Foum Zguid, Tata and Akka – and then further to **Bouizakarne** (507 km). Eastwards, Rissani and the Tafilalet are reached after a 250 km trip on the trail CT 3454 via Tazzarine and Alnif.

The *ksar* **Amezrou** is located beyond the Dra Bridge. It is renowned for its Berber jewelry (genuine if you're lucky). The craft was founded here by Jewish silversmiths, but today the work is carried on by Muslims.

The most interesting destination to visit in this area is the village of **Tamegroute**, 18 km to the southeast of Zagora. The Nassiriya brotherhood maintains a

Koran school and the **library** belonging to it. There are over 4,000 medieval manuscripts stored here including *hadiths* and Korans, books on the history of Fès and Alexandria, dictionaries and textbooks on astronomy, medicine and mathematics. An algebra book from the 13th century features the western Arabic numerals, which although now forgotten, inspired the development of our numerals via the universities of Córdoba, Granada and Sevilla. The collection's prime showpiece, sheltered behind mere window glass, is an interpretation of the Koran on gazelle hide dating from 1091. The scholar Sidi Mohammed Abdallah ben Nasser founded this collection of books in the 17th century. His grave in the adjacent mausoleum is sought out by infirm or feeble pilgrims hoping for a miraculous cure from the *baraka* of the library patron, who is venerated as a *marabout*. They take shelter in the interior courtyard of the 18th-century burial temple, which is also accessible to non-Muslims. The tall, opulently painted cedar gateway of the tomb, framed by stucco arabesques and Koran *suras*, may still today merely be passed by Muslims.

On the eastern edge of the town are the traditional **potters' workshops** in which time has indeed stood still: Under the skilled hands of the potters, articles for everyday use are made. They are covered with a silvery-gray manganese glaze and fired in archaic kilns, thus lending them their characteristic green hue. Women in black garb bring in the thorny brush used for firing the kiln.

On the continuing journey to **Mhamid** one can pay a visit to the **sand dunes of Tinfou**. To the south of them, the Oued Dra veers sharply to the west near **Oulad Driss**, an ancient *ksar* which the desert sand is threatening to overwhelm. These days, it is only in years of extraordinarily abundant precipitation that the waters of the Oued Dra make it as far as Tan-Tan and the Atlantic (750 km away).

RIVER OASES OF SOUTH MOROCCO

Accommodation

ER RACHIDIA: *MODERATE:* **Rissani**, Route d'Erfoud, Tel: 057-2136.
BUDGET: **Oasis**, Rue Abou Abdallah 4, Tel: 2519. **Meski**, Av. Moulay Ali Cherif, Tel: 2065.
ERFOUD: *MODERATE:* **Salam**, Route de Rissani, Tel: 057-6665. **Tafilalet**, Av. M. Ismael, Tel: 057-6535 (landrover rental).
BUDGET: **La Gazelle**, Av. Mohammed V, Tel: 6028.
RISSANI: *BUDGET:* **El Filalia**, Grand Place de Rissani.
MERZOUGA: *ABSOLUTELY BASIC:* **Des Amis**, at the edge of the sand dunes (no water!).
TINERHIR: *MODERATE:* **Saghro**, Tel: 1.
BUDGET: **Todhga**, Av. Hassan II 37, Tel: 9.
GORGES DU TODHRA: *BUDGET:* **Des Roches** and **Yasmina**, both in the Todhra Valley.
BOUMALNE: *MODERATE:* **El Madayec**, Tel: 31.
BUDGET: **Soleil Bleu**, in front of the market complex.
GORGES DU DADES: *BUDGET:* **Auberge Ait Oudinar**, in the upper Dades Valley, 23 km from Boumalne.
EL KELAA DES M'GOUNA: *MODERATE:* **Les Roses du Dades**, Tel: 18.
BUDGET HOTELS along the Route du Ouarzazate.
OUARZAZATE: *LUXURY:* **Club Karam**, Bd. Prince Moulay Rachid, Tel: 2225. *MODERATE:* **Belère**, Bd. Prince Moulay Rachid, Tel: 2803. **Azghor**, Bd. Prince Moulay Rachid, Tel: 2612. **Riad Salam**, Rue Moh. Diouri, Tel: 2206. **Tichka Salam**, Av. Mohammed V, Tel: 2206. *BUDGET:* **La Gazelle**, Av. Mohammed V, Tel: 2151. **Es Salaam** and **Royal**, both on Av. Mohammed V.
ZAGORA: *MODERATE:* **Tinzouline**, at the northern City Gate, Tel: 22, **Club Reda**, on the west bank of the Dades River, Tel: 149.
BUDGET: **La Fibule du Dra**, at the east end of the Dades Bridge. **La Vallée du Dra**, **Des Amis**, **La Palmeraie**, all on Av. Mohammed V.

Weekly Markets

ER RACHIDIA: Sundays, Tuesdays, Thursdays. **ERFOUD:** Daily. **RISSANI:** Sundays, Tuesdays, Thursdays (with livestock market). **TINERHIR:** Mondays. **BOUMALNE:** Wednesdays. **EL KELAA:** Wednesdays. **SKOURA:** Mondays. **OUARZAZATE:** Sundays. **ZAGORA:** Sundays and Wednesdays.

MARABOUTS AND MOUNTAIN PEAKS

MARRAKECH

TINMAL

OURIKA VALLEY

TELOUET

TOUBKAL TREK

OUKAIMEDEN TREK

JEBEL SIROUA MULE "TREK"

MARRAKECH

"Marrakech, the pearl cast over the Atlas" – this poetic metaphor was coined by the Andalusian poetess Hafsa Bint El-Hadj in the 12th century. And in fact the city of Marrakech, which is also named "The Red" for the hue of its buildings, is to this day indeed one of the finest pearls of Morocco; though no virginal one by any means, rather one pierced, to stay true to the graphic yet floral language of the Orientals. The *marrakshi* have a grasping (in the true sense of the word) way about them: An attempt to take in the sights at the Jemaa el Fna (famed for its itinerant entertainers) and the bazaar without the protection of a *guide officiel* can easily turn into a frantic race through a gauntlet of self-proclaimed guides, snake charmers and touts. Of course, that's all part of the flair of this Berber city, which one either falls head over heels for, or hates.

History

In the middle of the wide Haouz Plain, before the immense silhouette of the

Previous pages: The Jemaa el Fna magically attracts tourists, street entertainers, storytellers, and swindlers. Left: This man selling water is dressed in Rifi garb.

High Atlas (snow-capped until May), Abu Bekr, the first great commander of the Almoravids, had a gigantic tent-camp set up for his troops around 1060 on the location of present-day Marrakech. These camel riders, inspired by the jihad (the Islamic Holy War) and a somewhat less religious greed for booty, were, as Sanhadja Berbers, related to the Tuaregs and called themselves *al murabitun*, the "men of the *ribat*" (castle of an order).

Under Sultan Youssef Ben Tashfin, Abou Bekr's camp developed into a city sometime around 1070. Following ben Tashfin's decisive victory over the Christian troops of the Spanish King Alfonso in Andalusia, and benefitting from the rich spoils that victory brought, Marrakech became capital of an empire that soon extended from Algeria to the Atlantic and from the Ebro to the Senegal. The Almoravids had quite a number of Andalusian-influenced mosques and palaces designed and built, surrounded the city with a 12-km long wall and had an extensive palm grove planted all the way around it. These oasis gardens were watered by *khettaras*, subterranean groundwater collection channels which were installed at depths as great as 50 m.

In 1222 the fanatic preacher Ibn Toumart turned up in the city. Having accused the Almoravids of decadence and

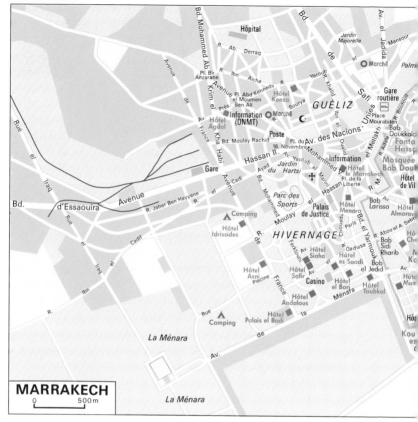

MARRAKECH

0   500 m

La Ménara

heresy, he was forced into flight by the irate rulers. He found refuge in Tinmal in the High Atlas among Masmouda Berbers and called on them to wage a holy war against the Almoravids. Their first attempt to take Marrakech in 1130 miscarried, however. The self-styled *mahdi* (one led by god himself) died, and it wasn't until a full 16 years later that his favorite pupil Abd el Moumen succeeded in the conquest, though only with the aid of the traitorous Christian palace guard.

The new rulers called themselves *al muwahiddun,* "confessors of the divine unity", and proceeded to tear down all the buildings of their predecessors with all the vim and vigor of fanatics. The Almohad Abd el Moumen assumed the title

Amir el Mumin, "ruler of the faithful", thus claiming to be head of all Muslims. In fact, even the present day King Hassan II still bears this title. Abd el Moumen also ruled an empire which encompassed the entire Maghreb as far as Tripolitania and half of Spain.

The Almohads, concernded with the looks of their city, erected some significant buildings in Marrakech, such as the Koutoubia Mosque, a large kasbah, walls and gates, deep cisterns, e parks and new city quarters. They summoned important scientists of the time to their court, including the famed Moorish Aristotelian commentator and physician Averoes (Ibn Rushd), and also liberated the physician Avenzoar from his Almoravid dungeon.

1 Souk Attarine
2 Souk Teinturies

prosperity, evidence of which remains in the ruins of the El Badi Palace and the Saadian tombs. Ahmed I, the most note-worthy sultan of the Saadian Dynasty, conquered the gold-trading cities of Timbuktu and Gao in 1591, taking rich booty and bearing from that time on the appellation *el mansour*, "the victorious" and *ed dehbi*, "the gilded".

The Arabic Alawi dynasty, which succeeded the Saadis in the 17th century, was no longer centered in Marrakech, having relocated its seat to Meknes, Fès and Rabat instead. Despite this, however, Alawi sultans continued to maintain palaces in Marrakech as well and even built new complexes such as the Palais de la Bahia and the Dar Si Said.

In 1907, the city stepped into the center of political events once more as Moulay Abd el Hafiz, supported by Madani el Glaoui, leader of the powerful Glaoua Berbers, had himself proclaimed sultan in Marrakech and drove his incompetent brother Abd el Aziz from the throne. But he too would soon have to abdicate real power following the signing of the protectorate treaty in Fès on March 30, 1912. In the same year, a revolt in Marrakech organized by the religious warrior El Hiba gave the French a convenient excuse to march into the city. Thami el Glaoui, Madani's successor and pasha of the city, put his men at the disposal of the French as a police force and thus rose to become the absolute ruler of the South.

El Glaoui thrived in an atmosphere of fabulous wealth. In his luxurious city palace he received film stars, aristocracy and world leaders, and the dissipation of his parties filled the pages of tabloids at the time. However, his urging of the French to send Sultan Mohammed V, who was striving for independence, into exile on Madagascar in 1953 turned out to be his undoing. When, in the wake of bloody riots, Morocco finally did achieve independence under Mohammed V in 1956, el Glaoui lost both power and for-

Tribal revolts and palace intrigues finally led to the dynasty's downfall at the beginning of the 13th century. In 1269, Marrakech was taken by the Merinids, a Berber tribe from the eastern steppes of Algeria, and the sultans' court was moved to Fès. As a result, the Berber city in the High Atlas lost importance, depopulated and, at the beginning of the 16th century, even became a target of the Portuguese, who had established themselves on the Atlantic coast.

In 1521, the Arabic *Saadis* moved into the city without encountering any serious resistance, having already conquered Fès and the Sous territory. They settled on Marrakech as their new capital. This signalled the beginning of a new period of

tune. The once-splendid Glaoua kasbah of Telouet has been condemned by the Alawis to fall into decay.

Jemaa el Fna

The square **Jemaa el Fna** is without a doubt the pulsating heart of the medina, the fountainhead of the city's vigor. The Saadian sultan Ahmed el Mansour originally wanted to construct the Mosque Jemaa el Hana at this site. Due to a series of unfortunate events, however, the sultan was unable to realize his plans before his death. Therefore, the square was named Jemaa el Fna (Mosque of Ruins). Later, the heads of execution victims were set out on display, thus the name of the square came to be translated as "assembly of the dead". Today, all around the square, cafés with roof terraces provide a vantage point from which to enjoy the somewhat more uplifting, modern-

Above: Storytellers are actors, preachers, mimes, and clowns – all in one.

day comings and goings. Best photos are taken just before sunset.

The Jemaa el Fna teems with humanity at any hour of the day. In the mornings small businessmen, including barbers, cobblers and dentists set up shop here. They are joined in the course of the day by fruit sellers, orange juice squeezers and street peddlers. By late afternoon there is a throng of the density you would expect at a fairground. One must simply dive into a vast mass of humanity in constant motion.

The plaza looks like some sort of open-air circus. There are certainly some picturesque figures to be found here. The first dirham is usually snared by the rather photogenic **water sellers** in their traditional red Rifi costumes with wide-brimmed straw hats – not for the precious wet stuff in the goat-skins they carry, but rather for the "royalties" they exact from passing shutterbugs. Equally professional photographic models include the **snake charmers**, who also let scorpions crawl across their foreheads for variety. The visitor who grabs for his camera will almost certainly be presented with an aggressive cobra – and if the reptile is too languid, its master will step on its tail! Should the spectator fail to cough up a coin or two, the kindly snake charmer comes threateningly closer – and he has the convincing argument in his hands!

Muffled-sounding drums accompany the sharp clacking of iron rattles: the *gnaoua,* black musicians, are making their appearance. The dark-skinned men are clothed in long white *ganduras* (shirt-dresses). Their heads are graced with a shell-embroidered cap from which hangs a long cord with tassel, swinging back and forth to the rhythm. They whirl madly around in a circle with iron rattles in both hands. The eldest beats the drum while the youngest, a charming little fellow with a faithful gaze (and sinewy fingers) collects money from the audience. The *gnaoua* belong to a mysterious brotherhood which is said to be involved in nocturnal spirit conjury, a rumor that may loosen a superstitious purse string or two.

But the square has even more to offer. Red-dressed **acrobats** form living towers and perform furious somersaults. They are members of the Sidi Aulad ou Moussa Brotherhood, whose center is located at Tiznit. Their members also appear in the circuses of Europe.

A "**game of chance**" promises a quick dirham or two: lying on a box is a piece of cord with two loops in it. Whoever can guess which of the loops closes when the cord is pulled is the winner. Pushed into playing along, the first hesitant (and usually European) spectator wins 100 dirham with his first try. Of course, he is simultaneously pressed to continue playing. The bet is fifty dirham, and just as quickly he has lost fifty of his hundred. Naturally enough the con-men have no change, so the mark has to play further, losing again. In another second or two he's reaching for his own wallet. The more alert player disappears like a flash with the first bill. Then all the swindler's curses are useless – even they can have tough days sometimes.

The **storytellers** are the true heroes of the square. They lure the biggest audiences, being actor, preacher, pantomime, jester and acrobat all rolled up into one person. And they can tell beautiful tales, like the one of the herdsman who disappeared in the forest and had a peculiar story to tell on his return. While searching for his lost cows he encountered a woman with small children. When he asked her about his cows, he was suddenly surrounded by ghosts. One of these ghost women was nursing her child. She offered him her other breast and took him in as her son. For a long while the herdsman stayed in the forest with the ghosts, where he wanted for nothing. However, he grew ever more homesick and eventually wanted to come back among people. The ghosts wouldn't let him have his way for a long time. Only after he had promised to return to them one day did they let him go, but not before he had spoken a magic incantation which gave the spirits power over him forever. In return, he received the gift of being able to perform beneficial deeds. After the herdsman had returned to the people he continued to watch the cattle as before, but one thing had changed: Because of his *baraka* (power of benediction) he was now capable of helping the people. Many of them asked him for advice, and he aided them by writing down their problems on a piece of paper and wrapping the coins he was offered in it. He then buried the packet at the foot of a tree, and when he looked again a little later the money had disappeared – but in return, the solution was now on the paper. However, when his mother was dying his powers failed. Could it have been that the ghosts wanted to get him back?

After nightfall, the scents of food waft across the market square. Fish-friers and soup-cooks lay claim to the areas where

the street-performers and jugglers were, covering them with tables and benches and then imploring the onlookers – who have become hungry by now – to take a seat.

Medina

To the north of the square is the bazaar quarter of the *souks,* which can be thoroughly explored in a stroll of about three hours. The **Rue Souk Smarine**, near the Ouessabine mosque, was once the rush-weavers' market; textiles have now become dominant here. After 200 m a short alleyway turns off to the right, leading to the **Place Ragba Kedima**, the old slave-market and one of the most picturesque places in the medina. Spices, carpets and Berber cosmetics are on sale; all around the square apothecaries specializing in natural remedies offer such

Above: Death is free, a snake picture never. Right: Medersa Ben Youssef was once a university of theology.

aphrodisiac medications ranging from dried thorn-tail lizards to the more common Spanish fly.

Past the turn-off to the Place Kedima the **Rue Souk Smarine** forks into the **Souk Attarine** (left) and the **Souk el Kebir** (right). If you keep left again at the start of the mixed Souk Attarine, you come to the **Souk des Teinturiers,** or dyers' lane, where colorful bundles of dyed wool hang over the street to dry, just asa they have for ages. Back again to the Souk Attarine, next come the markets of the *babouche*-makers and the iron and coppersmiths. Turning right along one of the *kisseria*-alleys with textile stores, the Souk el Kebir (jewelers, silversmiths) is reached. Traders in leather goods display their wares in the Souk Cherratine.

The souk comes to an end in front of the **Ben Youssef mosque**, the former Friday-mosque of the Almoravid sultan Ali Ben Youssef. It dates from 1120, but was altered in the 16th and 19th centuries. The **koubba** (grave) **El Baadiyin** is located to the south of the mosque. It wasn't excavated until 1960 by French archeologists and, like the mosque, dates from the 11th century. Its function isn't entirely clear. The building consists of a dome with ornamental ribs and may well have contained a fountain for some ancient form of ritual cleansing.

The neighboring **medersa Ben Youssef**, founded by the Merinid sultan Abu el Hassan (1331-1351) is a real must. In 1564 the Saadian sultan El Ghalib extended it to the largest medersa in the Maghreb. In its heydey more than 900 students received instruction in Islamic administration here. There are 150 cells lined up around one large and seven smaller interior courtyards. The complex need not shy from comparisons with the structures in Fès on which it it was modelled. The academic activities of the medersa continued almost uninterrupted until 1960, after which it was transformed into a museum.

The center of the main atrium is dominated by a rectangular marble basin. The profusion of ornamentation on the walls consists of a series of colorful geometric tiled mosaics at the base, surmounted by arabesque Koran suras, pine cones and seashells in stucco work or carved in cedar. Peculiar depictions of animals decorate the marble pool of a fountain at the stairway leading up to the students' cells. The windows of these rooms on the first floor provide interesting perspectives of the stuccoed walls of the courtyard.

Continuing further northwest now, you come upon an old *fondouk* (inn). Here stands a beautiful monumental **fountain**, which is named, tellingly, *Ain khrob ou khof*, "drink and admire".

Passing through the **Bab Taghzout,** you come upon the **zawiya of Sidi Bel Abbes** and the most highly revered burial sanctuary in Marrakech. Sidi Bel Abbes (1130-1205) was the most important of the city's seven patron saints. During the reign of Moulay Ismail, the ritual developed of seeking out their seven *koub-bas* (graves) as part of a pilgrimage. Today they are also well-suited as orientation points for a city tour.

Marrakech's second patron saint is Sidi Ben Slimane el Jazouli, whose zawiya is located a short distance from that of Sidi bel Abbes. The holy man lived in the 15th century and was considered a descendant of the Prophet.

By crossing the Rue Riad el Arous and following the Rue Dar el Glaoui, one arrives at the **Dar el Glaoui**, which was the seat of the Thami, Pasha of the Glaouase Berbers until 1955. The palace was built in a traditional Spanish-Moorish style in the early 20th century and is not open to the public. Another striking building in the northern part of the medina is the **Bab Doukkala mosque**, founded in the 16th century by Lalla Messaouda, the mother of Sultan Ahmed el Mansour. The **Sidi el Hassan ou Ali Fountain** with its three domes and magnificient ornamental tile mosaics is part of the mosque.

To the east, the Rue Bab Doukkala opens into the Rue Mouassine, which

175

leads to the **el Mouassine Mosque**. It was constructed in 1573 under the Saadian sultan Abdallah el Gahlib. It was financed, however, by the wealthy merchant family Mouassine. The roof, which spans seven aisles, has a carved wooden ceiling of astonishing beauty. Outside the mosque stands the profusely ornamented **Mouassine Fountain** with an ornate columned porch and seven basins.

Located at the end of the Rue Mouassine is the **zawiya of Sidi Abd el Aziz**, the city's third patron saint. If you continue to stroll south, you will come upon the **marabout of Sidi Moulay el Ksouras**, the fourth patron saint of Marrakech. From the Place Bab Fteuh one arrives back at the Jemaa el Fna once again.

The Koutoubia Mosque

From the "Square of the Dead" one can already see the city's landmark, the minaret of the venerable **Koutoubia Mosque**. It was named after the **souk el koutoubiyyin**, the bazaar of the book-traders, which is nearby. It might well be noted that this market originated in the 12th century, a long period during which a Christian European would have been hard-pressed to write the word *book*. The hall-type mosque has 17 aisles and 112 columns covering a total floor area of 5400 sq.m and is thus among the largest of its kind – 25,000 faithful can say their prayers within it. At the end of the prayer hall is an ornately carved *minbar* (pulpit), which is supposed to be a remnant of the Almoravid mosque destroyed by the Almohad builders of the present edifice. The pulpit is thought to have come from Córdoba; its donor is believed to have been the Almoravid sultan Ali ben Youssef (1107-1143).

The square **minaret**, which wasn't completed until the reign of Yacoub el

Right: The traditional bags of the Atlas Berbers are richly embroidered with silk.

Mansour (1184-1199), was the direct model for the Giralda in Sevilla and the Hassan Tower in Rabat. It is considered the ultimate structure of its kind. The tower is 69 m in height, its lateral length 12,8 m. Six rooms one above the other, constitute the interior; leading around them is a ramp, by way of which the muezzin could ride up to the balcony. The tower is adorned with four copper globes. According to legend, they were originally made of pure gold, and there were once supposed to have been only three. The fourth was donated by the wife of Yacoub el Mansour as compensation for her failure to keep the fast for one day during the month of Ramadan. As an expression of penitence she had her golden jewelry melted down, from which the fourth globe was fashioned.

The Kasbah District

The **Bab Agnaou**, constructed of bluish limestone, is considered the most beautiful gateway in Marrakech. It didn't serve for the defense of the city, having been instead the main portal to a well-fortified residential quarter that the Almohad sultan Yacoub el Mansour had built and that today encompasses the big Kasbah Mosque, the Saadian Graves, the el Badi Palace and the Dar el Makhzen, the present-day royal palace.

Hidden behind high walls on the south side of the Kasbah Mosque is one of the special jewels of art history: the **Saadian Graves** (Tombeaux des Saadiens), an indeed magnificent necropolis from the era of the Saadian sultan Ahmed el Mansour (1578-1603).

In contrast to the Kasbah Mosque, the burial grounds are a museum and may be viewed by the public. Sultan Abdallah El-Ghalib (1557-1574) had the first permanent tomb constructed. Ahmed el Mansour was the man ultimately responsible for the site being expanded into a necropolis in which all the rulers, family mem-

bers and dignitaries of the Arabic Saadian Dynasty could be interred. Envious of their architecture, the Alawi sultan Moulay Ismail had the Saadis' palaces destroyed. He spared the graves, but had them surrounded by a high wall. After that the complex became overgrown and fell into oblivion. The necropolis wasn't explored again until 1917, when French archeologists made a separate entrance by breaking through the wall, since the original way through the adjacent Kasbah Mosque was forbidden to Christians.

The complex houses two mausoleums. The first, just to the left of the entrance, is the largest and most beautiful, consisting of three halls. The **prayer hall** with the *mihrab* (prayer niche) in which the Alawi ruler Moulay el Yazid (1790-1792) lies buried was not originally intended for interments. The second room, named the **Hall of Twelve Columns**, houses the grave of the great Saadian sultan Ahmed el Mansour (1578-1603). It is among the most sumptuous structures Maghreb artisans and craftsmen ever created. Twelve columns of Carrara marble connected by horseshoe arches support a dome consisting of countless gilded *muqarnas* (prisms), creating an effect reminiscent of a crystal cave. In the third room, the **Hall of the Three Niches**, the sultan's children are interred; it is extraordinarily rich in ornamentation as well.

A pavilion in the midst of the cemetery garden shelters, among others, the **grave of Lalla Messaouda**, Ahmed el Mansour's mother.

The most costly of this ruler's ostentatious buildings was the nearby **El Badi Palace,** which was financed with the plunder from his raids on the gold city of Timbuktu. All that has been preserved of the 18-hectare palace complex are the peripheral wall, pavilion ruins, gardens and a subterranean dungeon, since for ten years during the 17th century, Moulay Ismail used the buildings as a "quarry" for his ambitious construction plans in Meknes. Today the grounds serve as a grandiose backdrop for the annual **folklore festival**. Towards the end of spring,

the best of Morocco's folklore groups can be seen for ten days of evening performances. Bordering the west side of the El Badi Palace is the **Dar el Makhzen**, the present-day royal palace, which, understandably enough, is not at all open to the public, but can of course be observed from a distance.

Located only a few hundred meters from the El Badi ruins is the **Bahia Palace**, which can be toured if Hassan II's servants don't happen to be staying there at the time. The palace was constructed at the close of the 19th century for Si Moussa, the grand vizier of Sultan Abd er Rahman. His son, Bou Ahmed, grand vizier of Sultans Abu Ali Hassan I and Abd el Azis, resided there as well. Later, the palace served for a time as the base of a protectorate's administration. The magnificent oriental edifice, which is

Above: Almohad architects created the minaret of the Koutoubia mosque in the 12th century. Right: Those with courage may join in the dance.

concealed behind unassuming external walls, was erected in the course of seven years by one French and one Moroccan architect. It bears its appellation *bahia* (beautiful, lustrous) with every right: it features painstakingly landscaped *riads* (court gardens), loftly staterooms ornamented in Moorish style, a mirrored hall, a large harem court with adjoining garden and a refreshing blue-and-white-tiled palace mosque.

Departing the Bahia Palace, one can follow the direction signs to the **Dar Si Said Palace**, which now houses the **Museum of Moroccan Folk Art**. This exquisite building was constructed at the end of the last century for Si Said, a vizier of Sultan Abou Ali Hassan. The four rooms of the ground floor contain exhibits of Berber jewelry, household articles, clothing and daggers, sabres and muzzle-loading guns.The upper floor, the main appeal of which is its splendid ceiling of carved wood, holds a wedding throne on which the bride of a wealthy man accepted her bridal gifts. The walls are hung with exquisite rugs from the main production regions including Chichaoua, Beni M'Guild, Rabat and Glaoua. At the rear of the grounds tall cedar gates are on display. Graced with arabesques and geometric ornamentation these gates come from kasbahs of the Dra Valley.

City Gates and Gardens

The **Bab Doukkala** is the best place to start out on a tour of the medina. The city's first wall was laid out in 1127 by the Almoravids and is still in good condition in spite of difficult centuries. It was lengthened from 9 km to 12 km under the Almohads. Reddish clay served as building material. The wall is between 6 m and 9 m high and ranges from 1,4 m to 2 m in thickness. The **koubba of Kadi Ayad ben Moussa** (1613-1624), the fifth of the city's seven patron saints, is hidden at the northern tip of the medina wall.

Passing around the northeastern point of the medina wall, it leads after a while to the the horseshoe-shaped Almohad gateway **Bab el Khemis**, where a livestock market is held on Thursdays. Next comes the **Bab Debbagh**, the tanners' gate; its terrace affords good views of the Tanners' Quarter. At the **Bab Ailen**, the Almohads suffered a devastating defeat on their first attempt to take over Marrakech from the Almoravides.

The Christian Almoravid militia is said to have admitted the Almohad forces to the city through the **Bab Aghmat** in the year 1146, the next gateway on the itinerary. The largest cemetery in Marrakech is located before the portal. Standing next to it is the **zawiya of Sidi Youssef** (died 1197), the sixth of the city's seven patron saints. He lived in a cave here with people afflicted with leprosy. The 18th-century **Bab Ahmar** (the red gate), through which the sultans entered the city in former times, leads directly to the Dar el Makhzen, the present royal palace. By following the road one reaches the outer and inner *mechouar*, courtyards which were used by the guard as assembly and exercise grounds.

From the inner *mechouar* you can enter the **Agdal**, the former sultanic garden of the Almohad rulers of the 12th century. The grounds are over 3 km long and almost 1,5 km wide. Garden is actually the wrong designation, since it is more of a fruit plantation with olive, citrus, pomegranate, fig, plum and pear trees as well as numerous grapevines. All are irrigated with water from the High Atlas; the place is named after the two large pools used to collect that very valuable water.

If you then continue along the medina wall, you come to the **Bab Ighli**, pass by the koubba of Sidi Amara and thus reach the **Bab Ksiba**. This gate leads to the palace area and is therefore well-guarded if Hassan II happens to be in town. Next comes the **Bab er Robb**, the "gate of condensed grape juice". It was presum-

ably constructed during the reign of the devout Almohad sultan Yacoub el Mansour (1184-1199). The cultivation of grapevines was and is broadly disseminated in Islamic countries. In earlier days the juice of the grapes was boiled down to a syrup and used as a sweetener, although it was sometimes covertly fermented into alcohol – though this is quite explicitly forbidden in the Koran. To trust is good, control, however, is better – in former times grape juice entering the city was indeed strictly monitored at the Bab er Robb, presumably by the Almohad equivalent of a prohibition officer. Situated in one graveyard to the west of the "grape-gate" is the **koubba of Sidi es Soheyli** (1115-1185), the last of the city's seven holy men.

Not far past the **Bab el Jedid**, the "new gate", stands the **Hotel Mamounia**, the most renowned luxury hotel in Morocco. It was built in 1923 by the French in Neo-Moorish Protectorate style and has accommodated more than a few VIP's from around the world. In the forties and fif-

ties, British statesman Winston Churchill spent many a night in room 300, drawing inspiration for his painting from its tremendous view of the High Atlas Range. Those curious about the discreet charm of the bourgeoisie should by bo case miss sipping a cup of coffee here. By the way, the hotel even has its own golf course in the adjacent park, which was laid out in the 16th century as a sultanic garden of the Saadian Dynasty.

To the west, far beyond the medina walls, a vast ancient olive grove stretches out near the airport – this is the **Menara Garden**, established back in the 12th century under the Almohads. The Alawi pavilion wasn't added until the 19th century; reflected in a large irrigation pond, the pleasure seat is a pretty subject for a photo backed by the Atlas Range.

Located to the north of Marrakech is the historic **palm grove** of its Almoravid

Above: Don't rush – there is always time for a "Moroccan whiskey". Right: Alaouitian weekend residence from the 19th century.

founders, extending over an area of 13,000 hectares clear out to the Oued Tensift. Another horticultural delight, albeit a less august one, is on the way. The **Jardin Majorelle** is a small botanical paradise created by Louis Majorelle (1859-1926), a French painter and also cabinet-maker who lived in Marrakech for many years. Today the garden is the property of fashion-designer Yves Saint Laurent, who has reshaped it into an avant-garde work of art.

New Town: Gueliz

After 1912, the French laid out a spacious city quarter at a respectful distance from the Muslim old quarter. It was reserved for Europeans and named **Gueliz** after the nearby hill on which the Legionnaires' barracks stood. This is where to look for the modern Marrakech. Those with a taste for fixed prices, hard drinks and elegant restaurants with international cuisine are in the right place in the *Ville Nouvelle*. Large hotels with nightclubs, bars with liquor licenses, the new convention center, the railway station and lively boulevards, along which the idle saunter lazily, in short the entire westernized city quarter is centered around the **Place du 16 Novembre**, site of the main post and telegraph office.

Following the **Avenue Mohammed V** (the district's main business street, it comes out of the medina and cuts across the plaza) toward the northwest, one arrives at the **Place Abd el Moumen ben Ali**, where, in addition to cafés, confectioner's shops and ice-cream parlors the *Office Nationale Marocaine du Tourisme* (O.N.M.T.) is located.

Into the Highlands

An excursion into the mountainous region south of Marrakech, an alluring landscape steeped in history, starts out at the Bab er Robb, the stand for the om-

nibus taxis serving route S 501 via Asni up to the 2,092-m high **Tizi n'Test Pass**. The road first passes through the intensively irrigated Haouz Plain and is lined with small water-driven grain mills. Beyond Tahanout, the **Moulay Brahim Gorge** forms the "gateway" to the High Atlas range. The route, blasted intrepidly right into the cliffs and abounding in blind curves, takes some strong nerves – one rule of thumb is to always consider the approaching tourist bus from Taroudannt as the mightier opponent!

Zawiya Moulay Brahim

After 47 kilometers, trail P 6037 branches off to the right towards the **zawiya of Moulay Brahim**. The grave of the holy man, perched on a spur of rock at an altitude of 1,300 m, is the scene of a *moussem* (pilgrimage festival) which attracts more than 50,000 believers every year on the seventh day after *mouloud* (Mohammed's birthday). The pilgrims perform their ritual ablutions at the spring below the village, climb **Jebel Khelout** (1,545 m), Moulay Brahim's place of meditation, and make a sacrificial offering of a sheep at the burial mosque above the village. In particular, married couples, who are still without a son participate in this pilgrimage hoping to benefit from the fertility-promoting blessings of the *marabout*. A visit here is indeed worthwhile for the mountain panorama alone, which stretches from the Adrar n'Oukaimeden (3,273 m) and Angour (3,616 m) in the east to the Toubkal Massif (4,167 m) to the south. Simple village restaurants serve mutton shish-kebabs and *tajine* (stew). The modest pilgrimage lodge is also open year-round.

Back again on the S 501, the river-oasis of the Oued Reraia with its abundant fruit trees creates a close-to-nature summer resort for the citizens of Marrakech trying to escape the heat. A kasbah towers above **Asni**, the main town in the area, where a weekly market is held on Saturdays. The refined **Grand Hotel du Toubkal**, situated at 1,200 m altitude,

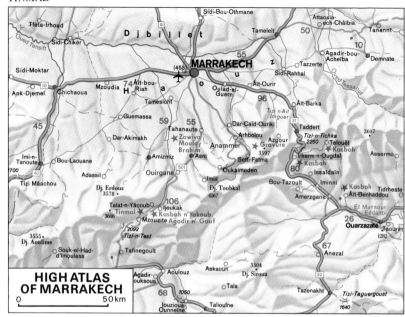

**HIGH ATLAS
OF MARRAKECH**
0   50 km

gets along without air conditioning for the most part – even in August.

Continuing uphill, there's the choice of turning left on the trail through the Mizane Valley to Imlil, a small Berber village sheltered under nut trees. This is the starting point for Toubkal ascents. Otherwise, after about 64 km the little town of **Ouirgane** is reached. It is particularly well-known for its restaurant **Le Sanglier qui fume** – the smoking wild boar in the name is of course only consumed by non-believers! Salterns at the edge of the town are an indication of the rock-salt deposits in the outcrops of Jurassic limestone. Now the road follows the Oued n'Fiss, the bed of which repeatedly narrows to a gully. Along this stretch, always beware of the trucks transporting copper and galenite from the mines of Takhbart down in the valley. Past Ijoukak, the **kasbah Talat n'Yacoub** appears on your right, followed soon afterwards by the **agadir**

Right: The farmers from the Toubkal region come to Asni on market day.

n'Gouf. Around the turn of the century, these were mountain citadels of the Berber Goundafa clan, who at that time controlled the caravan routes and thus trade with the south.

TINMAL

The imposing walls built out of rammed earth which soon appear to the right, protected the Almohad **stronghold of Tinmal** in the 12th century. In order to get to the ruins of the mosque, turn right at kilometer 104 and head down to the Oued n'Fiss, which can only be crossed on foot. When the water is high, this can be a risky business, since the makeshift catwalk is frequently washed away by the swollen flows.

In 1122, Ibn Toumart, a Berber from the Sous region, returned from religious studies in Syria and began to give instruction in the Koran to the Masmouda Berbers of the High Atlas. The core of his teaching was that there was only one God and that those professing the faith should

be governed by the strict doctrines of the *sharia*, which he then translated into the Berber Tashelhite dialect, which is still spoken today. He commanded the respect of his students in the Tinmal *ribat* (castle of an order) through the liberal use of the whip. Once the local tribes named Ibn Toumart *imam* (religious leader) and *mahdi* (guided by God), the holy man had become a powerful one in a more worldly sense. In 1125 he declared a *jihad* (holy war) against the Almoravids, who as Sahara Berbers were the traditional arch-enemies of the Atlas Berbers and whose rule extended from the Senegal River to the Ebro. The Almoravids' counter-attack, failed at the walls of Tinmal. After the mahdi's death in 1130, his favorite student, Abd el Moumen, commanded the Mamouda horsemen with great success, taking Marrakech in 1146, and followed up that relatively small victory with the conquering of Algeria and Andalusia, and then designating himself caliph (successor of the Prophet) in 1162. Although he relocated his administrative

seat to Marrakech, he had the sultanic treasury stored in Tinmal and ordered a huge mosque built here in 1154, which served as model for sacred buildings in Marrakech (Koutoubia), Rabat (Hassan Tower) and Seville (Giralda).

Sheltered behind the mosque's restored outer wall is the nine-aisled prayer hall, the roof of which has not been rebuilt, so that the Friday prayer services (still held here when the weather is good) take place under open skies. The *sahn* (forecourt) with its square *sadirvan* (purification basin) is located on the west side of the classical court mosque. The east wall is formed by the *kibla* (prayer wall), which faces toward Mecca. At its center is the ornately crafted *mihrab* (prayer niche). The cupola of the niche, decorated with *muqarnas* (plaster prisms), rises above a pentagonal base, tapering to an octagon and the luck-bringing Solomon's seal – a genuine masterpiece of Almohad architecture. The niche is decorated with interlaced friezes of geometric ornamentation and arabesques, optically supported by

capitals of columns graced with acanthus and palmaceous motifs. The square minaret rises above the *kibla* (usually opposite); those who climb the tower are rewarded with a magnificent view over the Jebel Tazaghart (3,843 m), often covered with snow into May.

The remaining 32 km to the head of the pass are quite tough. The road isn't paved throughout, turning into a gravel track and passing the **kasbah Tagoundaft** and the village of **Idni**, beyond which it winds its way up in tight curves to the **Tizi n'Test** pass (2,092 m). On the way, the **Ouanoukrim Massif** (4,088 m) is clearly visible to the east. The tremendous panorama, which then opens up to the south, is worth the drive. From this point, the trip can now either be continued southwest into the Sous Valley, Agadir and the Anti-Atlas or eastwards to the Jebel Siroua and to Ouarzazate.

Above: The upkeep of the fields of Anammer is hard work. Right: The south ramp of Tizi n'Tichka.

OURIKA VALLEY

After about one day in Marrakech, running the gauntlet through cordons of self-proclaimed guides with their insistent "Voulez-vous visiter la medina?", most people have already had enough of the hectic ambience of the city. Having narrowly escaped being run down by kamikaze-style moped drivers and sweating buckets in the "four star" hotel because the air conditioning is out of order again, are some indications that it's high time for a trip into the **Ourika Valley**. Just 33 km south of the city on the S 513 you have already left the sweltering behind in its dust, and, if it's a Monday, you can pay a visit to the weekly market of **Dar Caid Ourika**. Here the High Atlas opens up before you: the *Oued* Ourika, which originates on the west face of the Angour (3,616 m), has, in the course of millions of years, created a notch valley, which was settled very early on by the Shluh Berbers. The reddish-brown soil which lends the steep slopes their color is called *hamri* by the Berbers. They have planted vegetable gardens in the valley's wider places, irrigated with the help of *seguias* (open canals). They were perfectly happy to sell parcels of land on the river bed for the villas of French jet-setters and wealthy Moroccans, fully aware that sooner or later the dry years would be followed by wet ones: the devastation caused by flooding from the spring melts of 1988 can be seen along the whole stretch upriver to Setti Fatma.

Holm oaks, a part of the primary vegetation, flourish on the surrounding slopes, and more recently the Berber thuja (arborvitae) has been reforested to stem disastrous landslides. The prickly-pear cacti found near the villages are a Spanish souvenir introduced from South America. In the springtime, olive, cherry, plum and apple trees bloom in the oases, and since they are exotic in Morocco, apples fetch a high price.

Further up the valley, the first bends in the road are lined with potters' booths selling ceramic bowls and unglazed *tajine* pots. About 46 km from Marrakech, the well-run hotel restaurant **Ourika** at an altitude of some 1,000m, is rather popular among skiiers in the winter and as well among heat refugees in the summer. The obliging and courteous hotel staff, for the most part Berbers from the surrounding villages, can be of helpful assistance in organizing hikes of several days. At **Arhbalou** (Thursday market), route A 6305 turns off to the right toward **Oukaimeden**. The skiing area features ski-lifts, hotels, prehistoric rock engravings and an outstanding view of the Atlas Range and Haouz Plain.

Back to the Ourika Valley, a bridge nine km past Arhbalou opens the way to a three-hour excursion on foot to the high-altitude village of **Anammer** (1,650 m). From there one can make a two-day trek, accompanied by a guide familiar with the area, to the worthwhile Neolithic rock engravings (depictions of weapons, carts

and African game) in the nearby **Yagour Massif** (altitude: 2,726 m).

If you drive further south along the S 513, then after altogether 65 km, just short of **Setti Fatma** (1,500 m, *moussem* in August), the asphalt road ends. A trail goes the remaining distance to the village. On the slope opposite it lies the **grave of the Lalla Setti Fatma,** recognizable by its pyramid-shaped roof with green-glazed tiles. A narrow path winds its way through an extended grove of walnuts and chestnuts to a small waterfall. Starting out from Setti Fatma, hikers can follow the Ouriaka River to the west and continue to Imlil in a march of three whole days, crossing the **Tizi n'Tacheddirt** pass (3,230 m) and passing through splendid alpine scenery.

Tizi n'Tichka and Telouet

Route P 31 to the Tichka Pass is the approach to the Glaoua kasbah of Telouet. It is also the road leading on to the south to Ouarzazate. You depart Marrakech south-eastwards and crosse the Zat River (raging in springtime) at Ait Ourir. There is a French restaurant at the bridge. With the **Tizi n'Ait Imguer** (1,470 m), a pass with a beautiful view of the R'dat Valley and the **agadir of Arhbalou**, you have reached the High Atlas. Through the endless curves which follow you should be prepared for the heavy-weight manganese ore carriers that rumble down from the mountains. Holm oaks, Aleppo pines and junipers flourish on the precipitous slopes. After 88 km, the village of **Taddert** (1,600 m) appears. It is surrounded by tall walnut trees and has simple cafés and a restaurant with a terrace as well as the only alcohol license in the area.

With replenished energy, the traveller must now deal with the narrow serpentine curves that follow, arriving after 104 km at the head of the **Tizi n'Tichka** (2,260 m) with its commanding views, flanked to the west by Jebel bou Ourioul (3,573 m) and overlooking the Asif Mellah Valley in the south. The Atlas Mountains have an abundance of minerals, but the so-called "amethysts" sold by the numerous traders here are frequently little more than tinted quartzite. Calcite druses are also manipulated in a thousand-and-one ways. The also offered strings of "semi-precious" stones are unfortunately for the most part imported.

TELOUET

A few kilometers beyond the head of the pass, the narrow, but asphalted P 6802 turns off to the east. The imposing **kasbah of Telouet** (1,800 m) appears after some 22 km. This adobe structure, strategically situated on the Timbuktu-Fès caravan route, was erected in the 19th century by the Glaoua Berbers. In 1953, these feudal lords of the Atlas, under the leadership of Thami el Glaoui, the pasha

of Marrakech, were powerful enough (with French collaboration) to send Sultan Mohammed V into exile. The original source of their immeasurable wealth lay in the subjugated oasis villages of southern Morocco and in their corner on the grain market. Later on, however, these were eclipsed by their interest in the production of manganese and of antimony being exploited by French mining firms. On his triumphal return in the year of 1955, Sultan Mohammed V deprived the Glaoua clan of power. Ever since, their former ancestral castle has decayed visibly and now merely a few of their former black servants are still living in the old servant's quarter.

An idea of the former splendor can be gathered in the *salle de réception* continue to leve in the old servants' quarters. The iron cross bars of the doors are inlaid with silver damascene; the tall folding doors are decorated with carved and painted geometric designs. Multicolored faïence mosaics on the walls depict variations of magical numbers, framed above by plaster friezes featuring Koran suras Crystalline *muqarnas* – prisms of wood and plaster – painted cedar ceiling, which is crowned with a dome. A horseshoe-shaped opening in the window latticework provides a splendid view over the valley and the nearby village.

Departing Telouet, a rather adventurous mountain trail, the **CT 6803**, leads to Ait Benhaddou. First, howerver, it heads east to the kasbah Anemiter, then to the south, passing high above the gorge of the Assif Ounila and via narrow, steep gravel, covered hairpin bends down to the **kasbah of Tamdaght** (worth seeing) and, finally, on to the showpiece **ksar Ait Benhaddou**.If you decide instead on the considerably more comfortable P 31 for the continuing journey south to Ouarzazate, on the way you can take a look at the tamped-earth granary of the mountain farmers of **Ighrem n'Ougdal**, one of the last agadirs still in use in the Atlas.

Right: Fun is guaranteed on the Toubkal trail with Lahcen, the guide from Imlil.

Hiking in the High Atlas

Jebel Toubkal, at 4,167 m the highest mountain in North Africa, draws those interested in ski-tours in winter and alpine hikers in summer. Approaching it from Marrakech on the S 501, turn to the left past Asni and follow the P 6038, an adventurous, landslide-afflicted trail, along the picturesque river oases of Mizane, to **Imlil** (1,800 m). The rickety omnibus taxis from Asni also run here. This mountain village, has a lot of what the trekker's heart desires, for example simple terrace café with unassuming little rooms to let, a CAF (Club Alpin Français) hut and a private camping field (left at the village entrance). Small shops sell such staples as bread, cheese, vegetables, oil, meat and camp-stove gas, and with luck a 1:50,000 hikers' map. The parking area is guarded. State-examined mountain guides - among them one named Lahcen, a good-natured linguistic whiz – can be hired at negotiable daily rates. If desired they can organize the entire trek. On the other hand, the drivers of the pack-mules work for fixed, though not unreasonable tariffs. Now and then one may also ride the astoundingly sure-footed mules to shorten the walking time. It's no problem for the drivers, who enjoy the enviable physical condition of marathon runners! It's a good idea to bring along a tent, since rental tents are of limited availability and lodging can't always be found in the villages.

TOUBKAL TREK

A hike around Jebel Toubkal with an ascent to the summit can be done in five to six days. On the other hand, Toubkal stormers in a big hurry take a six-hour ride up to the **Neltner refuge**, spend the night there, knock off the summit in four hours, ride back to Imlil and drive back to Marrakech the same night to nurse their chafed behinds in the hotel. However, the best part of this trek – experiencing the Berber culture in the high-altitude river oases behind the main range of the High Atlas – requires more time.

187

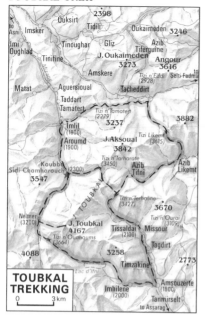

TOUBKAL TREKKING
0   3 km

Starting from **Imlil**, follow the trail (now no longer drivable), which, after passing through a series of steep hairpin bends, heads south high above the left bank of the Mizane River. After about half an hour the village of **Aroumd** appears on the other bank. It's built in a manner typical for the Shluh Berbers of the region. Nestling on an outcrop at an altitude of some 1,900 meters, the rough-stone buildings, built terrace-style into the slope, are equipped with south-facing balconies on which women can be seen knotting their carpets. Further up the valley the route crosses the Mizane and after a good four hours arrives at the **koubba of Sidi Chamharouch** (2,300 m). The *baraka* (blessing) of the holy man can drive away *gnuns* (evil spirits) and cure infertility. Small shops sell soft drinks and cookies, but the big movers are the devotionals. A small resting place on the streambed can hold four tents if need be,

Right: Lac d'Ifni emerged 10,000 years ago, an ice aged moraine lake.

although for the sake of altitude acclimatization it's a better idea to climb up to the Nelter refuge situated at 3,200 m (following the Mikane; another four hours). The hut has cooking facilities and 30 beds, which are usually filled up in July and August. The manager sells beverages, but no food. Snow can be expected until the end of April, sometimes until May.

Break out for **Jebel Toubkal** before 7 a.m. to make use of the cool of morning, climbing a good three hours over piles of boulders and scree to the summit ridge. The highest point (4,167 m) is marked by a three-legged trigonometric symbol – no cross in the land of Muslims! – put up in 1931 by the Moroccan section of the Club Alpin Français. On a clear day the Anti-Atlas can be discerned to the south. From this altitude, its 2,000-m peaks appear rather flat. Behind them are the strata of the Sahara's northern edge; in the east, at about 50 km distance, is the crater edge of the extended volcanic Siroua Massif (3,304 m). In the foreground to the northeast is Tichki (3,627 m); behind it, Angour (3,616 m); to the north, Adrar n'Oukaimeden (3,273 m) and only three kilometers further west, Jebel Ouanoukrim (4,088 m).

Back at the Neltner refuge one can either indulge in a lazy afternoon and spend the night, or continue with the hiking tour, just short of two hours up the valley to the **Tizi n'Ouanoums**, a pass that crosses the main ridge of the High Atlas at an altitude of 3,664 m. On the way, there are visible traces of the last Ice Age, which ended 10,000 years ago: The terminal moraine climbed at the beginning consist of rock debris bulldozed by a glacier. Snowfields often last here until June. The three-hour descent to the deep-blue moraine lake **Lac d'Ifni** (2,312 m) isn't just uncomfortable for the mules, but the pleasure of swimming in its cool, crystalline waters is worth the trouble. There are tenting sites on the west and northeast lakeshores.

Passing by the lake to the north and descending the slope of the terminal moraine, after approximately 1.5 hours you come to the valley of the Tifnoute, the headstream of the Sous River. The village of **Imhilene** (2,000 m) provides the opportunity of spending the night in a Berber home. This romantic river oasis has an abundance of walnut tree between which barley, maize, and also vegetables flourish. A half hour further downstream lies Amsouzerte (1,800 m): some intrepid truck drivers coming in from Aoulouz (to the south) occasionally negociate the rutted trail CT 6855 thus far.

The stage which follows, over the **Terhaline Pass** to Sidi Chamharouch, requires 12 hours' hiking time and doesn't have to be knocked off in one day. Hiking northward along the idyllic **Tisgui Valley** on a comfortable track, you pass by the villages of Timakine, Tagdirt und Missour, which are located on the opposite slope. During their centuries of toil, the Shluh Berbers have laid out terraced fields on the mountain, irrigated by *se-guias* (open canals). Since the tillable area cannot be expanded, many of the villagers have gone to France as foreign laborers. At the end of the valley in **Tissaldai** (2,100 m), lodging is available from the hospitable village residents.

The steep ascent to **Tizi n'Terhaline** (3,427 m) becomes mercilessly hot toward noon, so it's a good idea to set out early in the morning after a good night's sleep in Tissaldai. Having reached the head of the pass, there is the option of expanding the six-day tour by choosing the 2.5 days trekking back to Imlil, the starting point via Azib Tifni, Azib Likemt, Tizi Likemt pass, the village of Tacheddirt and the Tizi n'Tamatert pass.

Now, the route, ascending to the northwest, crosses the saddle of the Tarharat massif (roughly 3,700 m) and arrives, on the north face of Tichki, at the pass **Tizi n'Tarharate** (3,450 m). On the descent – 2.5 hours through rubble and scree (beware of loose stones!) – you can look forward to the foot-bath in **Sidi Chamharouch**. Arriving back Imlil after

189

another three hours in the mountains, the sleepy village seems more like a hectic outpost of civilization.

OUKAIMEDEN TREK

Like the Toubkal tour, the four-day hike around the Oukaimeden and Angour Massifs starts out in **Imlil**. It is, however, a little less strenuous. The highest point is the Tizi n'Tacheddirt at 3,230 m In case you hire a pack-mule (recommended!), its driver usually can also serve as guide through the region.

On the southern edge of Imlil you cross a ford shaded by walnut trees and follow a trail on the other side of the Mizane that leads uphill eastward to the village of **Tamatert**, and the grave of the *lalla imitaza*. That the Atlas Berbers venerate holy women is condemned by the *ulema* (Koran scholars) as a dubious pre-Islamic custom. The dirt road then starts to wind

Above: Knotting rugs in the Berber village of Imlil is still the domain of women.

its way along hairpin bends, which can be cut across to the **Tizi n'Tamatert** pass (2,279 m). A solid two hours should be estimated to achieve this hike.

At the pass you turn to the east and follow an easy trail (no change of altitude) with a great view over the Imenane Valley and beyond to Jebel Oukaimeden (3,273 m) in the north. This road was constructed for the planned exploitation of the area's barite deposits. After another 1.5 hours the path descends to **Ouanesekra** (2,050 m) and then contines up the **Imenane Valley** to the nearby village of **Tacheddirt** (2,280 m). The latter has provided lodging for more than a few hikers in its day; a **CAF lodge** has room for 15, and offers kitchen facilities. Tenting is scarcely possible since the village is surrounded by intensively cultivated terraces. There is no store here, although bread can be obtained from the farmers.

Sworn campers continue their hike uphill to the northeast. After about 1.5 hours, the low wind-break walls of an *azib* provide a camping spot (at approxi-

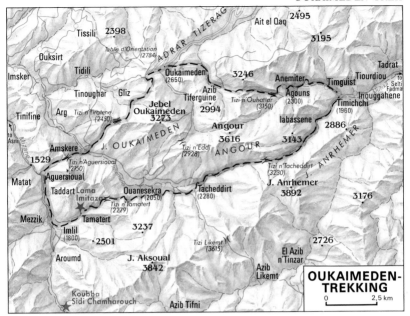

mately 2,600 m). The herdsmen encountered frequentliy here in April sometimes offer mutton for sale. This meat, roasted on a spit, immediately restores the energy used to get here. The sheep's head is indeed a prized delicacy among the mule drivers and herdsmen!

In another two hours the highest pass of the entire tour, the **Tizi n'Tacheddirt** (3,230 m), is finally reached. This is followed by a three- hour descent along the narrow valley of the Assif Iabassene, passing the archaic-looking village of **Iabassene** on down into the **Ourika Valley**. There is a rarely-used CAF cabin in **Timichchi** (1,960 m). Deviating from the tour one can, at this point, easily head down the valley and after a good half day arrive Setti Fatma and also the asphalt route S 513 to Marrakech.

Now, if you go without deviating, the hike goes upriver, passing **Timguist** and **Anemiter**, to the small Berber village of **Agouns** (2,300 m). There is a camping spot located to the southeast of the village on the main *seguia* (irrigation channel).

On the next day it's a three-hour climb up to the **Tizi n'Ouhattar** (3,150 m). From the top, **Angour** (3,616 m) can be seen. Descending westwards, the vegetation, which has been scanty up to this point, changes noticeably. Moist air masses coming in all the time from the Atlantic have created lush meadows here.

After about two hour's worth of descent you arrive at the winter-sports center of **Oukaimeden** (2,650 m). Particularly with its seven ski-lifts on Jebel Oukaimeden (3,273 m), it is without equal in North Africa. The restaurant **Chez Juju** as well as the hotels **De l'Angour** and **Imlil** are only open in winter and high summer. On the other hand, the campground (on a small lake) and the thoroughly comfortable **CAF refuge,** equipped with 160 beds, cooking facilities, hot showers and even a bar (!) are open year-round. Prehistoric rock engravings of ritual daggers and cattle well over 5,000 years old can be viewed just behind the hotels. An orientatation plaque near the radio tower at altitude 2,784 names the

191

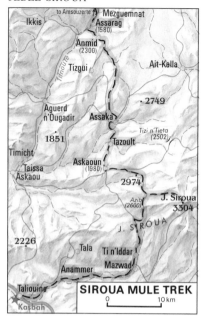

SIROUA MULE TREK

0   10 km

mountains and ranges of the surrounding panorama: from Angour to the southeast, on to Jebel Oukaimeden and the Toubkal Massif and out to Marrakech in the north. A rather curvy road constructed especially for the benefit of tour busses leads down into the Ourika Valley.

Leaving the ski area early in the morning heading southwest, follow an alpine path (2,500 m) to the **Tizi n'Tiratene** (2,450 m), then descend and cross the Imenane River at **Amskere**. After the ascent to the Tizi n'Aguersioua (2,150 m) in the west, the route drops to **Aguersioul** in the Mizane Valley. Finally, following trail P 6038 southward, you arrive at the village of **Imlil** again after a total of ten hours.

JEBEL SIROUA MULE "TREK"

Following the Toubkal tour described above, it is possible to leave the route at **Amsouzerte** and set your sights on the little-travelled variation to **Taliouine** via the **Siroua Volcano**. Considering the lengthy passage over desolate, arid pla-

teaux, this is really only a tour for mule-riders with plenty of stamina! The first day's ride passes along the Tifnoute River heading south, arriving first **Assarag** (1,580 m, shops, possibly a mule-driver familiar with the locality). At the other end of town, turn left onto the small trail **CT 6836**, passing by the rather biblical-looking village of **Anmid**. The unpaved road winds its way up to a sparsely inhabited plateau (2,300 m). Having followed the trail for a total of 35 km, passing by the villages of **Assaka** and **Tazoult**, one arrives at the market-town of **Askaoun** (1,980 m, overnight accommodations available at the restaurant).

Leaving the village, turn east onto the CT 6801, which you leave again after (about 10 km) by the **Aghbalou n'Oulid Spring** to follow a path heading off to the southeast – local guide required! The path goes right along the Timighad Valley, passing Ifard n'Magous (2,974 m), and after another 10 km reaches the volcanic rocks of the northwestern edge (2,700m) of the **Siroua Massif**. It takes a good two hours to ascend the 3,304 m summit of this volcano, which became extinct in the Tertiary Period. Once back at its northwestern foot, a two-hour hike further to the southwest brings you to an alpine meadow with an *azib* (herdsmens'camp), a pleasant tenting spot at an altitude of 2,600 m.

After an 8-km descent through the Tizguy Gorge, in the village of **Ti n'Iddar** (Glaoua rugs are hand-knotted here), one comes upon a trail which – via the village of Mazwad, passing by **Anammer** and after about 30 km (within sight of the **Taliouine Kasbah**) – connects with the major Route P 32 running from Agadir to Ouarzazate. The town of Taliouine has the comfortable three-star **Hotel Ibn Toumart** as well as a small auberge whose owner, Ahmed, frequently organizes trekking tours. In closing, it's worth mentioning that this tour can be undertaken the other way around.

MARRAKECH

Accommodation

LUXURY: **Mamounia**, Av. Bab Jedid, Tel: 48981. **Mansour Eddahbi**, Palais de Congrès, Tel: 48222. **Es Saadi**, Av. Quadissia, Tel: 48811. **Semiramis-Meridien**, Rte de Casa, Tel: 31377. *MODERATE:* **Andalous**, Av. Jnane el Harti, Tel: 48226. **Les Almoravides**, Jnane Lakhdar, Tel: 45142. **Le Marrakech**, Pl. de la Liberté, Tel: 34351. **Imilchil**, Av. Echouhada, Tel: 34150. **Sahara Inn**, Semlalia, Route de Casa, Tel: 34388. *BUDGET:* **Foucauld**, Av. El Mouahidine, Tel: 45499. **Hotel Ali**, Rue Moulay Ismael, Tel: 44979. **CTM**, Jemaa el Fna, Tel: 42325.

Restaurants

MOROCCAN: **Dar Marjana** (very exclusive!), Derb Sidi Ali Tair 15 (near Bab Doukkala), Tel: 45773. **Dar Es Salam** (folklore), Derb Jedid 95, Tel: 43520. **Chez Ali** (with *fantasia*), 12 km in direction of Casablanca, turn left after Tensift Bridge, twon office: Rue Ibn Aicha 2, Tel: 32187. *FRENCH:* **La Rive Gauche**, Bd. Yacoub El Mansour, Tel: 30297. **La Fontaine**, Rue de la Liberté 3, Tel: 34984. *INEXPENSIVE :* Restaurants and street kitchens around Jemaa el Fna.

Nightlife

Night club **Stars House**, Place de la Liberté. Discotheques in the Hotels **N'Fis**, **Sofitel**, **Le Marrakech**, **Mamounia**.

Sports

TENNIS: **Royal Club Tennis**, Rue Oued El Makhazine, Tel: 31902. *GOLF:* **Hotel Mamounia**. *RIDING:* **Club Equestre**, Route d'Asni (4 km), Tel: 48529. *HUNTING AND FISHING:* Permits from the **Ministère d'Eaux et Forêts**, Rue Abou El Abbas Essabti, Tel: 42143. *SKIING:* **Skiclub**, Av. Mohammed V, Tel: 34026 (skiing region Oukaimeden).

Shopping

Market: Marché Central, Av. Mohammed V. **International Press***:* Newsstand at the Marché Central and in front of the Hotel CTM. **Crafts:** in the Medina, bargaining essential; fixed prices at the **Ensemble Artisanal**, Av. Mohammed V. (near the Place de la Liberté).

Transportation

AIR: Aeroport Marrakech-Menara, 5 km southwest, Tel: 30939. **Royal Air Maroc**, Av. Mohammed V, Tel: 34338. **BUS: Gare Routière**, Place El Mourabitène (near Bab Doukkala), Tel: 34402. **RAIL: Gare**, Av. de la Marche Verte, Tel: 47768, to Casa, Fès, Tanger. **RENTAL CARS**: **Avis**, Av. Mohammed V 137, Tel: 33723. **Hertz**, Av. Mohammed V 154, Tel: 34680. **Interrent**, Bd. Zerktouni 63, Tel: 31228. **TAXI:** Long-distance taxis (blue) at the Jemaa el Fna, near the Club Med.

Hospitals

Hôpital Ibn Tofail, Rue Ibn Aicha/ Abdelwahab Derraq, Tel: 48011. **Avenzoar**, Rue Sidi Mimoun, Tel: 42019.

Pharmacies

Pharmacie Centrale, Av. Mohammed V 166, Tel: 30158. *NIGHT SERVICE:* **Pharmacie de Nuit**, Rue Khalid Ibn Oualid, Tel: 30415.

Tourist Information / Post

ONMT, Place Abd el Moumen Ben Ali, Tel: 48906. **Syndicat d'Initiative**, Av. Mohammed V, Tel: 32097. *POST:* **PTT**, Av. Mohammed V (Ville Nouvelle); Jemaa el Fna (Medina).

HIGH ATLAS OF MARRAKECH

Accommodation

MODERATE: **Ourika Hotel**, Vallée de l'Ourika, Tel: 4-33993. **Ramuntcho**, Vallée de l'Ourika, Tel: 119. **Chez Juju**, Oukaimeden, Tel: 59005. **Hotel Imlil**, Oukaimeden, Tel: 59113. **Grand Hotel du Toubkal**, Asni, Tel: 3. **La Roseraie**, Ouirgane, Tel: 4. **Au Sanglier qui Fume**, Ouirgane, Tel: 9. *CLUB ALPIN FRANÇAIS HUTS (Refuges Du Caf):* **Imlil** (1800m, sleeps 38), **Neltner** (Toubkal, 3200 m, sleeps 35), **Lépiney** (Tazarhart, 3000 m, sleeps 22), **Tachdirt** (2300 m, sleeps 23), **Oukaimeden** (2600 m, sleeps 80). Reservations: CAF, Casablanca, BP 6178, Tel: 270090, CAF Marrakech, BP 888.

Weekly Markets

TAHANNOUT: Tuesdays. **ASNI**: Saturdays. **OUIRGANE**: Thursdays. **IJOUKAK**: Wednesdays. **OURIKA :** Mondays**.**

Trekking Information

Hotel Ali, Rue Moulay Ismael (near Jemaa el Fna), Tel: 44979 (ask for a guide from Imlil). **Club Alpin Francais**, Casablanca, BP 6178, Tel: 270090, CAF Marrakech, BP 888. **ONMT**, Marrakech, Pl. Abd el Moumen, Tel: 48906. *MAPS:* **Division de la Cartographie**, Rabat, Av. Moulay Hassan 31, Tel: 7-65311 (mornings only; scale 1:50 000 and 1:100 000). **Hanoud du Lahcen**, Imlil.

ARGAN TREES
AND
FORTIFIED
GRANARIES

ANTI-ATLAS
JEBEL BANI
ANTI-ATLAS TREKKING
WESTERN SAHARA

ANTI-ATLAS

Rising southwest of the High-Atlas, the Anti-Atlas with its southern ranges of the Jebel Bani and Jebel Ouarkziz leads to the Western Sahara, a formerly Spanish area, which Morocco has been claiming since 1976. Geologically, the mountains of southern Morocco are considerably older than the northerly Atlas range. This is why tectonic stress occurs time and again in the border zone under the **Sous Valley**, particularly affecting the region around Agadir. The last major earthquake, in March 1960, took the lives of more than 50,000 people.

The geological history of the Anti-Atlas goes back as far as the Precambrian, a era of geology some 500 million years ago. Consequently, the climate changed several times und the effects, mainly caused by the changing intensity of erosion, formed soft-silhouetted highlands as well as a few steep canyons. Granite boulders characteristically accentuate a dry mountain landscape, with an average rainfall of hardly more than 250 mm annualy. On the not very fertile granite debris soil, a small number of shluh-berbers

Previous pages: Tioulit was built at a protected location, as many villages in the Anti-Atlas. Left: Storerooms in Agadir Tasguent.

grow barley as a main staple food, but their harvest is meager, what gives them a tough struggle for their daily bread. Only some very small river oases offer fertile soils and limited but sufficient water for irrigation agriculture. Nowadays, a small number of *agadirs*, the fortress-like granaries most typical for the entire Atlas, that used to be vivid in former centuries, are still in use and maintained by the villagers. A tasty, reddish oil comes from the orange-colored, olive-like fruits of the thorny argan-tree. Argans even grow on the dry, rocky slopes oft the Anti-Atlas, where no other trees could survive and can get hundreds of years old.

Sous Valley

The **Oued Sous** waters a fertile plain on the northern edge of the Anti-Atlas stretching from the Atlantic coast eastwards to the foreland of the **Jebel Siroua**. The lower Sous Valley was once one of Morocco's flourishing economic regions. During the rule of the Saadis in the 16th and 17th centuries, sugar cane was cultivated and high prices obtained - until, that is, the sugar markets of the Caribbean and South America were opened up. Afterwards, the economic situation of the Sous went downhill. Today, attempts are being made to revert to the old ways by

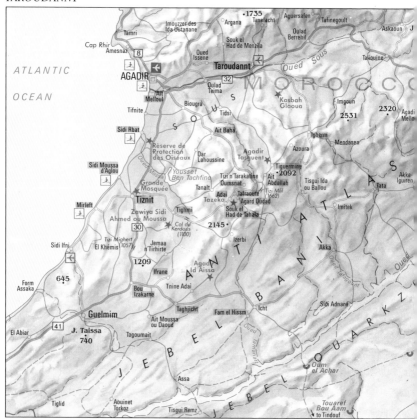

cultivating tropical and subtropical fruits and vegetables. These are then exported from the harbor at Agadir. A thriving orange-processing industry has developed, producing juice, preserves and candied orange peel made from the bitter Seville oranges, which is still in demand. Because of the mild climate, even banana trees do well in greenhouses. The inhabitants of the Sous area, the *soussi*s, are considered to be very skilled in business, but also extremely miserly – two not necessarily mutually exclusive qualities.

Taroudannt

This small town has about 20,000 inhabitants and is the economic center of the Sous region. Taroudannt presents a self-contained townscape, its imposing surrounding wall dating from the 18th century. Although there are no outstanding sights, the picturesque souks make the visit worthwhile. From the **Place Assarag**, where there are many streetside cafés as well as the bus station, you can enter the cool, shady alleys of the **medina**. After passing the stands of the peppermint dealers, you will find stores with cosmetics and vdarious types of Moroccan medicine crowded together in the narrow passageway. The jewelry and carpet dealers usually have more spacious stores and wait for people on a day's outing from Agadir. After all the hubbub, and with tired feet, it is best to let a horse-

It is worth your while taking a walk in the oasis gardens of Tioute, where there is an abundance of henna bushes. The henna powder produced from the leaves and stems is green; only when mixed with limewater does the characteristic reddish-brown color emerge. Besides being a popular cosmetic dye, henna is used to paint symbols of luck on the hands and feet of Moroccan brides.

An impressive hike can be taken in the gorge of the **Oued Sdas**: It starts at a wide course ford through the **Oved Sdas**, 3.5 km to the east of Tioute, and leads north along the river to the archaic stone villages Tazenntat and Tifnout.

From Taroudannt to Tafraoute

After passing expansive fruit and vegetable plantations, you reach **Ait Melloul** on the improved RN 32 westbound for Agadir. The S 509 forks off here to the south and climbs up into the mountains of the Anti-Atlas. The luxuriant green of the Sous plain is quickly replaced by sparsely-covered mountain slopes and stony fields showing little yield despite the hard work of the farmers. Trees, some of them with extremely bizarre shapes, grow everywhere. These are *argan*, solely found in southwestern Morocco. In spring and summer they bear fruit similar to olives, harvested by the inhabitants and made into a savory oil. It has a nutty taste and is either used as a garnish for the flat bread or eaten mixed with honey and ground almonds as *hamlou* – a high-calorie snack. However, the argan trees are better known for fact that goats that sometimes climb nimbly into the highest treetops in order to eat the fresh leaves and sprouts there. In some parts this has already led to the over-grazing of the trees and even endangers their existence. Behind the small market town **Ait Baha**, the narrow road ascends in tight curves, high above the impressive **Oued Ait Baha Gorge**. The yellow blossoms of

drawn cab take you to the **Hotel Salam**. It lies idyllically in the southeastern corner of the old city wall, framed by palm trees and bougainvillea. At the horseshoe-shaped "Moorish" swimming pool, you can order a Berber cocktail and then watch the storks at work on their nests high up on the battlement of the wall.

From Taroudannt it is possible to make an excursion to the old **Glaoua Kasbah** of the **Tioute Oasis**. The village boys are quite willing to guide visitors through the splendid, now dilapidated buildings. Artfully painted ceilings of cedarwood and the herringbone pattern of reed-thatching testify to the affluence of earlier pashas who bled the population and drove them to poverty.

spurges line the way. En route the ancient oil mills with which farmers produce olive oil and arghan oil in the traditional manner can frequently be seen in the villages. After crossing the 1,500 m high **Tizi n'Tarakatine** pass and the **Tizi Mlil** (1,662 m), which soon follows it, the winding road leads down into the **Valley of the Ammel**n. The first blocks of granite now appear, reminiscent of giant wool sacks because of their rounded weathered forms. They are characteristic of this landscape.

Only the small town of **Tafraoute** offers accommodations for those who want to spend the night. It is also suitable as a starting point for one-day excursions and walking tours in the surrounding high valleys of the Anti-Atlas. You can stock up on fresh fruit and vegetables at the town's Wednesday market, which is well worth the visit for its own sake. **Hotel Les Amandiers**, built high above the city in kasbah style, offers a wonderful view of the extensive rock face of nearby Jebel Lekst (2,359 m). As the muezzin of the nearby mosque calls for evening prayer, the slowly setting sun imparts reddish tinges to the granite.

Walk to Oumsnat

Start at the center of town in Tafraoute and walk in a northerly direction, past the public *hammam* (steam bath) and the Koran school, from which, every morning, comes the loud, but rhythmic voice of children as they recite the versesof the Koran. On a small footpath, passing grain fields, you will come to a little cemetery. In rural areas, sharp stones mark the head and foot of the graves. The dead are buried at a depth of scarcely one meter, wrapped only in a cloth. The corpse is laid on its side with drawn-up legs, the face directed towards Mecca. There is no

grave decoration in the Islamic countries. Instead, bowls are broken on the graves for the use of the dead in the next world.

The scattered arghan and almond trees offer little in the way of shade. Asphodel and fragrant lavender bloom at the edge of the path. The narrow footpath now climbs up to an easy pass. At the end of the valley, nomads pitch their tents (*khaimas*) until early summer. Their goats and sheep graze in the surrounding area. From the pass, there is a splendid view of the valley of the Ammeln. At every location where springs flow from the steep rock face of **Jebel Lekst** on the other side, the Ammel – Berbers of the Schluh tribe – once built well-fortified villages and fertile oasis gardens. Since the yield from agriculture today can no longer ensure the livelihood of quickly-growing families, most of the men from these areas have had to leave their families and native surrounding to find work in the large Moroccan cities of the north, or as foreign workers in Europe. With their hard-earned money, they have lavish houses built in their villages. For the most part, only the old people, women and children live in them.

Oumsnat, the most visited place in the valley of the Ammeln, is two hours on foot to the east of the pass. It can also be reached directly from Tafraoute on route 7147. Like most of the villages in the region around Tafraoute, Oumsnat has a newer section with fine, modern houses, even villas, and an older section built in a protective location higher up the mountain-side. The old houses are made of natural stone bonded with loam. Some of the older fortified dwellings still have the traditional *lokba* facades, which are unfortunately falling into disrepair with the houses. They are formed using small black slate tiles and decorate the wall above the low entrance door. Traditional magical protective symbols of the Berbers are included as geometrical ornaments: as diamonds, triangles, squares,

Right: The Ammeln village of Oumsnat is situated on a spring oasis in the Jebel Lekst.

and rectangles. Typically, Ammel houses – in addition to beautifully adorned ancient wooden doors – have inner courts, which can be covered, and extensive roof terraces, which serve as sleeping areas during the hot summer months. The inhabitants are protected from the evil eye and the *gnun*, evil spirit, by having cooking pots turned upside down on the whitewashed battlements of the walls.

In many places there are little streams flowing through the gardens in which barley, vegetables and fruit are cultivated. Because of the elevation of over 1,000 m, temperatures can fall below freezing in the winter. For this reason, dates grown in the area cannot achieve the best quality. In contrast, the almond trees that bloom in January and February do very well here. The blossoming of the almonds is celebrated in January and February.

Excursion to Aguard Oudad

The route CT 7147 runs south from Tafraoute to a picturesque village by the name of **Agard Oudad**. With its pastel-colored, trim little houses, it stands at the foot of a mighty granite rock commonly called **Napoleon's Hat**. If you follow a small trail, which branches off here in a southwesterly direction, you will reach a magnificent landscape of granite blocks painted in garishly bright colors: the work of the Belgian landscape artist Jean Virame. As in all works of art, one can argue about taste; but in any case, the violet, red and blue of the boulders – set off by the occasional green of the arghan trees sets a contrast definitely presents an unusual photographic motif.

Excursion to the Agadir Tasguent

In order to visit the archaic fortified granary of Ida Ou Zekri in **Tasguent**, an automobile with high clearance is sufficient during the dry season. After it has rained, however, it is better to charter a Land-Rover taxi in Tafraoute.

First drive up the S 509 to **Tizi Mlil** and, beyond the head of the pass, turn in

the direction of Igherm onto the CT 7040, which is asphalted at the start, following the main ridge of the Anti-Atlas through the semi-arid mountain landscape eastward. Having passed the village **Ait Abdallah**, do not continue straight ahead when you reach the *douar* **Tiguermine**. Instead, 37 km after the fork from the S 509, turn towards the north and follow CT 7040 in the direction of Taroudant. After about 7 km, a trail to the agadir Tasguent (1,500 m) branches off at Douar Alma. Reckon with at least six full hours for the excursion.

The actual **agadir of Tasguent** lies just before the village of the same name in a small side valley and is among the finest intact fortified granaries in all of Morocco. It stands on a table mountain and is a number of stories high. The entire edifice is made of natural stones without connective clay and the storage rooms are grouped around three inner courts. At the

Above: The "siyala" tattoo on the forehead should offer protection from the "evil eye".

entrance of the agadir there is a watchman (*amin*), who opens the mighty door with his wooden notched key when given a good tip. He is appointed to this post of confidence by the villagers, who still store their provisions there today, and is actually only allowed to let in people he knows well. The storage cells of the individual farmer families are built above each other to a height of up to seven stories. All of the rooms have their own wooden doors, often decorated with magical fertility symbols, bolted with carved drop-pin locks. Access is possible over large stone slabs sunk into the walls which follow each other in a sequence similar to that of stairs.

Not only are grain, olive and arghan oils, legumes and dried fruit stored here in the storehouse fortress of Tasguent; political meetings of the village council (*jemaa al amma*), the head of which is the village elder (*amghrar*), also take place here. In times of war, the fortress served the villagers as a refuge. Since the agadir of Tasguent also has a mosque and includes the burial sites of several holy men and women (*mrabtin*), it is considered to be a sacred place.

From Tafraoute to Tiznit

Continuing the drive to Tiznit, you can visit the pretty village of **Adai** at the end of the valley of Tafraoute. Its pastel-colored houses and imposing mosque, surrounded by mighty granite boulders, are among the loveliest motifs of the area. A small track across the fields opposite leads past almond trees to the remarkable prehistoric petroglyphs of Tazzeka. Neolithic ancestors of the Berbers carved a gazelle and a rock goat – it could perhaps also be a cow and a mouflon – into a steep granite face; researchers are not in complete agreement as to age and interpretation. These rock engravings presumably served as invocation of luck for the hunt and the fertility of the herds.

Beneath the cliff there are some beautiful old carob trees. From the long pods, the natives make a chocolate substitute, which has abecome a specially in many western health-food stores. The kernels of the carob are called *karat* in Arabian. They are constant in weight, do not take in any moisture even when it is damp, and therefore were used in earlier times as a unit of weight for gems.

After **Souk el Had de Tahala**, the granite rocks disappear and the roads winds in numerous curves through valleys and barren plateaus. From **Col du Kerdous** (1,100 m), you have a wonderful view to the west. The head of the pass is "embellished" by an unfinished and since ruined, kasbah-like hotel with a tea room, where a Berber serves refreshing peppermint tea, an agreeable refreshment for those preparing to proceed to the valley.

Acrobats and Marabouts

Just behind the Col du Kerdous begins the tribal region of the **Tazeroualt**. The farming villages perch like aeries on the steep cliffs, high above the bare grain terraces. Fragrant herbs (thyme, wild mint, fennel and lavender) bloom at the edge of the road in spring.

At the bottom of the valley, behind the small market town **Tighmi**, a road forks off to **yawiya Sidi Ahmed ou Moussa**. The acrobats in red garb who perform on the Jemaa el Fna square in Marrakech, building human pyramids, are trained here, where the Sidi Ahmen Brotherhood is based and from where, between the 16th and 19th centuries, it exercised considerable political influence on the whole area and in the Sous valley. Every year, on the third Thursday in August, numerous Berber families particularly from the remote valleys make a pilgrimage to the holy sites in order to be closer to the divine power (*baraka*) of the living and dead holy men. As everywhere in Morocco, there is no admission to the tomb mosque for non-Moslems.

In the winter route 7074 on the ford of the **Oued Assaka**, shortly before Tiznit, often becomes a dead-end. After rainfall in the mountains, the water gushes down mountain slopes almost devoid of vegetation, into the valleys, making the dry wadis and rivulets swell into raging rivers within hours. Those wishing to drive on to Tiznit in such conditions without a cross-country vehicle can either hope for a quick sinking of the water level or turn back to Tafaoute in order to reach their goal via Ait Baha and Agadir.

Tiznit

On a desert-like steppe between the Anti-Atlas and the Atlantic lies the city of **Tiznit**, surrounded by a mighty red loam wall. It was founded in the year 1881 as a garrison town for the troops of the Sultan Moulay el Hassan, who fought against the rebellious Berber tribes of the region. Even today, the military has a very strong presence in Tiznit.

Narrow alleys of the old town lead past trim loam houses to the **Great Mosque**, its distinct minaret with protruding wood pieces reminiscent of the architecture of the Sahel. Directly next to it is the **Lalla Tiznit Spring**. This local holy woman is said to have given the water healing powers, which is why the spring pool (more closely resembling an old, completely algae-covered pond) has indeed the status of a pilgrim's destination. On the way to the **Place du Mechouar** marketplace, you can buy fresh mint leaves in a small shop; mint from Tiznit is said to be the best in the land.

Berber Silver and Talismans

Around the Place du Mechouar, the **souks of the silversmiths** once attracted especially rich customers, since Tiznit was on the caravan route from Maure-

Above: The garmet clasps made by the Berber women are created in the workshops of Tiznit. Right: On the beach at Sidi Ifni.

tania to Marrakech. Jews dominated the jewelry business in the whole of North Africa until 1956. It was the migration after the founding of Israel that ushered in the decline of this trade.

In the displays of the stores it is conspicuous that there is almost no gold jewelry on offer: It is considered to be corrupt by the Berbers. The materials that dominate are then silver, semiprecious stones and enamel. If it is to cost somewhat less, then "Berber silver" is used, an alloy of silver, nickel, and lead. On the shelves and in the display cases the dealers present arm bands, earrings, talismans, chains and brooches. Many pieces show stylized traditional symbols of the Berbers, since Berber women do not wear jewellery solely to be attractive: gazelle and dove feet, snake and ram heads, salamander, fish and turtles have the function of protecting from the evil eye, from witchcraft and frome magic as well. The continuously recurring motif of the magical number five (*khamsa*) in the form of dots or as the "hand of Fatima" is said to protect the wearer reliably. Red coral branches keep children from having accidents, enhance male potency, and increase the milk flow for nursing mothers. Amber and tropical resin from the West of Africa as well as musk are concealed in some particular amulet lockets and talismans – as an aphrodisiac with both healing and protective powers.

When buying jewelry, however, keep in mind that not everything which shines like silver actually is silver!

Beaches, Flowers and Flamingos

On the pebble beach of **Sidi Moussa d'Aglou**, west of Tiznit, the fishermen live in former Berber cave-dwellings during the fishing season. In contrast, the hippies of the seventies preferred the several secluded sand bays of **Mirleft** further south. Half-way between the two towns of Agadir and Tiznit lies the beau-

tiful dune beach of **Sidi Rbat**. There the **Oued Massa** flows into the Atlantic.

The mouth of the Massa is steeped in legends: a whale is said to have disgorged the biblical prophet Jonah on dry land here. Around A.D. 682, the Islamic conqueror Sidi Oka ben Nafi reached the Atlantic here with the words: "There is no more land to conquer in the west!" The *mahdi*, redeemer of the world and proclaimer of the last judgment, is also expected at the mouth of the Massa. Unmoved by all this, the pink flamingos, wild ducks and other water birds continue to feed in the delta, which has been designated as a bird sanctuary and is rich in fish. On the various kilometer-long sand beaches, carpets of violet, yellow and white marigolds cling to the ground. Beach lilacs – which bring a high price in Europe as dried flowers – grow here in great numbers because of the considerable fog and dew forming above the cold surging waters of the Canary stream in the ocean's waters. A little further inland, euphorbias (spurges), frequently taken

for cacti because of their form, thrive behind the high sand dunes.

In the dry climate of the Sahara foreland, plants and animals have absolutely to adjust to the extreme environmental conditions in order to survive. Creatures have the advantage that they are mobile and can avoid the hot sun. Animals such as the jerboa and the desert fox (fennec) mostly spend the hot part of the day in underground burrows and first go hunting in the cool of the night. In contrast, plants cannot change their position at all and the need for protection from overheating and drying out becomes essential to survival. Dwarfism and thorns reduce the surface from which water can evaporate and protect the plants from being eaten by the starving herds.

The phenomena of the "desert blossoming" – the *acheb* – occurs because the plant seeds can wait for decades for adequate precipitation and then explode into bloom. One of the most important forms of adaptation to the dry climate is the so-called succulence, the long-term storage

JEBEL BANI

During the Western Saharan conflict, the main road P30 was improved for use as a transportation route for military supplies. Accompanied by light, but extensive arghan forests, it crosses the western foothills of the Anti-Atlas beyond **Tiznit** at the 1,057-m high **Tizi-Mighert** and thereby reaches **Bou Izakarne**. The road forks in this small oasis town. To the south, the relatively well-built P41 facilitates the drive via Gouelmim, Tan Tan and Tarfaya into the Western Sahara. The P31, on the other hand, turns to the east and leads to the spring oases of **Fam el Hissn**, **Akka**, and **Tata** in the western Jebel Bani, and then via **Foum Zguid** to **Zagora**. It is only partially asphalted. Because of the border dispute with Algeria and the military conflict with the Western Sahara liberation movement Frente Polisario, this stretch has been closed to foreign visitors for varying periods of time during the past few years. You should, therefore, first ask the authorities in Bou Izakarne about road conditions and current prohibited zones.

On the trip through barren, desert-like terrain, river valleys with fertile oases are the only diversion. The larger of the few villages function as administrative centers of the very sparsely-populated region, and used to be important resting places for the caravans.

Fam el Hissn lies on a once important north-south artery betweenTafraoute and **Tindouf** in Algeria (currently closed, no border-crossing possible).

Between **Akka**, where tasty date varieties grow on the wadi of the same name, and the oasis **Tata**, a road which is first rather bumpy, later at least asphalted, leads on through **Igherm** to Taroudannt. In **Foum Zguid**, a street forks off to **Agdz** in the upper Dra Valley and to **Tazenakht** at the foot of **Jebel Siroua**. **Bou Azzer** with the largest manganese mines in Morocco lies on this stretch.

of water in the thickened roots, stems, and leaves. Since it is a matter of the best possible ratio between the surface and the volume, the sphere-shaped and cylindrical succulents like the euphorbias are the most common.

Inland, the Massa River is dammed to form the **Youssef-Ben-Tashfin Lake** at the western edge of the Anti-Atlas. By an extensive distribution system, the newly-allocated farmland was to give a new existence to farmers leaving the dry high valleys of the mountains. A lack of information, strict cultivation regulations, and unfavorable weather conditions with unforeseen night frosts meant that the plan to export fresh fruit and vegetables to Europe almost failed. The region was simply unfit for intensive agriculture. Many of the canals are now filled with sand; most of the farmers have returned to traditional methods of cultivation.

Above: The Reguibat Berbers were feared caravan marauders in earlier times. Right: Functional male adornment.

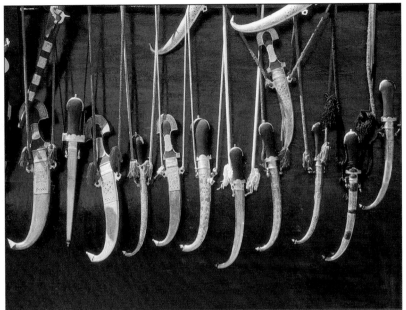

Places of interest in the region are mostly to be found away from the main route, but anyway it is worth planning the time to see them.

Foums and Fortified Graneries

In the valley of the **Oued Ifrane**, some 15 km to the east of Bou Izakarne, there are a number of idyllic oasis villages. The main town of **Ifrane de l'Anti-Atlas** has a *mellah* (Jewish Quarter) that is worth the visit. In the Jewish cemetery, a grave-stone with a 2,000-year-old inscription was found which is said to prove that the first Israelites fled here as early as during the reign of King Nebuchadnezzar in the 6th century B.C., at the time of the Baby-lonian captivity. The palm gardens of the oasis are inviting to take long strolls in. The contrast between the barren rock walls and the green of the gardens makes the importance of water for the plants, an-imals and people of this region very clear.

Even further to the east, the geological form of the *foum*, also called *kheneg*, ap-pears for the first time in the oasis **Tagh-jicht**. *Foum* translated means "opening in the cliff". Its creation goes back to high depressions existing during the Palaeo-zoic era, into which the rivers of the Anti-Atlas flowed. Jebel Bani served as a nat-ural barrier for this. In the course of time, the dammed lakes formed in this manner searched for a runoff and created open-ings. Such *foum* oases can be seen along the entire route to Zagora.

In the upper **Seyad Valley**, 30 km northeast of Taghjicht, stands the impres-sive **agadir Id Aissa.** Like the agadir of Tasguent, it is among the finest fortified graneries in Morocco. The citadel-like building crowns a table mountain, acces-sible by way of a a steep path. Tunnel-like passages lead to the individual sto-rage rooms; remnants of stone bee-hives can still be seen. During times of siege, the now-dry cisterns made survival pos-sible. The storage fortress was protected by merlon-reinforced walls and watch towers. The Berbers with a settled life-style built such strongholds to protect themselves from the raids (*razzou*) of the still nomadic Reguibat Berbers. In earlier times, these camel breeders frequently attacked the oases of the Dra Valley, the Anti-Atlas and Jebel Bani. They were after the farmers' crops. When such was the case, entire villages stayed in the Agadir in order to protect both their lives and their possessions.

From Agadir Id Aissa, there is a good view of the canyon-like valley of the **Oued Seyad** with its green band of oasis gardens and the low loam houses. Rocks and stones are polished smooth by the sand storms of the Sahara. Their surface is shiny black. This phenomenon is called **desert varnish**. As in all the old mountains of southern Morocco, iron oxide and manganese oxide are present in the rock. Because of the high ground temperature, which can reach 70°C in summer, the water in the capillaries of the stone rises to the surface and causes a black oxide layer to form.

Petroglyphs and *maader* Culture

In the Moroccan-Algerian border area of the lower Dra Valley there are many Stone-Age rock engravings. The largest collection is in **Oued Tamanart**, which can be reached from **Fam el Hissn**. However, interesting engravings can also be found in **Oued Tafagount**, 75 km to the south of **Akka**. The easiest of all to reach are the **Lybica-Berbères engravings** (eastern Jebel Bani): from Tinsouline in the Upper Dra Valley, an 8-km long trail makes its way to this Neolithic cult site located at the edge of a dry wadi.

Before undertaking such an excursion, it is absolutely necessary to check in advance with the police or the mayor (*kaid*) of the oasis towns as to whether the trails are open to tourists. There you can hire a

Right: Cliff drawings at Tinsouline depict mounted particularly warriors, camels and a panther hunt.

knowledgeable guide, without which the rock pictures can hardly be found.

The petroglyphs of the northwestern Sahara are without exception – and in contrast to the color petroglyphs of the Algerian Sahara – engraved into the rock with chisels. The oldest are up to 10,000 years old and presumably the work of hunters and gatherers; the newest ones are from about 5,000 B.C. and were probably created by cattle-raising herdsmen. Through the magic of the pictures, hunting luck was to be evoked or, depending on the case the herds protected from wild animals. The portrayals range from the large wild animals of the African savannah, via heavy-handed portraits of human beings (with rudimentary round heads) to stylized cattle and Libyan chariots.

The petroglyphs of the Oued Tamanart and the Oued Dra were created in the more recent phase. Elephants, rhinoceros, giraffes and ostriches are all surrounded by magical symbols which still have not been interpreted. Another group shows cattle and animals which were hunted, as well as the two-wheeled chariots of the legendary Garamants, whose exploits were chronicled by Greek historians. Whether these rock engravings were once in colored can no longer be established today.

During the winter – half of the year, these excursions often reveal barley and lentil fields in areas completely devoid of people. The fellahs of distant villages frequently make use of the fertile alluvial land in remote river valleys and, after rainfall has temporarily filled the usually dry river beds, plant particularly quick-growing crops there. This type of field tillage is called *maader* or *feija*. At harvest time, the villagers who are setting off on the arduous journey to the remote valleys are sent off ceremonially with baskets of provision. This tradition goes back to the times when the oases were terrorized by nomads and such journeys held quite a number of dangers.

ANTI-ATLAS TREKKING

The eight-day trekking tour of the Anti-Atlas described here leads through a high plateau southeast of Tafraoute without prominent peaks. With precipitation of often less than 200 mm a year, desert-like vegetation predominates, and yet the Shluh Berbers do plant barley in irrigated valleys during the winter rains and graze their goats on the barren slopes.

The best trekking months are in springtime March and April, in autumn October and November: warm during the day and frost-free at night.

About six hours' walking time is the daily norm; the trail runs at elevations between 1,000 and 1,850 m, with ascents and descents in the range of 350 m.

It is definitely not advisable to try the trek without competent help, as the terralin is often difficult. Ask the innkeepers or police in **Tafraoute** about a competent guide; he hires the mule drivers with suitable pack animals, is helpful in putting together the equipment, familiar with the rules of courtesy when dealing with the villagers – and is respected by their children. All provisions must be bought in Tafraoute; the busy Wednesday market is the ideal place to buy kitchen utensils, a water canister, cooker and camping gas. Remember to take along oil, spices, tea and sugar, and solely drink water which has been boiled or treated. Moroccan oranges are especially delightful and inexpensive, that's why they are ideal for trekking as citrus fruit which both nourishes and quenches thirst. Solid walking shoes, a tent, sleeping bag and insulation mat should be brought along from home and ballast left at the hotel.

A Land-Rover collective taxi takes you through the **Valley of the Ammel** directly to the **Tizi Mlil pass** (1662 m) and on over the bumpy trail 7040 to **Ait Abdallah** (1,500 m). At the police station you find out in which hospitable Berber house you can spend the night (1st night).

Next morning, you walk alongside the barley fields to the hamlet **Amzaout** and then up to an broad high plateau (1,850 m). Before the descent into a side valley, a lush green spring hollow is an inviting place for your midday break.

Well-fortified, you now reach the main valley of the Assif n'Ait Fiid and follow its dried-out bed to the camping site near the little village **El Medina** (1,550 m, 2nd night). Wadis generally contain water merely after heavy rainfalls, but seepage frequently provides ground water which the natives draw via their wells. Camp sites are usually near the latter.

After breakfast you climb up a winding path behind the village to the 1,700-m high plateau. Looking back at the oasis, the houses of El Medina (built closely together for security) and the rock-covered round threshing floors upon which the mules thresh the stacked grain as they walk in circles are all visible. Above, reddish-brown, folded strata of rock stretch al the way to the horizon.

When the weather is clear, wonderful panoramas open up above the magnificent rock landscape to the frequently snow-covered massif of the **Adrar n' Aklim**, the highest elevation of the Anti-Atlas with 2,530 m. The "contrary" Atlas is one of the oldest mountain ranges in the world. The forces of the earth have solidified and pressed it together, folded and faulted it, transformed its structure and mineral contents and continually eroded it. The variety of forms, colors, and weathering in the sediment formed from earlier lakes, seas, and depressions is just as astonishing as its composition: One finds limestone and marl, sandstone, conglomerates and quarzite, slate, mica schist and phyllite.

The very varied appearance of the dead material corresponds to the diversity of the plants. Since the slopes and plateau surfaces appear barren from a distance because of their lack of trees and bushes, when you hike past them it is a surprise to

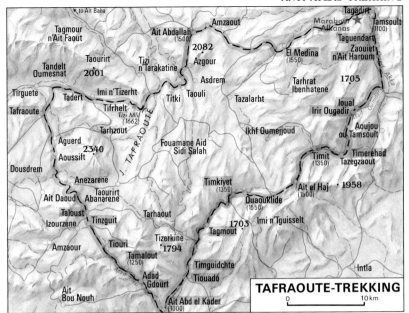

TAFRAOUTE-TREKKING

0   10 km

see how many colorful flowers blossom here in the only apparently deserted land. Between lavender, thyme, sage, rosemary and wormwood, there are also some grasses that serve as food for the goat herds. Next to grazed-down grass patches, poisonous plants such as asphodel, henbane and spurges assert themselves.

A steep descent leads from the plateau back down to the valley of the Ait Fiid River, where palms at the marabout of **Alkanas** (1,200 m) do provide the ideal shade for a lunch break. Now you can follow the gravel valley with its sparse vegetation all the way down to the two villages of **Tagadirt** and **Tamsoults** (1100 meters) that lie at the confluence of the Fiid and the Oued Akka (3rd night). The tarred road number 7085 runs along the eastern side, connecting Taroudannt with Tata and Akka.

Further along the Akka Valley southwards, the roadway crosses the river bed. It is best to follow the charming path on the east side of the wadi, leading past fields and groves through the villages

Taguennart and **Zaouiet n'Ait Haroum**. In such fertile valley oases, the Berbers carry on the cultivation of crops under irrigation by diverting the life-giving waters of rivers or wells into a system of open canals, the *seguias*, which lead to gardens and fields. Barley (as a grain for bread), potatoes, onions, vegetables and melons are all cultivated in the oases; alfalfa is planted for the livestock.

A grove of date palms at the point where the Oued Akka abruptly turns to the east invites you to rest. The excavation shafts of the underground *khettaras* (old irrigation tunnels that conduct the ground water from the side valleys to the valley wells) are conspicuous here.

You now leave the Akka Valley. If you follow the gorge-like Assif Oumder up-valley, you will find a suitable camping site between the villages of **Ioual** and **Irir Ougadir** at a fresh spring (4th night).

After traversing the gorge, you will discover charming villages with shady groves at the foot of stony slopes. On exposed rock spurs stand fort-like build-

211

ings, the fortified granaries of the Berbers. The agadir of **Timerehad** is still in operation, while the community storage facility of **Tazegzaout**, somewhat further up the valley, is already dilapidated. In these community-run *agadirs*, the villagers used to store their grain, oil, nuts, dates, plows, hoes, scythes and valuable items of all sorts, even sewing machines. There, where the plundering nomads once were a frequently recurring plague for the farmers, even the farmhouses squeezed onto the narrow ridge under the refuge. Since there have been no more robbery raids since the thirties, the Berbers now settle in more comfortable locations at the edge of the river valleys and leave their *agadirs* to the ravages of time.

Along the upper course of the Assif Oumder, the path snakes upwards to **Timit** (1,350 m) with increasingly sparse

Above: The oil from the fruit of the arghan trees is produced in archaic mills in Tagmout. Right: The oasis Adad in the valley of the Issi River.

vegetation. Here you can turn to the southwest into the valley of the Assif n'Ait el Haj and then hike up the river to the remote village of **Ait el Haj** (1,500 m). A meadow dotted with palms and fruit trees provides a nice, comfortable setting to pitch a tent.

Most animals of the semi-desert can never really be seen, since they are only active in the dusk or at night, live underground, or are well-disguised. However, there is a myriad of birds, amphibians, lizards and insects (such as black ground beetles, grasshoppers, and also dragonflies) that do display themselves in public and during abusliness hours, so to speak. With some luck, you will also see rodents such as the jerboa,who hops around on oversized hind legs hoofed animals such as the gazelle, or predators such as the fennec and jackal. The only venomous snakes are: the horned viper and the Avicenna viper; adders, other vipers and cobras are usually harmless. The sting of the poisonous yellow and black scorpions is always unpleasant, but life-threatening at most for children and people with a poor constitution. Because of snakes and scorpions it is certainly not advisable to go barefoot or reach under rocks or into crevices with bare hands!

Now the path leads to the west out of the Haj Valley, extends over a barren high plateau (1,800 m), descends slowly down into the valley of the Assif n'Tagmout, and reaches the village of **Ouaouklide** (1,500 m). In the river oasis there is an inviting river forest beneath a vertical cliff wall, a very nice spot for a break. Such trees and bushes along the dry river beds reach ground water with their deep roots, while herb-like plants and grasses with their widely-branched root networks close to the surface are dependent on rainfall and morning dew. Characteristic plants along the border of the bank are – in addition to date palms – oleander, cistus, tamarisks, and willows. Olive, argan and almond trees are cultivated. Broom,

prickly pear and euphorbias grow wild. After a gorge-like narrowing of the Assif n'Tagmoute, a grove with ponds near the village of **Timkiyet** (1,350 m) will tempt you to bivouac (6th night).

On the seventh day, the hike leads down the valley to **Tagmout**. In the village there is a small mosque, numerous marabouts, circular threshing floors and oil presses. While the extraction of oil – as indeed farm work and the keeping of livestock – is man's work for the strictly Islamic Berbers, carpet knotting, blanket weaving, and making pottery are all part of a woman's household; both lively villages contain graves of holy men. **Timguidchte** and **Tiouado** (lying further south on the trail 7075) are reached by about noon. The walls of the houses are mostly whitewashed pink, brown, or ocher, the door and window frames have a white border to protect against the "evil eye". Small grocer's stores offer lemonade for sale. Following the trail to the south, you will pass through a stony wasteland on the way to **Ait Abd el Kader** (1,000 m), where the grocery stores are not just open on market day.

On the last day of the tour you hike along the winding bed of the deep Assif n'Issi. It is worthwhile along the way to make a detour to the clustered villages of **Gdourt** and **Adad**. Near **Tamalout** (1,250 m), the last village of the notch valley, a shady grove on a stream is perfect for the midday break. For the restless mountain climbers, the short ascent to the ruined village with the dilapidated *agadir* is recommended. This is somewhat to the south on a rock overhang.

After a last bend, the valley oasis of Assif n'Issi ends. The way leads further to the northwest on an elevated plain which is made accessible by way of a trail. You walk through the villages **Tiouri** and **Tinzguit** to **Taloust**, where at 1,600 m, two drivable trails meet up. Ask in the café about getting a ride to Tafraoute, which is 25 kilometers away. And last not least: Do not forget to hand over an appropriate bakshish to your guide and your mule-drivers.

WESTERN SAHARA

The Western Sahara, a Spanish colony until 1976, is indeed a sizeable piece of real estate (270,000 sq. km) stretching south from **Cap Juby** to **Nouadhibou** on the Mauretanian border. In the east there are "map borders" with Algeria. Since the country was completely annexed by Morocco in 1979, four provinces have been created: **Laayoune**, **Boujdour**, **Oued Eddahab (Dakhla)** and **Smara**; all are very sparsely populated with a total of only about 200,000 inhabitants. Native nomad tribes include the Berber Reguibat, as well as the Tekna and Oulad Slim, who migrated from Arabia in the 13th century and still speak the Arabian *hassani* dialect today.

The area is of some economic significance. Western Sahara's long white sand beaches represent considerable tourist potential, and the coastal waters beyond them are extremely rich in fish. The largest deposits of phosphates in the world lie in the Western Sahara and it is presumed that there are also large deposits of petroleum and uranium beneath the desert sands. On the basis of these rich mineral resources, the political conflict as to the future of the former Spanish colony is understandable.

The Western Sahara Conflict

On November 6, 1975, as the Spanish dictator Franco lay on his deathbed, King Hassan II staged what was called the "Green March": hundreds of thousands of Moroccans went into the Western Sahara waving flags to support Morocco's claim to the area on the grounds that *sahraouis*, the nomads, had paid tribute to the Alawi sultans of the 19th century, and this somehow entitled them to a piece of this pie. When Franco died on November 20, 1975, the Spanish rashly gave their colonies independence. Morocco initially annexed the northern part of the Western Sahara, while Mauretania took over the administration of the southern third.

Morocco did not recognize the 1975 verdict of the International Court of Justice in the Hague stating that the Moroccan rulers had no rights whatsoever to the Western Sahara. When, in the year 1979, the United Nations recognized both the *Frente Polisario* liberation movement as the only legal representative of the Sahraouic people and the Democratic Arabic Republic of the Sahara *(DARS)* it had proclaimed, Mauretania soon pulled back out of the southern portion, thus leaving a power vacuum. Morocco then annexed that as well.

Since then, the uncompromising position of Morocco in the Western Sahara conflict has not only strained the national budget, but also the relation with Algeria: The Algerian town of **Tindouf** has become the headquarters of the Sahraouic government in exile and its freedom fighters, who have involved the Moroccan army in a trying guerilla war. This is why Hassan II had a 1,600-km long defensive wall built along the border with Algeria in 1981. Equipped with night-vision and various self-firing devices, it has claimed the last gazelles of the area.

The war had another side effect of some importance to the powers that be. It diverted attention from Morocco's domestic problems – food shortages and a chronic financial crisis – and brought the king the support of his people and even of the opposition. When the Maghreb nations of Libya, Tunisia, Algeria, Mauretania and Morocco formed the Union of the Arabian Maghreb, the Polisario lost its most important financial backer. The deadline for the referendum on the future of the Western Sahara (called for since 1981 by the UNO and the OAU) has been postponed time and time again because of the unacceptable preconditions set by Morocco. The most recent timetable was for January 1992.

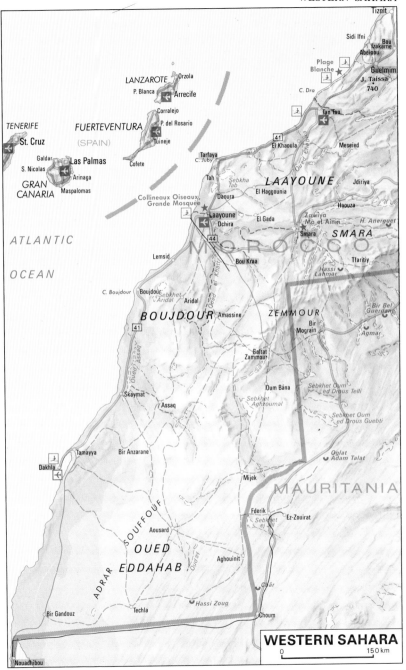

Tiznit

Sidi Ifni
Bou Izakarne
Abeïnou
Plage Blanche
Guelmim
J. Taïssa 740
C. Dra

LANZAROTE
Orzola
P. Blanca
Arrecife
Corralejo
P. del Rosario
FUERTEVENTURA
(SPAIN)
Tuineje
Tan Tan
41
El Khaoula
Meseied

Tarfaya
C. Juby

TENERIFE
St. Cruz
Tah
Sebkha Tah
Daoura
El Haggounia
LAAYOUNE
Jdiriya

Galdar
Las Palmas
S. Nicolas
Arinaga
GRAN CANARIA
Maspalomas

Haouza

Collineaux Oiseaux
Grande Mosquée
Laayoune
Dchira
El Gada
Zawiya Ma el Aïnin
Smara
H. Anerguet
SMARA

ATLANTIC

44
Smara

OCEAN

Lemsid
Bou Kraa
Tfaritiy

Hassi Lahmar

C. Boujdour
Boujdour
Sebkhet Aridal
Aridal
Bir Bel Guerdane

BOUJDOUR
Amassine
ZEMMOUR
Agmar

41
Bir Mograin

Galtat Zammour

Skaymat
Assaq
Oum Bána
Sebkhet Oum ed Drous Telli

Sebkhet Aghzoumal

Sebkhet Oum ed Drous Guebti

Tamayya
Bir Anzarane
Oglat Adam Talat

Dakhla

Mijek

MAURITANIA

SOUFFOUF
Fderik
Ez-Zouirat
Aousard
Sebkhet ej Jill

OUED EDDAHAB
ADRAR
Aghouinit
Ouday

Bir Gandouz
Techla
Hassi Zoug
Gâar
Choum

WESTERN SAHARA
0   150km

Nouadhibou

215

From Bou Izakarne to Dakhla

The P41 heading south from **Bou Iza-karne** was asphalted in recent years and now reaches Dakhla (1,060 km away). All the larger settlements of the Western Sahara yet have had sizeable financial support from Morocco since the Green March of 1975 and the underdeveloped infrastructure has been considerably improved. There are now regular flights from Casablanca and Agadir to Laayoune and Dakhla. The region is seldom visited by foreign tourists, however, owing primarily to weakness in that sector. There is inadequate hotel capacity and – except for the long sand beaches – few places of interest, and large areas inland are closed to civilians anyway. The construction of beach hotels is planned and a pilot project in Laayoune has already shown initial success.

Above: The sandy and shining beaches of Plage Blanche have yet been spared from the construction of hotels.

The small sleepy market town of **Guel-mim** no longer awakens Saturday mornings to the penetrating sound of camel calls at the beginning of the weekly market, but rather to a stream of people on day excursions from Agadir. The once-proud **Blue Men** – descendants of the Reguibat Berbers, once feared as caravan robbers – today sell postcards, tinny armbands and glass beads. Their indigo-blue garments, the *guedra* (the ecstatic knee-dance of the Berber women) and the camel market once made Guelmim famous. Today, the greatness of the nomadic culture can only be sensed during the popular summer *moussem*. Its downfall can be attributed to the drought and the war.

In the village of **Abeinou**, 13 km north of the town, you can enjoy $40^{o}C$ ($104^{o}F$) sulfur springs. If you prefer to swim in the ocean and have a cross-country vehicle, you can take the bumpy trail to the **Plage Blanche** on the Atlantic ocean: sabout 65 km southwest of Guelmim, a much-praised white dune beach stretches over dozens of kilometers.

The capital of the province, **Tan Tan**, with its 42,000 inhabitants, many stores, and numerous simple hotels, is among the most ambitious places in southern Morocco. Towering over Tan Tan is the **koubba** of the revered sheik **Ma el Ainin** (1831-1910)**,** who ruled large parts of Morocco at the turn of the century and heroically fought against the French.

The estuary of the **Oued Chebika**, some 50 km southwest of Tan Tan on the Atlantic, is an area of picturesque sand dunes and white beaches, the habitat of flamingos and other water birds. The trip is worth the effort.

In 1958, the Spanish returned the area between Tan Tan and Tarfaya, which they occupied in 1916, to Morocco.

The former border town of **Tarfaya** lies on **Cap Juby**. The Canary Islands are only 100 km away and play an important role as a trading partner. Test drillings done by oil exploration companies just off the coast on the continental shelf have been very promising.

Laayoune, the provincial capital, grew from 6,000 residents in 1960 to a population of 100,000 in the course of Moroccan occupation. Chosen as the place to show off Morocco's commitment in the Sahara, modern quarters have expanded into the desert. In addition to the **Great Moulay Abd el Aziz mosque**, the main attraction is the bird park **Colline aux Oiseaux** with its cactus gardens. Besides promoting the export of phosphate, there is to be intensified investment in tourism at **Laayoune Plage** 25 km west of the city. The former Spanish parador was renovated into a luxury hotel to accommodate the king during his visit in 1985.

The provincial capital of **Smara** is a desert nest plagued by sandstorms, the sole place of interest there being the ruins of the rebel sheik **Ma el Ainin's zawiya**, destroyed by the French during a punitive expedition in 1913.

The phosphate mining area of **Bou Kraa** lies 100 km southeast of Laayoune. On the longest conveyor belt in the world, 1.5 million tons of raw phosphate are transported annually to the coast, and exported from the harbor of Laayoune.

National highway P41 ends in **Dakhla**, until 1975 the Spanish Villa Cisneros, and today the capital of the **Oued Eddahab** province (formerly Rio d'Oro) founded in 1979. Dakhla lies at the end of a 40-km long headland bordered by white, virgin sand. It has approximately 20,000 inhabitants and lives primarily from the export of sea-food to the Canary Islands. Tourism is also slowly starting up here. There are small hotels available to vacationers who want to swim and fish on the magnificent beaches of the **Baie de Rio d'Oro**.

South of Dakhla, a trail leads on to Mauretania. This is still closed to tourists owing to the continuing instability in the region. Still plans have been hatched to open up the border to transit travelers.

ANTI-ATLAS

Accommodation

TALIOUINE: *MODERATE:* **Ibn Toumert**, Tel: 29. *BUDGET:* **Auberge**, Route de Ouarzazate (eastern edge of town, north of the kasbah).

TAROUDANT: *LUXURY:* **La Gazelle d'Or**, Route de Marrakech (1 km), Tel: 085-2039. *MODERATE:* **Salam**, Tel: 2312. *BUDGET:* **Saadiens**, Borj Annassim, Tel: 2589. **Hotel de Taroudant**, Place Assarag, Tel: 2416.

TAFRAOUTE: *MODERATE:* **Les Amandiers**, Tel: 8. *BUDGET:* **Tanger**, **Redduane**, **Du Soleil**, both hotels in central location.

SIDI RBAT: *BUDGET:* **Club Balnéaire** (beach at the Massa estuary).

TIZNIT: *MODERATE:* **Tiznit**, Rue Bir Inzaran, Tel: 086-2411. *BUDGET:* **Paris**, Pl. du Mechouar. **Mauritania**, Rue de Guelmim, Tel: 2092.

SIDI MOUSSA D'AGLOU: *BUDGET:* **Motel Aglou** (at the Tiznit beach).

MIRHLEFT: Very basic accommodation in private houses. Limited camping facilities at the bays, but no road access for vehicles.

SIDI IFNI: *BUDGET:* **Belle Vue**, Place Hassan II Nr.9, Tel: 5072. **Ait Ba Amran**, Rue de la Plage, Tel: 087-5173. **Suerte Loca,** opposite the gendarmerie. **Beau Rivage.**

FORT BOU JERIF: 30 km south of Sidi Ifni, basic rooms in a former French fort. Restaurant and camping at Oued Assaka, 10 km from the beach.

BOU IZAKARNE: *BUDGET:* **Anti-Atlas**, Route de Guelmim, Tel: 087-4134.

GUELMIM: *BUDGET:* **Salam**, Route de Tan Tan, Tel: 087-2057.

TAN-TAN: *BUDGET:* **Etoile du Sahara**, Rue El Fida 17, Tel: 087-7085. **Royal**, Centre Ville, Tel: 7186.

TATA: *BUDGET:* **Renaissance**, Avenue des F.A.R. 96, Tel: 42.

WESTERN SAHARA
Accommodation

LAAYOUNE: *LUXURY:* **Al Massira**, Rue de la Mecque 12, Tel: 224225. **Parador**, Rue Okba Ibn Nafi, Tel: 224500. *MODERATE:* **Nagijr**, Place Dchira, Tel: 224168. **El Alia**, Tel: 222231. *BUDGET:* **Residencia**. **Lakuara**, Tel: 223326. **Marhaba**, Av. Hassan II.

DAKHLA: *MODERATE:* **La Sarga**, Place Hassan II. *BUDGET:* **Bahia**.

BOUJDOUR: *BUDGET:* **Boughaze**, Bd. Massira.

TARFAYA: *BUDGET:* **Hamma**; **Marche Verte.**

FATIMA'S DAUGHTERS

The fate of Moroccan women today is the fate of the all Moslem women: apparently powerless, they drift towards an uncertain future while surrounded by a seething society that forces them to remain silent and be infinitely small in the face of the infinitely large totality.

Chouma means shame: a banal word for those who do not comprehend its genuince significance and power. However, it is a magical word for a young girl who tries to go beyond the rigid old boundaries of "what is proper", upon which family honor depends. The word *chouma* just has to be spoken and the girl will recoil and remorsefully beg Allah for forgiveness: for leaving the house of her parents, for having lived with a man and lost her virginity, for example. She will believe that evil spirits, *gnuns*, are driving her. These must be exorcized through prayer – that Allah understand and help – and through witchcraft – so that the neighbors never find out.

For much too long a time, women in oriental society have not been able to obtain respect. Some traditionally-oriented husbands expect the wives to kiss their hands when they come home. She bears a heavy burden as spouse. As a young girl she is subject to lustful stares. The birth of a daughter does not cause tears of joy throughout the house for two days afterwards, as does that of a son. Instead, there is silence: just a daughter – one more hungry mouth. She must also be watched so as to ensure her virginity when she one day marries the bridegroom selected for her will be the one who brings a good bride price. She is an empty frame for her family, hung up in order not to be touched, careful not to provoke any sort

Previous pages: Knotted dreams await buyers. Fantasia, the skillful art of feint attacks. Right: The roles of men and women are clearly defined in the Anti-Atlas.

of scandal – even just the sound of the word causes trembling: scandal means *chouma*. Most important, never fuel the ridicule of the neighbors; for they could point their fingers. If necessary, things are concealed, lies are told, stories invented. Every means is justified in order to avert shame to the family honor. And who is interested in the fate of the daughter? No Star of Bethlehem will guide her, but rather her father who locks her in. The mother will be very strict and take pride in seeing that the light of her virtuous daughter shines brighter than that of the neighbor's daughters.

In traditional Moroccan society, the woman as daughter is the slave in her parents' house and as wife she is the slave of her husband. She often has to tolerate a mother-in-law disappointed by life, who asserts the right to hit her, to decide matters for the married couple, to question the marriage, and even to destroy the marriage contract. What choice does a woman have when the alternative is to be rejected and unemployed? Her parents see it as a shame to have to take back their daughter. She is left to her fate, above all when she has the misfortune of having children to feed.

Female tragedies mostly do not take place in the so-called "good families" of the bourgeoisie, but rather in the more modest homes of the middle and working class. There, fear and oppression can be found. Breaking out of the family yoke leads often enough to prostitution.

The word "freedom", obvious for most young European and American women, is foreign to the Moroccan woman of the same age group. The young Moroccan woman then asks why she doesn't have the same right to this freedom, the freedom to go out, to live her life as she sees fit. The mass media and fashion, but particularly university study, naturally have a lasting influence on the behavior of modern Moroccan women. In an intolerable marriage situation, a more educated

woman who works at her own profession will hardly ever hesitate to leave her husband's house and establish her independence elsewhere in order finally to live the life that appeals to her.

Yet, even the woman with a university degree will not have an easy time marrying again. The Moroccan man looks for an "easy victim", for women he can rule without effort because he is allowed to do everything: he can lock her in, mistreat her, and leave her without paying any alimony. He is ultimately the boss and has the right to their mutual possessions. If he has the financial means, he can also have four wives and as many concubines as he wishes. However, mistreated women are starting to organize themselves; newspapers have begun to break the taboo and criticize the barbarian practic which, at the end of the 20th century have become indefensible even in Morocco.

Where is the religion in all this? The man has "his" mosques and "his" god. Here, as in everything else, the woman is merely a second-class citizen. While it is true that Moroccan women have increasingly started to wear their hair covered in recent years, this is less a sign of religious fanaticism than an expression of exhaustion in the year-long struggle for equal rights. And yet, they will continue to fight and try to propagate their ideas within the family and with friends. They no longer fatalistically accept their destiny today. With great patience, engaging smiles, and much charm they will perhaps reach their goal some day .

In the cities, meantime, the veil has fallen. The modern townswoman no longer hesitates to say what she thinks and wants to make up for lost time – in view of the unlived life of her mother. She sits at the wheel of a car, smokes cigarettes, takes care of business and goes alone to the restaurants of the elegant hotels of Casa, Rabat and Agadir.

Berber girls in the back-country also dream of freedom in Casablanca – but the fascinating independence of avant-garde city women will remain unattainable for them for quite some time to come.

223

CHILDREN

Children enjoy a remarkably high status in the Islamic society of Morocco; sons are in particular important for the prestige of the family since they are expected to provide for aged parents in later life. However, the enormous annual population growth of almost three percent has so changed the age pyramid in recent years that more than half of the Moroccans are now younger than twenty years of age. Six to eight offspring is normal in the rural areas: in the cities, the average is four children. Married couples without children are pitied, childless married women are considered the ultimate failures and can be repudiated.

Boys and girls are brought up in accordance with their later roles in society. Daughters are included in the housework and care of other children at an early age

Above: Girls are introduced early to house and field work. Right: These foreigners are somewhat peculiar...

since they are to be prepared for their future role as housewife and mother. In contrast, sons are treated like little pashas. Their lapses are more likely to be forgiven than those of their sisters. In the absence of the father, the oldest son takes over a representative function at an early age; all the women in the family must show him great respect.

At the age of about seven years, the boys are accepted into society through the act of circumcision. A large celebration is held on this occasion, representing a high point in the life of a Moroccan male, is second only to his wedding. The opposite tends to be true of the act of circumcision itself. Even today in more rural areas the "operation" is performed by barbers who work without the use of anesthetic or other gifts of modern medicine such as hygiene.

Moroccan society is divided into a world of women and a world of men. After reaching puberty, the boys are abruptly excluded from meetings with their aunts and female cousins or with other women, with female neighbors and with friends of their mothers. They must then soon learn the rules of the male world, above all as regards the Islamic-patriarchal term of "honor", and cut their ties to their mothers. Girls are first recognized by society when they marry.

School education often starts for little Moroccans in a Koran school, which represents a type of voluntary preschool religious instruction. There, they learn the main principles of Islam and also the Arabic language. Subsequent schooling within the state-financed educational system comprises general compulsory attendance for at least seven years. Despite this, it frequently happens in rural areas that girls are not sent to school at all, or are just sent for a few years. This is particularly noticeable in the older generations of the population, where there is a considerable educational divide between women and men. Thus, in the middle-aged generation, more than 90 percent of the women cannot read and write.

During the first two years of instruction the classroom language is Arabic, then later it is Arabic and French. The style of instruction is based on memorization and is authoritarian. (Berber children have another language usually, that of their tribe, which they speak at home). Many of the cities in Morocco then offer some form of further education.

Child labor is widespread in the lower and middle classes. Even during their younger years children often have an important economic function within the family; they are indispensable as care-takers for their smaller siblings and assistants in the household, and as helpers on the farm or in workshops.

Along the tourist routes, children often beg very aggressively – a behavior which hardly exists in areas not touched by tourist traffic. "Un dirham, un dirham!" and "Bonbon" are the words heard most frequently from the street children in Morocco. But, before you let yourself be pushed to a generous gesture, you should remember that children who are successful at begging will often be encouraged even more by their parents to do so and no longer go to school. Their future subsequently becomes dependent upon the charity of the tourists. And that is a rather difficult seasonal form of employment. Social conflicts also occur in the families because of begging. A farm worker in the south earns about twenty dirhams, somewhat more than two dollars, a day. Children can beg such amounts within a few minutes from a "generous busload". If you really want to help the children, then you can go to the mayor or an institution like the SOS Children's Village near Marrakech. It is also possible to take on a sponsorship for Moroccan children.

In their leisure time, Moroccan children are very creative. It is normal for them to build their own toys. Racing cars and small fortresses are magically put to-

gether from plastic bottles, old tires and branches. Marbles and coins do belong to their basic equipment.

It is often conspicuous that small children have a long tuft of hair on an otherwise shaved head. This is called the "tuft of Allah": when a child dies, which happens quite frequently with social conditions being what they are, even the Moroccans of today assume that Allah pulls it into Paradise by this tuft.

Christmas for the Moroccan children takes place on *achoura* day, the tenth day of the Islamic New Year month of *moharrem*. It is the anniversary of the death of Hussein, grandson of the Prophet. In Schiite Islam, it is celebrated as a day of mourning with processions and self-flagellation. In contrast, in Sunnite Morocco this day has become a festival for the children in which they receive presents.

On the day of the *Id el Kebir*, when the pilgrims in Mecca and all Moslems of the entire world celebrate the large mutton festival, the offspring are presented with new clothes.

MOROCCAN CUISINE

The cuisine of Morocco is generally easily digestible, not too fatty, and only rarely very spicy. Secret of good taste is the correct seasoning: Even back Europe of the 10th century, the exquisite spices of the Moors were known as an expensive delicacy. Nowadays, dealers in the souks create gaudy spice pyramids, their colors ranging from light ocher to diverse tones of yellow, orange and red.

The showpiece spice is the *rasel hanud*, which could be translated as the "coronation of the store". This is a mixture of at least 15 different spices. Turmeric, cumin, coriander, paprika and aniseed are its most important ingredients and at the same time the most common taste refiners in Moroccan cuisine. Saffron is popular, but very expensive. The word is derived from the Arabian *saffaran*, which means "to make yellow". Gram for gram, saffron is extracted from the inflorescence of a crocus, that a tedious job, that justifies the high price of 10 dirham per gram. It is cultivated in southern Morocco at the foot of Jebel Siroua.

In the mornings on the city streets you can see girls carrying long trays on their heads with bread dough made of barley or wheat, marked with the family stamp. They are going to the bakehouse to have this staple food baked. The Arabs call the resulting fresh flat breads *khozba*, the Berbers refer to them as *aghrom*. They are an important part of every meal..

Morocco's diverse agricultural products constitute the basic ingredients of its cuisine. Potatoes, carrots and tomatoes are made into tasty soups and stews. The people who can afford it eat meat, preferably lamb and beef; although camel meat is no longer quite as fashionable, in a salted state it is still a delicacy for the residents of Fès.

Right: Bismillah - Mechoui is served from a mud oven on Id El Kebir.

If there is a typical dish in the Moroccan kitchen, then it is *tajine*. This refers to the characteristic earthen cooking pot with its pointed cover as well as to the dish itself. Tajines are traditionally placed on small charcoal stoves to simmer. Ingredients vary according to the season of the year. There are recipes containing vegetables and meat, with a spicy or sweet character.

A popular recipe for the fall is as follows. Diced potatoes, onions and carrots, small pieces of tomato, pickled lemons and mutton are layered and sprinkled with fresh coriander, cumin, turmeric and salt. Quince cut into eighths and raisins are put on top. Before the tajine lands on the charcoal stove, meat broth and olive oil are added and the cover is put on. All is then stewed for about two hours. The tajine is put in the middle of the table, the lid solemnly raised, and all of the guests at the table use small pieces of bread to scoop the morsels out of the pot.

The preparation of a *tangia* reveals an unusual method of cooking. A large piece of beef or mutton is put into an amphora-like clay jug with some vegetables and meat broth and seasoned with *rasel hanud*. The container is then firmly closed with a piece of tanned raw hide and taken to the public bakery. When the baker is done with his daily work, he puts the tangia into the baking oven, which is no longer heated but still remains hot; it cooks for about twelve hours. Once you have experienced the opening of such a tangia pot, have seen the expectant faces and smelled the seductive aroma, you will find it hard to understand how such a simple thing as half a day in an earthenware jug can produce such a mirade. Albert, this kind of "slow food" is not unknown to other cultures on this planet. The crock pot fad of not so long ago is nothing more than an extension of this.

Couscous is known far beyond the borders of North Africa. The main ingredient of this dish is durum wheat semolina,

which is cooked for a long time in special steam pots and mixed time and again with olive oil. It is served with a stew made of vegetables and meat. If you like it "hot", there is a scorching red pepper sauce called *harissa* served as a garnish. Moroccans take some couscous between out-stretched fingers and form it into a sphere about the size of a table-tennis ball by rolling the hot mass back and forth. It is important that the couscous have enough oil in it to hold together.

Every Moroccan likes quick-broiled food from the charcoal grill - as much at beloved picnics with the family as *en passant,* that is while strolling and shopping. Grilled meat skewers (*brochettes*) and ground-meat balls (*kefta*) are eaten together with freshly-baked bread and a cold tomato sauce.

A particularly delicious specialty is lemon chicken (*poulet au citron*). To prepare it, the Moroccans use lemons which have been pickled in brine. They then still taste lemony but no longer sour. This gives the dish a special character.

Bastilla comes from Fès. Thin sheets of pastry are filled with raisins, vegetables, egg and the meat of boiled pigeon (alternatively, use chicken breast), baked in an oven and dusted with confectioners' sugar and cinnamon before serving.

For special occasions such as weddings, *mechoui* is prepared: a lamb, roasted on a spit or in a loam oven built especially for this purpose. A Moroccan gala dinner with *mechoui* is called *diffa*.

The most common soup, *harira*, is made with fresh coriander and chickpeas. It is also called Ramadan soup because it is the first thing eaten at the end of a long day of fasting. Like all the people of the Mediterranean, the Moroccans also love sweets of almost every kind. Dates, honey and almond baked goods conclude the tasty meal. Marzipan-filled" gazelle horns" (*cornes de gazelle*) and *chebakia*, a brown, sugar-sweet honey pastry are both very popular. Finally, the Moroccan national drink is called *thé à la menthe* (in French) very sweet china green tea flavored with fresh mint leaves.

THE ART OF BARGAINING

It is very difficult to establish general ground rules for the age-old procedure of bargaining. Every sales situation ist new, and indeed every initial offer by a trader differs in character.

The timelessness of this business is shown by *Elias Canetti's* bazaar experiences in the fifties. In *Voices from Marrakech* he writes: "In countries of the price ethic, there where fixed prices rule, there is no art whatsoever in buying something. Every dumbbell goes and finds what he needs, every dumbbell who can read numbers manages not to be cheated. With the souks, however, the price first named is an incomprehensible riddle...One might think that there were more different sorts of prices than different people in the world...".

Buying and haggling in Oriental countries has always been and is still an art in

Above: When they start to haggle, the merchants' hearts take a leap.

and of itself. According to experience, foreign visitors divide into three groups in this respect: natural talents, who not only see this process as an endeavor to achieve a favorable price, but also recognize in it an interesting form of communication; those who have been instructed and often desperately try to turn sales negotiations in their favor; and those who fundamentally refuse to involve themselves in the back and forth of offers and counter-offers. First and foremost, one should differentiate between the various branches. For food and objects of daily use, the prices have in the meantime become established throughout the country. The *villes nouvelles* of the larger towns and cities already have supermarkets. However, the small Moroccan shops, the *épiceries*, still continue to enjoy the largest patronage. Many of these grocery stores, which are often open until the late hours of the night, belong to people from the south. They mostly come from the Sous Valley or the area around Tafraoute. Because of their business acumen and their economic success, there are many jokes about the stinginess of this professional or regional group.

At the weekly markets (*souks*), there are usually signs with the prices per kilo for the goods. Because of the ancient scales, however, it is quite often more than difficult to check on the amount purchased, so that foreigners possibly have to reckon with paying a few dirhams more. Despite this, it is highly recommended that you shop at these markets: There is an overwhelming amount of fresh fruit and vegetables, spices and local products offered here.

The art of bargaining is generally required for goods that are especially produced for tourists, or that are interesting for this target group. This includes in particular carpets, kelims, leather goods, ceramics, daggers, jewelry, minerals, fossils and hand-engraved trays.

Every transaction takes time! The locals always open their negotiation procedure with general set phrases. They first inquire as to the well-being of the business and private spheres and only then does the exchange of first offers occur. In this process, the buyer and the trader both follow their proven strategies: the person interested in buying criticizes the quality of the product and laments the high price, the seller advances dramatic tales of bankruptcy and the threatening financial ruin of his family.

The first offer and/or counter-offer is decisive. As a general guideline, one third of the initial offer made by the trader is valid, but there are also situations where this rule already sets the price too high - a fifth is usually more appropriate in the *souks* of Marrakech. If there is a lovely piece which you like very much, it is better to avoid showing your interest too much. Bazaar traders observe their customers with unabated attention! If the salesman notices that a customer is really interested in a certain item, much of the negotiating latitude is then already lost.

Pretending to leave the store can surprisingly lower the price.

Tourists who start haggling and making specific price offers but then suddenly lose the desire to buy something violate an unwritten law of the oriental bazaar and draw the righteous anger of all traders – for the last offer is considered consent to make a purchase and is seen to be the purchasing price. If you don't want to buy anything but would like to have an approximate idea of the price of an item, you should only ask for the price but never start the negotiating process.

Transactions with street hawkers generally are very risky: They mostly offer items of poor quality and have relatively high basic prices since they only sell to fully solvent tourists.

For the little things that are already relatively cheap you should not bargain down to the last centime. Haggling about small amounts is unseemly for us "rich" foreigners. But when you are in the final stages of a larger purchase, it is important not at all to let yourself be phased by the trader's lamenting and by one of the countless other unusual sales strategies.

Previous information about the general price levels can be obtained at the government artisan office. This is particularly important if you want to buy valuable objects like carpets, kelims, jewelry, and antiques. You should always be particularly critical when dealing with "old" pieces, since fakes are nothing out of the ordinary. Haggling can be much fun. Whoever is able to assert themselves in regard to what price they want to pay rises in the esteem of the locals.

As an aside, the word "*khamsa*" (five) is a tabu for many Moroccans since it is considered to be defensive magic and – when uttered while speaking to another person – presumes that they have malevolent intentions. This is why it is so very often described as "the fingers of your right hand" during negotiations carried out in Arabic.

KNOTTED DREAMS

The assortment of carpets in Morocco is, without exaggeration, enormous, presenting much more than just the "department-store Berbers" that are offered more cheaply in other countries than in that of their origin. Incidentally, the original of these deep-pile carpets in the natural colors of the sheep's wool was the traditional tribal carpet of the semi-nomadic Beni M'Guild from Azrou (Middle Atlas).

In Morocco, three different forms of knots are used in carpet knotting: the Turkish *gördes* and *senneh* knots, which include two warp threads, and the Berber knots with four warp threads. Low-pile carpets *gtifa*, have a considerably lower number of knots per square meter than Persian rugs. Woven carpets are produced all over the country; they are called *hanbel*. Often they are decorated with

Above: A Kelim with embroidered diamond shapes brings good fortune. Right: Rug weaving at home creates jobs in rural areas.

embroidery according to traditional *sumakh* technique. In this, the embroidery threads are neither shortened nor sewn up on the back. All Moroccan carpets are striking in their diversity of symbolism: magical Berber ornaments, religious motifs (*mihrab*), animal types (*wasm*) and naive or stylized portrayals, landscapes, animals, plants, vehicles and utensils.

The colors vary according to the region. Wool from the sheep can be white, brown or black, goat's wool is black. There is camel wool in various tones of brown. And, just as is the case with felt, colors added to wool tend to be particularly brilliant. Colors available today are primarily chemical in origin and application. However, the old art of making dyes from plants has not been lost: some of the carpet schools in the country have retained the traditional methods of dyeing. *Alkanna*, which produces color tones from red to brown, is extracted from the roots of the henna bush. Blue tones are made with the help of indigo: the leaves of the indigo bush are fermented in limewater, the pigment is dried and then traded in cube form as so-called indigo white. The wool fibers are soaked in this, first turning blue upon oxidation.

The Arabian-influenced, *tapis royal* (royal carpet) of the cities of Rabat, Salé and Mediouna has an oriental pattern on a red ground. A medallion is surrounded by ornamental borders and plant decorations. The ceiling price set for king's carpets by the government is based on four levels of quality, according to the number of knots: *extra supérieur*: 1,600 knots per sq. m; supérieur: 900 knots per sq.m; *moyenne*: 625 knots per sq.m; *courante*: 400 knots per sq.m. Other official parameters are that the carpets in the high price ranges be of wool, their colors, dyes must be of good quality, and a special distinction is granted to those carpets whose weft and warp are made of wool, and when the preliminary tasks such as dyeing and spinning was done by hand.

In terms of folklore, the specialties of ethnic groups outside the large cities are even more interesting: red and brown *chichaoua* carpets with a pile of up to 15 cm are produced by the Arabic tribes of the *Chiadma* and the *Rehamna* in western Haouz. Their trademarks are *wasm* symbols based on old animal types. The Berber tribes of the *Zaiane* and the *Zemmour*, who live in the Middle Atlas and on the central plateau, are masters of kelim weaving. Fine geometric embroidery decorates their prayer mats. Experts also value the saddlebags and capes (*tamizart*) bordered with many small shiny silvery discs (*muzun*). From the wintery climes of the Atlas Mountains come the *handiras*, which, with their long wool threads on the backs are used as sleeping pads or else as capes. The *akhnif*, the woven and embroidered cloak worn by the semi-nomads of the Central High Atlas, is similar to the well-known *burnous*, the hooded cloak of the Bedouins..

Tazenakht carpets with their characteristic color combinations of orange, yellow, and black are typical for the region between Jebel Siroua and the upper Dra Valley. From the High Atlas south of Marrakech come precious woven and knotted *glaoua* carpets with the geometric Berber symbols such as diamonds, crosses and triangles.

The valuable wedding carpets of the Oued Zem Berbers can tell entire stories. Despite the Koran's prohibition of pictures, they feature naive representations of mosques, people, domestic animals, tents, tea pots, trucks and even, on occasion, pregnant camels.

Despite the government ceiling on the prices of knotted carpets which every dealer must display, tough bargaining is still required. It is wise to stick to specially stores when buying a carpet, but beware, in spite of the congenial appearances and treatment. Barganining may be on the order of the day. For, along with fairy-tale legends about the origin – the Tuaregs do not live in Morocco and do not knot carpets! – the prices dreamed up by dealers are also pretty incredible.

NOBLE HORSES

Colorfully-decorated *horses* prance nervously at the other end of the sand lot. The guests sit comfortably on soft cushions under a tent and wait – after a good meal with a glass of peppermint tea – for the climax of the festivities.

A beautiful horse neighs, strident, guttural Arabic words fly back and forth; the air is filled with heat and dust, stirred up by pounding hooves. The tension slowly increases. Suddenly, as if given an invisible signal, the riders and horses spring into wild action and, with loud shouting, threateningly rush in a closed formation precisely towards the area where the unsuspecting guests are sitting. The warriors pull up their guns, a volley of shots cracks, and ... less than five meters from the guest tent, in a cloud of noise and dust, the charging horde comes to a standstill just as abruptly as it started.

Above: The silver rifles are loaded – calm prevails before the storm.

The fantasia is presented to welcome guests of honor, to *moussems*, or to weddings: a mock attack true to the *ghaswa*, a robbery subject to certain laws and considered an honorable deed among nomads. If the rider attack is performed to honor a freshly-married couple, the bridegroom should under no circumstances make the faux pas of even batting an eyelid. Yet, it is not easy in the face of a horde of riders who rival each other to bring their horses – accompanied by a single bang from all the muzzle-loaders – to a halt immediately in front of the guests.

Any tourist can experience this war game in Morocco today. In Marrakech, for example, where the fantasia is staged under open skies in front of tent restaurants as a folklore spectacle. More fantasia can be experienced in Tissa, a small market town at the southern edge of the Rif Mountains. Oulad Aliane and Oulad Ryab tribes migrated here from Arabia in the 12th century and every year, in autumn, hold a *moussem* with a large horse market and rider games. It takes place at the *marabout* of the Sidi Mohammed ben Lahcen.The Meknes and Moulay Idriss pilgrimages are also accompanied by equestrian games.

In Morocco – as in the Islamic world as a whole, and in fact in all those countries where the horse served man in all walks of life – there is a particular relationship between people and their horses, since "Allah gave his favor to the horses". One of the loveliest legends told in Morocco about horses gives evidence of the esteem in which the Moslems hold the "daughters of the wind" and "drinkers of the air": "When God wanted to create the horse, he spoke to the South Wind: "Condense yourself, I want to make a new being out of you to honor my saints and to degrade my enemies". The South Wind spoke:"Create it, O Lord". God then took a handful of the South Wind, breathed on it, and created the horse".

The legend of the "El Khamsa al Rasul Allah" is said to indicate the origins of *asile* (thoroughbred) Arab horses. On the *hedschra*, Mohammed's flight from his enemies, the Prophet reached a watering place with his followers. The horses, close to dying of thirst, plunged towards the cool water. Yet before they even had a chance to drink, Mohammed noticed that he had fallen into an ambush and let the signal to leave be sounded. However, only "the five" (Arabic: *khamsa*) returned without drinking and thereby saved the Prophet's life. He blessed them and gave them the names of Koheila, Saklavia, Hamdania, Hadba, and Obeya. Although there is no evidence that the main stock of Arab horses can be traced all the time back to the mares of the Prophet, the frequent recurrence of the term "el khamsa" is nevertheless conspicuous.

The German Karl Schmidt went to Arabia at the beginning of the 20th century and shared the life of the nomads in the desert for 7 years. They called him "Raswan", a name he took on after the death of an Arab stallion. He developed a system of differentiating thoroughbred and non-thoroughbred horses, and referred to the "el khamsa". The classification ultimately three basic types: the "classic" breeds of Kohaylan and Saklawi, and the somewhat coarser type called Muniqui.

The Prophet Mohammed even gave the horse religious significance in the Koran, having recognized the value of the speedy mount for the propagation of his religion: "As God created the horse, he spoke to the splendid creature: I have made you to be without equal. All of the treasures of this earth lie between your eyes. You will subjugate my enemies under your hooves; carry my friends upon your back. This is to be the seat from which prayers rise to me. You shall be joyful upon the entire earth and preferred above all other creatures, for yours shall be the love of the master of the earth. You shall fly without wings and conquer without a sword".

Even the rudiments of horse breeding were regulated through the Koran. A generous award was promised to the Moslem who raised a horse with which he could go off to the holy war. Horses were never spared in battle – with one exception. An unwritten law allowed a pregnant mare to be taken out of the battle under certain circumstances in order to bring her foal into the world without danger. "I recommend to you the care of the mare", says the Prophet, "for her back is a place of honor and her body conceals inexhaustible treasures".

Usually only mares that had withstood battle were used for breeding. Stallions were considered unsuitable for war since they gave themselves away through their loud neighing. They tended to be more of a burden, which is why just a few of the best were raised and used for breeding. While owners could usually tell long stories about their mares and the names given to them, less attention was paid to stallions. Mohammed is said to have ridden for a time on "El Mortadshis", the

"beautiful neighing." The names are in most cases given according to the origin, to mutual characteristics or coincidental occurrences. The name "Kohaylan", for example, comes from *el khol*, a black powder that women use as make-up for their eyelids. Animals of the Kohaylan line, on the other hand, are distinguished by a blue-gray coloring of the skin around the muzzle and eyes. "Mu'niqui" means "long neck" in Arabic.

Although export of noble horses was banned in general, a Moroccan stallion from Moulay Ismail's stables became famous in Europe in 1730 when it was presented to the court of Louis XV. by the Beys of Tunis. Spurned by the French king, the horse first worked as a carthorse in the streets of Paris. There it was discovered by a British dealer, who then sold it to the Englisch breeder Lord Goldophin. As "Goldophin Barb", the noble

Above: Only the best Berber stallions are used for breeding. Right: A beard – often sign of a Koran scholar.

stallion eventually became one of the forebears of British thoroughbreds, siring the "Matchem Line" of innumerable successful racehorses.

The Berber horses were already known to and highly valued by the Romans, who admired their robust constitution and exceptional speed. It so happens that it was bred in Morocco long before the Arabians achieved their high rank there. The Berber horses also influenced – through breeding – the evolution of the Spanish horses, particularly the Andalusians. In look, Berber horses mostly differ quite markedly from Arabs due to their rather arched muzzle, strong lower jaws and flattened croupe. However, they do possess the same robust foundation and friendly temperament.

In the Haras of Meknes, a stud farm run by the Moroccan ministry of agariculture, both Arab and Berber horses are bred; if you want to take a photo of one of these marvellous animals, ask one of the housekeepers to display a stallion for you (bakshish recommended).

MOROCCAN LITERATURE

The literary life of Morocco is based today mostly on the works of 20th-century authors who grew up during the colonial era, and often witnessed first hand the difficult steps into independence. Their self-administered task is often to glue a picture of Morocco in its clinch with modern life, or to differenciate it from other cultures. In Morocco, many things are not what they seem at first sight: the friendly, helpful student turns out to be a tout; the obliging city guide transforms directly into a vulture when the tourist wants to present him with a supposedly generous baksheesh. For the poor majority of the people, life is a singular struggle to survive, which does not forgive weakness and is full of chasms appearing without warning. The struggle for existence and the search for identity between Western and Islamic values are the topics of contemporary literature in Morocco. Social criticism is directed at the suppression of the opposition, the lack of freedom in the traditional role of the woman and the situation of Moroccan foreign workers in France. Literary forms range from the humorous satire via the novel of character development to autobiography; the language of the writers varies from Maghrebi dialect to classic Arabic and polished French.

In *A Life Full of Pitfalls*, Larbi Layachi (under the pseudonym of **Driss ben Hamed Charhadi**) portrays the world of a young herdsman who finds work as a bread delivery man in the Tangier of the wild forties. But the wealthy owner of the bakehouse cheats him out of his rightful pay. In order to earn money, Ahmed fells trees in the government forest with his friend and – unconscious of the illegality of the act – tries to sell them to Spaniards on the *souk* (marketplace). The police arrest and maltreat him; he lands in jail for the first, but not the last time. Again and again he is cheated or betrayed by false

friends. The culturally pessimistic core statement of his autobiographical account is a saying his mother gave him on his difficult life's path : "If you see a Moslem who has had luck, then you know that no other Moslem was with him". The illiterate Larbi Layachi did, however, finally get lucky: it was no less than the American **Paul Bowles**, the "Titan of Tangier" who in 1963 translated the stories into a tape recorder in his Moroccan dialect of Arabic – as he died with the stories of **Mohammed Mrabet** (*M'Hashish* and others).

The book written in classical Arabic by **Mohammed Choukri**, *The Hard Bread*, was also translated into English by Bowles in 1973. It tells the story of a farmhand who worked on a Spanish farm during the protectorate period.

Bowles' own novel, *The Spider's House*, is of value in terms of contemporary history. In 1954, the independence party Istiqlal called upon Morrocans to boycott the sacrifice holy to Moslems on the holiday of Id el kebir since the French protectorate masters had sent Sultan Mohammed V into exile exactly one year before. In Fès, the young Amar experiences bloody battles between the opposition and the French police and the identity crisis of the traditional Moslems faced between loyalty to Allah and the independence movement.

The forties in the gray zone of Tangier, which was international at that time, are portrayed by Paul Bowles in *Let it Come Down* (1952). The American Dyar is entangled in currency smuggling, sinks more deeply into the decadent world of the whites and finally kills a Moroccan while *m'hashish* (full of hashish). In Bowles's existential novel, *The Sheltering Sky* (1949), an American couple flees to North Africa from the boredom of affluence and the purposelessness of their lives. In their search for their lost love, the two drive into the Sahara, where illness, death and insanity await them.

The writer **Abdellatif Laabi** was arrested as director of the literary magazine *Souffle* in 1972 and spent eight years behind bars as a political prisoner. His book *Kerkermeere*, published in the year of 1982, deals with his own time in prison, characterized by torture and degradation, companionship and hope in despair. He wants to be the "wandering seismograph in the jungle of the 20th century" with his literature as the "proclamation of being alive. It is the guarantee that the human outcry is never silenced."

The early works on **Driss Chraibi** were forbidden in Morocco for a long period of time; today they grace the window displays of every book store. Chraibi graduated from the élite school Lycée Lyautey in Casablanca in 1947 and subsequently studied chemistry in France. It was in France in 1954 that he published *Le passé simple* (The Simple Past), a bitter reckoning with his despotic father and

the traditional feudal society that does not recognize human rights. In the process he gained a great number of enemies in his homeland. In his second book, *Les boucs* (The Bastards, 1955), he criticized in a strident manner the miserable situation of North African immigrants and foreign workers in France.

In contrast, a much more reconciliatory tone and refreshing humor is found in his *The Civilization, Mother!* (1972), his wishful thinking about the emancipation of his mother in the Casablanca of the forties. The traditionally-raised Arab woman presumes there is a spirit in her newly-installed radio, the younger generation's pride and joy, and names it Monsieur Ktö. "Monsieur Ktö became the man she had never known, the husband who recited love poetry to her, the friend who gave her advice and told her about this world outside, of which she knew absolutely nothing."

Driss Chraibi's masterwork is the political satire *Une enquête au pays* (An Investigation in the Countryside, 1981). Police go to a Berber village on the Algerian border in order to track down a suspicious intellectual who is supposedly preparing attacks against the government. The wanted person turns out to be a blind man who had worked – illegally – in Algeria and had returned to his home village for health reasons. Chraibi portrays the Moroccan-Algerian border as a senseless relic of colonial times and thereby plays with international fire.

The internationally best-known author of today, having published seven novels and seven books of poetry in the French language, is **Tahar Ben Jelloun**. He spent the early years of his youth in Fès, studied philosophy in Rabat in the sixties, and worked as a teacher in Casablanca. His novel *Harrouda* (1973) is, among other things, an individualistic description of the political and mystical history of the city where he was born. The witch *Harrouda* is the embodiment of feminine

Right: Calligraphy – words of the prophet chiseled in stone (Fès: Attarine).

sexuality, ruling the excessive fantasies of the young men of Fès. "Harrouda was then the *Schehersâd* who gave love medicine to the spectators, the matron, the *Scheicha* who lets her belly talk,...the spider woman who breaks into the dreams of youth..."

In 1971, Tahar Ben Jelloun emigrated to France, studied social psychology in Paris and, in 1975, published his psychological studly *The Deepest of Loneliness*. In it he investigates the social, emotional and sexual misery of North African emigrant workers in their "guest land".

The Memory Tree was published in 1978: the story of Moha, the fool and wise man (a well-known rogue figure in the Maghreb), who once sits as a flute-playing beggar in front of a bank, tearing up dirham bills. "Money makes you so ugly. I know what money is. I was sent by the Prophet to stop its circulation. I take it in the evening and tear it up in the morning...I stop the money. I stop the circus."

Ben Jelloun was awarded the literature prize of the French anti-discrimination movement *SOS Racisme* in 1985 for his novel *Son of her Father*. A *fassi* (resident of Fès) who is already the father of seven daughters but still no son one days reveals to his pregnant wife: "The eighth birth will be a day of joy...The child that you bring into the world will be of the masculine sex, a man, and he will be called Ahmed, even if it is a girl!" With this work, the author questions the rigorous Moslem patriarchy. The following volume of this novel of inner development bears the title *The Night of Innocence* and depicts the emancipated liberation of the girl who was raised to be a man. Tahar Ben Jelloun received the *Prix Goncourt*, the highest French literary prize, for this work in 1987.

Overall, like much African literature, the literature of Morocco is refreshing in its narrative and inventive in its themes. The country's history, the florescence of the language, the people's very particular brand of humor and emotional expression is perhaps best found here, in its most compact form.

Nelles Maps ...the maps, that get you going.

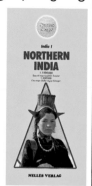

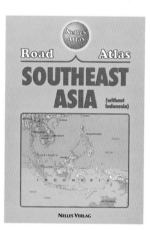

- Afghanistan
- Australia
- Bangkok
- Burma
- Caribbean Islands 1 / Bermuda, Bahamas, Greater Antilles
- Caribbean Islands 2 / Lesser Antilles
- China 1 / North-Eastern China
- China 2 / Northern China
- China 3 / Central China
- China 4 / Southern China
- Crete
- Egypt
- Hawaiian Islands
- Hawaiian Islands 1 / Kauai

Nelles Maps

- Hawaiian Islands 2 / Honolulu, Oahu
- Hawaiian Islands 3 / Maui, Molokai, Lanai
- Hawaiian Islands 4 / Hawaii
- Himalaya
- Hong Kong
- Indian Subcontinent
- India 1 / Northern India
- India 2 / Western India
- India 3 / Eastern India
- India 4 / Southern India
- India 5 / North-Eastern India
- Indonesia
- Indonesia 1 / Sumatra
- Indonesia 2 / Java + Nusa Tenggara
- Indonesia 3 / Bali
- Indonesia 4 / Kalimantan

- Indonesia 5 / Java + Bali
- Indonesia 6 / Sulawesi
- Indonesia 7 / Irian Jaya + Maluku
- Jakarta
- Japan
- Kenya
- Korea
- Malaysia
- West Malaysia
- Nepal
- New Zealand
- Pakistan
- Philippines
- Singapore
- South East Asia
- Sri Lanka
- Taiwan
- Thailand
- Vietnam, Laos Kampuchea

TABLE OF CONTENTS

TRAVEL PREPARATIONS

Conditions of Entry

No visa is required of citizens of the European Community, Switzerland and Austria. Upon presentation of a passport which is valid for at least six more months, visitors receive an entry stamp entitling them to a three-month stay in the country. Children under 16 can be included in the passport of their parents or can enter with their own passports in the accompaniment of their parents. If you are bringing a dog with you, it needs a current official veterinarian health certificate (not older than 10 days) with an attest that the obligatory rabies vaccination has been given (at least one month before, at most eight months before).

Vehicle papers: national driver's license and automobile papers are accepted. The obligatory green insurance card must be validated for Morocco. A *carnet de passage*, in which a camper inventory (where applicable) must also be listed, is necessary for trailers and boats. Vehicles and valuables are noted in the passport and checked when departing in order to prevent illegal sale of the vehicle in the country. The "black market" sale of an automobile, necessarily connected with passport falsification, is punished with a long-term jail sentence, which, may the trespasser beware, is no picnic in Morocco.

Climate and Travel Season

With its beaches, mountains and deserts, Morocco has various climates and is therefore in season all year long. The rainy season theoretically lasts from November to April. It can be interrupted by long dry periods or not take place at all; weeks of rain are very rare. Precipitation decreases from west to east and from north to south, with much more occurring in the Atlas Mountains than on the plains. In January and February, ski lifts are in operation in the Rif Mountains and the Middle and High Atlas. There can be night frosts at the palm oases of the south as well as in the desert. 4°C were measured in the room of a four-star hotel in Boumalne one January. Therefore, pack your down sleeping bag!

After Christmas, the ocean temperature in Agadir sinks to 16°C, which doesn't appear to disturb the beach tourists. Ski tours are possible in the High Atlas until the beginning of March, then the trekking period, which lasts until October, starts. The ideal round-trip time is in April. The country is green at the end of the winter rain period, the grain fields are almost ripe for the harvest and there are even spring flowers in the stony desert. People sensitive to heat should avoid the region south of the High Atlas from June to September, since you can reckon with 50°C (122°F) in the shade and sandstorms (medium daily high in Tata in July: 43.3°C). During this period there are also vehement afternoon thunderstorms in the High Atlas.

The swimming season on the Atlantic coast to the north of Essaouira lasts from June to the end of September; because of the cold upsurging water of the Canary stream, it can be foggy in the morning and also decidedly cool even in summer. Swimming season on the Mediterranean is from May to September.

Clothing

"The desert is a cold land in which it becomes very hot", is what General Lyautey, the first resident general of Morocco, is alleged to have said. When, in extreme cases, January temperatures in the hammada reach almost 30°C and sink to below freezing at night, it is necessary to wear warm pajamas! Such extremes can easily overstrain a northern body. You can best counter them by wearing clothes according to the onion-skin principle; from November to April a warm jacket and a rainproof garment should be accessible.

Strong hiking boots are necessary for trips to the mountains. Mountaineers should pack items made of down during the colder season: The thermometer can indicate 20°C below freezing during the winter in the High Atlas at 4,000 m. Ideal hiking weather prevails in the heights above 2,000 m as of May. In the south, a sun hat can delay the dwindling of the senses from April to October. However, a turban is more practical in a sand storm since it can be pulled in front of the face.

Health Precautions

There are no vaccinations required of travelers from Europe. However, it is recommended that you have immunization against typhoid fever, polio, hepatitis, tetanus and cholera. A dog bite can transmit rabies. In the southern river oases, there is some danger of malaria during the summer, the water there is thought to contain bilharzia, and flies can transmit the eye disease trachoma.

AIDS ("SIDA" in Morocco) is prevalent in the country; the same rules of prevention apply as everywhere, that is, either abstention or with condom, in which case you should be equipped.

Travelers are most frequently affected by diarrhea. Ice cubes made of tap water, non-disinfected drinking water from pipes or wells, salads and unpeeled fruit are all avoidable sources of infection. Luckily enough, you can purchase bottled mineral water almost everywhere; non-carbonated in plastic bottles (Sidi Harazem, Sidi Ali), carbonated in glass bottles (Oulmès). Meat and fish can be spoiled even in four-star hotels during the summer and caution is therefore advised. First-aid kits should include intestinal therapeutic agents, electrolyte, antibiotic dusting powder and eye drops, mosquito-repellent lotion, antihistamine ointment, anti-insect-sting tablets, sun protection, lip ointment, and throat lozenges. Simple hospital treatment (without medication) is free of charge, but established doctors do expect cash payment. It is therefore sensible to have foreign health insurance which also covers return air transport back home in the event of serious illness or injury.

Money

It is forbidden to import or export the dirham (DH), Morocco's national currency. Foreign currencies can be brought into the country in any amount, but a declaration may be required for sums over approximately US$ 1,700. Keep your currency exchange receipts in order to change back unspent dirhams at the end of the trip (max. 50% of the amount exchanged). German marks and French francs are the best-known foreign currencies, but all of the most common international currencies are accepted without complaints. The exchange rate (1991: US $1 = 3.60 DH) is set by the government and is the same in all hotels, exchange offices and banks. Traveler's checks and Euro-checks (ceiling amount of DH 2,000) are now being accepted by most banks; however, exchanging traveler's checks in higher amounts (above $200) can still be a problem in the south.

During the peak season, the supply of dirham in hotel exchange offices often runs out. Some of the airport exchange offices only exchange cash. Large souvenir stores – particularly carpet dealers – and hotels also accept credit cards (mostly American Express and Diner's Club). Money should be kept in the hotel safe or in a money belt, chest or calf pouch when traveling. The same rule as in most countries applies: Avoid brandishing your money when in public places.

Although dirham coins are constantly required for tips, they are rare and should therefore be requested when first exchanging your money. As you will be using them up with fair frequeny, always keep a little supply handy in a convenient but thiefproof pocket.

Morocco in Figures

Area: 458,730 sq. km; with Western Sahara 710,850 sq. km. Agricultural area: 84,000 sq. km; population density: 34.6 inhabitants per square kilometer; urbanization: 45% = two-thirds of the population lives in one-tenth of the country's area; population: approx. 25 million; Berbers: approx. 40%; portion of population under 25 years: 61.5%; life expectancy for men: 59 years, women: 63 years; calorie intake per inhabitant and day: 2,729 (= 113%); inhabitants per doctor: 4,900; inhabitants per dentist: 106,000; population growth: 2.6%; illiterates over 15 years: 66%; gross domestic product: DH 180 billion; foreign debts: US$ 22 billion; income per capita: US$ 560 (1986); employment structure: agriculture and forestry with fishing 39.7%, production and transportation 28.5%, trade 7.6%, service sector 7.1%. Around 70% of the population is – because of the large families and chronic under-employment – dependent upon agriculture.

Return Flight

Charter and scheduled return flights with Royal Air Maroc are completely booked up during the season, especially after Easter. The most important official act of the trip is getting a confirmation for the booked date of a return flight – with a stamp on the ticket! – in one of the RAM offices (in all cities with airports) at least 72 hours before the flight home. Reckon with two hours for checking in. Because of the adjustment to daylight-saving time, the flight plan can be shifted one hour in spring.

TRAVEL ROUTES TO MOROCCO

Air: Morocco has seven international airports (Casa, Rabat, Tangier, Agadir, Fès, Marrakech, Oujda). The most important airport for scheduled flights is the Aéroport Mohammed V near Casablanca. The state airline Royal Air Maroc (RAM) flies from there to the capital cities of Western Europe, North America, North and West Africa, the Near East and Brazil. Flying to Paris, Frankfurt or Munich, and then connecting to Morocco is one convenient possibility. In cooperation with Air France, the RAM offers about 30 flights a week between Paris and Casa. From Frankfurt and Munich, the RAM and Lufthansa fly to Tangier and Casa. The leading charter airport is Agadir. Charter flights from Fès and Marrakech are offered by Air France.

Sea Routes: Car ferries to Morocco: Algeciras - Ceuta: 90 minutes (Transmediterranea, several times daily); Algeciras - Tangier: two-and-a-half hours (Transmed., Limadet Ferry; several times daily); Gibraltar - Tangier: 2.5 hours (Transtour, Gibline; daily); Malaga - Tangier: 6 hours; Sète - Tangier: 36 hours (Comanav); Sète - Nador (Comanav); Almeria - Melilla: 6 hours; Malaga - Melilla: 7 hours (Transmed.). Las Palmas - Agadir and Las Palmas - Laayoune: from November to July weekly (British Ferries/Orient Lines and Comanav).

Rail: Paris - Casablanca: 48 hours (twice daily in summer, coordinated with ferry connection). Geneva - Casablanca: 47 hours. Young people under 26 years of age can travel economically with Interrail or Eurorail tickets. Car sleeper trains: Paris - Madrid; Madrid - Algeciras; Düsseldorf - Biarritz; Munich - Narbonne; Barcelona - Malaga.

Bus: A touring bus of the Moroccan CTM travels twice a week on the route Paris - Bordeaux / Lyon - Tangier - Casa - Marrakech - Agadir - Tiznit (50 hours). The Europabus drives to the ferry harbor of Malaga.

Car: Although there are numerous car rental agencies in the country, according to the contracts their cars are not to be driven on gravel roads. Landrovers can only be rented with a driver; it is therefore practical for fans of remote mountain and desert trails to drive their own vehicle (Munich - Algeciras: approx. 2700 km, 3 days). The quickest and cheapest ferry connection: Algeciras - Ceuta (necessary to book in advance during the summer and at Christmas). Caution: in Spain, the brazen car burglars strike at gas stations even when the driver is standing next to the car! Morocco is safer in this respect. Traveling on to Algeria is possible at the moment but always depends upon the political climate between Morocco and Algeria. In case of doubt, your embassy in Rabat should be able to give you information.

TRAVEL WITHIN THE COUNTRY

Air: Inner-Moroccan flights with RAM and its subsidiary Royal Air Inter are economical. Inland flights from the airports of: Agadir, Al Hoceima, Casablanca, Fès, Dakhla, Laayoune, Marrakech, Meknes, Nador, Ouarzazate, Oujda, Rabat, Tangier, Tan Tan and Tétouan.

Rail: The rail network of Morocco's ONCF covers just 2,500 km; the south still has no tracks. The Interrail pass is accepted. The only express train runs between Rabat and Casablanca. Other train connections (slow but punctual): Casa - Rabat - Meknes - Fès; Fès - Taza - Oujda; Casa - Marrakech; Casa - Knouribga; Casa - Safi; Tangier - Asilah - Meknes: A monthly network ticket is offered. It is advisable to reserve seats. Rail-buses extend the network beyond Agadir to Laayoune.

Bus: The bus network of the country has no gaps and the ticket prices are reasonable. The most comfortable long-distance buses - partly equipped with video – belong to the Compagnie de Transports Marocaine – Lignes Nationales, in short the CTM-LN. It is most practical to make reservations at the bus terminal (Gare Routière), which is also served by private lines. Night buses are used for trips to the hot south.

Taxis: The network of collective taxis is excellent: they reach even the most remote village, are quicker than the buses, cost only about twice as much, but are often very tightly packed. The number of legal seats is recorded on the registration certificate and is the basis for price negotiations in case you want to charter such a *grand taxi* alone (mostly Mercedes or Peugeot, in the south also Landrover; color: blue or beige).

A *petit taxi*, mostly red with a yellow sign, is only allowed to drive within the cities and must be equipped with a taximeter. Since the tariff usually lags behind the rate of inflation, the drivers often refuse to turn on the clock. Decisive behavior or previous price negotiations are then necessary. A maximum of three passengers may ride along.

Rental cars: Branches of international and Moroccan car rental agencies are found in all the tourist centers. Prices can be discussed with the small local agencies; for round trips it is advisable to use the three-day or week flat rate without kilometer limitations. Because of the frequently high tax rates (up to 20%), read the fine print in the contract! Comprehensive insurance calms the nerves. Check the tires as well as the spare tire and jack (flat tires happen frequently), make a list of dents already in evidence, and never leave without taking a test drive! You should have the orderly return of the car certified.

With your own vehicle: Morocco is an El Dorado for drivers with four-wheel drive vehicles, campers and motorcycles. European automobile clubs and insurance companies offer a foreign insurance policy which you should not be without. If after an accident policy holders present police documentation, they can have repair costs refunded by the Touring Club Maroc in Casablanca (Ave. des F.A.R. 3; Tel: 9-279288).

There is no unleaded gasoline. Diesel only costs half as much as gasoline. The network of gas stations is adequate. Car-park attendants, recognizable by their brass badges, watch the parking lots on the streets of the big cities and in hotels – a very reassuring institution.

Prohibited Areas

The South Moroccan routes Fam-el-Hissn-Tindouf and Guelmim-Assa-Zag-Tindouf are closed. Although there appears to be an easing of tensions in the Western Sahara, only the routes Guelmim - Laayoune, Cap Boujdour - Dakhla and Smara - Tan Tan have been opened to traffic up to now. The Mauretanian trail might be cleared for use by tourists again at some point; current information can be obtained from the local police and police stations. Even if the tourist office in Rabat promises a clear road, the reality is often different. Be sure to remain polite during the police inspections, which happen frequently in the Western Sahara and the Algerian border area. There are also restrictions at the Moroccan-Algerian border, particularly in the south.

Traffic

The road system is – by African standards – very good. Cars drive on the right and regulations generally correspond with traffic regulations in Central Europe. In traffic circles cars from the right have priority. Your driving style should be defensive. Encounters with trucks and buses on narrow southern Moroccan roads are a matter of strong nerves. Drive to the right in time to avoid the whirled-up rocks. You are urgently advised not to drive at night: in addition to unlit cars, donkey carts, cyclists, pedestrians, mules, sheep, goats, and camel there are also deep potholes which cause incalculable danger. In the Rif, the Middle and High Atlas, snow must be reckoned with in winter. However, they seldom last more than a day. In the mountains and in the south, fords may be blocked for days after rainfall. Use of

horn on pass and bending roads as well as when passing is advisable. It may seem obnoxious, but it could save lives.

PRACTICAL TIPS

Accommodations

Moroccan hotels are annually rated in an evaluation system which extends from 1*B (simple) to 5*****A (luxury). Hotels are chronically overbooked in the peak Easter season, so always call a day before arriving to confirm and check in early (as of 2 p.m.).

Alcohol

As an Islamic country, Morocco has a difficult relationship to alcohol. The Koran forbids intoxicants; despite this, the country produces beer and wine in large quantities. Only spirituous drinks are imported and therefore expensive. Drunks are locked up. No alcohol is served to Moslems during Ramadan. Otherwise, Moroccans also visit the bars of the tourist hotels. Not all restaurants and only a few stores have an alcohol license. In the more provincial southern Morocco and in the Western Sahara, wine and beer can only be purchased in the large tourist hotels.

Beggars

The Koran stipulates that alms be given to the needy as a religious duty. A blessing for the giver is a certainty. When someone gives nothing, then they at least say "*ashib allah*" (may Allah give it to you). National insurance is a foreign word for most Moroccans and therefore the handicapped, ill and old can only beg if they want to survive. However, children should not be given anything since well-meant donations mostly lead to their skipping school. Their chances of being employed someday sink if they do not finish school, thereby making their path into criminality a foregone conclusion. Keep this in mind!

Business Hours

Banks: Mon.-Fri. 8:15-11:15 a.m. and 2:15-4:30 p.m. The exchange of money is possible on weekends at airports and in large hotels. **Post Office**: Mon.-Fri. 8:30 a.m.-12:15 p.m. and 2:30-6:30 p.m.; Sat. 8:30a.m.-12 noon. **Telegraph Office**: Mon.-Sat. 8 a.m.-9 p.m. **Government Agencies**: Mon.-Fri. 8:30 a.m.-12 noon and 2:30-4:30 p.m. **Stores**: According to the owner's wishes; mostly long lunch breaks. Many bazaar stores are closed Fridays. **Museums and Monuments**: daily except Tues. from 9 a.m.-12 noon and 2 p.m. or 4 p.m.-6 p.m. During Ramadan special arrangements have been made because of the shortened working day; museums and monuments: 10 a.m.-5 p.m., administrative offices usually just mornings.

Customs

Entry: the following items are duty-free: 200 cigarettes or 200 g tobacco; 0.75 liters spirits or 2 liters wine; two photo cameras or one film camera and a photo camera; one radio; one tape recorder; one typewriter; one portable television set; two musical instruments; sports and camping equipment; personal travel necessities. Video cameras are occasionally recorded in the passport. Writings by the Ayatollah Khomeini and political books on the Western Sahara conflict are confiscated.

Departure: all luggage will be checked. Souvenirs may be exported duty-free, but are subject to customs declaration at the home airport. Morocco is considered to be associated with the EC; EC countries a 14% importation sales tax on souvenirs worth more than approx. $70.

Drink

The national drink of peppermint tea (*thé à la menthe* or *latai b'nana*) is made of green China tea, fresh mint leaves and much sugar. The breakfast coffee served in large hotels is usually a catastrophe; in contrast, there is good espresso and *café au lait* available at bars and in street cafés. American soft drink varieties are quite widespread. Non-carbonated water is Sidi Ali or Sidi Harazem, and carbonated mineral water is Oulmès. Common brands of Moroccan beer include Stork, Flag and Heineken. Wine is only served in restaurants, but never at bars. Acceptable red wines, comparable with French table wine come primarily from the region of Meknes: Cabernet Président, Ksar, Guerrouane and Beni M'tir. The same wineries also produce rosé and white wines (*Cap Blanc*). Milk-shake drinks such as apple milk, banana milk and almond milk can be purchased in the *glacerie* (ice-cream parlor). According to Western standards, the *orange pressée* (freshly-pressed orange juice) is unbelievably good and cheap (starting at DH 2). Trying it in street cafés tastes better than in most of the hotels. For reasons of health, it is better to avoid the use of ice-cubes.

Drugs

Marijuana and hashish are offered for sale in the Rif Mountains in particular. No matter what the salespeople say, be careful: the possession, use and trading of drugs is severely punished. Numerous tourist sit in distinctly uncomfortable Moroccan prisons for this reason.

Electricity

Depending on the region, it is common to have voltages of 110 volts as well as 220 volts.

Emergencies

Emergency numbers: Police (*Police Secour*) Tel: 19; Fire (*Pompiers*) Tel: 15; Ambulance (*Ambulance*): Tel 15. Every larger city has a **night pharmacy** (*Pharamacie nuit*). **Hospitals** are found in all provincial capitals; the best are in Casa and Rabat. In remote areas, inform the next gendarmerie post in the case of an emergency; there is no helicopter service. For difficult operations, as well as after accidents, it is better to fly home. Take out an insurance policy before leaving to cover this eventuality!

Etiquette

Non-Moslems are not allowed to enter mosques, mausoleums (*marabouts*), brotherhood buildings (*zawiyas*) and some cemeteries. Moroccans who do not live from tourism are very polite, love extensive rituals of welcome and are extremely hospitable. When invited to a private home, one should appear well-dressed and remove the shoes before entering. In case the food is eaten in the traditional manner without knives and forks: eat only with the right hand since the left is considered to be unclean (toilet paper is unknown in the back-country). It is appropriate to bring a present for the host or hostess (no money).

When bothered on the street by touts, begging or even stone-throwing children, you must react energetically; reservedness is interpreted as a sign of weakness. On the other hand, when dealing with administrative representative it is best to be polite and patient, but resolute. Politics are not discussed in public if, indeed, at all.

Food

The national dish *tajine* is prepared from vegetables and meat with olive oil and a special seasoning mixture and then simmered in an earthen pot. According to the season, tajine is also prepared with quince or plums. *Couscous* consists of durum wheat semolina steamed over a vegetable and meat broth with which it is served. *Bastilla* is a delicious puff pastry which is best filled with pigeon meat, onions, almonds and honey and dusted with confectioners' sugar. *Meschoui* is a festive mutton roast, traditionally cooked vertically in conical clay ovens and eaten with cumin seasoning. *Kefta* are ground-

meat balls, *brochettes* are meat skewers broiled over a charcoal flame. *Harira* is a thick brown bean soup with mutton, traditionally served during the Ramadan nights. Spicy-seasoned fried sausages made of mutton or beef are called *Merguez*. The *cornes de gazelle*, literally gazelle's horns, are a seductive pastry filled with almond paste and refined in taste with rose water.

Fraud

The goal of all bazaarists is to obtain the highest possible price. When street traders offer "real" silver jewelry, you can be absolutely certain that it is a worthless alloy. So-called gems are often worthless industry products; yellow plastic balls are frequently offered at a high price as amber. There really are amethysts in Morocco, but that which is offered in the souvenir stores is often dyed. The mineral dealers at the Tichka Pass and in Midelt are particularly imaginative. In contrast, all the fossils are real. Yellow powder is rarely valuable saffron.

Before making larger carpet purchases, make sure you have seen the government ceiling price, which every trader must display. The eloquence of the carpet dealers is boundless, but the contents is mostly meaningless. True silk is also rare and expensive in Morocco and the kelims are practically never embroidered with it. The so-called natural colors, the origin of which can even be "ground turquoise" according to the eloquent salesmen, most often originates in the tanks of chemical factories. 99 percent of all salesmen who wear a blue *gandura* and the matching turban have never even seen true indigo or an authentic representative of the Tuareg tribe. Commissions for touts does not fall under the category of fraud in the Orient; it is calculated into the sales price as customer advertising costs. As *nasrani* (a Christian), one always loses when gambling at the Jemma el Fna in Marrakech.

Guides

Officially, organized travel groups may only travel in Morocco when accompanied by a licensed guide (with badge and identification papers). In the royal cities, a local guide provided by the *Syndicat d'Initiative et du Tourisme* or the *Office National du Tourisme* (ONMT) must also be hired. Check the current tariffs (approx. DH 50 for half a day, approx. DH 100 for a whole day) in order to avoid problems when paying the guide *!* For those traveling alone, a guide can also be helpful in the obscure little alleys of the older parts of towns. However, don't fall prey to the illegal touts – the most obtrusive of whom taint the *medina* of Marrakech – and only use the services of guides who are identified as such (note name and number of official badge).

Holidays and Festivals

Although Moslems are supposed to go to the mosques for midday prayers on Friday, Sunday is the official day of rest. National holidays are according to the Gregorian calendar we know: January 1, New Year's Day; March 3, anniversary of King Hassan II's ascent to the throne; May 1: Labor Day; May 23: *Fête Nationale* (full legal age of crown prince established to be 16 years of age); July 9: *Fête de la Jeunesse* (Hassan II's birthday); August 14: commemoration of King Hassan's journey to Dakhla in 1981; August 20: *Révolution du Roi et du Peuple* (anniversary of the exiling of Mohammed V in 1953); August 21: birthday of Sidi Mohammed (crown prince); November 6: *Marche Verte* (anniversary of the Green March); November 16: declaration of independence.

Religious holidays follow the Islamic calendar, which begins in A.D. 622 with the *hedschra*, Mohammed's flight from Mecca 1992 = 1413. The basis for calculation is the lunar year, about 11 days shorter than the solar year, which is why the beginning of Ramadan wanders backwards through our calendar. *Achoura*: the "tenth day" (New Year). *Mouloud*: Mohammed's birthday (candlelight procession in Salé). *Chabana*: beginning of the fasting month of *Ramadan*, in which drinking, eating and smoking is only allowed between sundown and sunrise. Opulent banquets every night. No limitations for non-Moslem visitors; however, the Moroccans are quite touchy during the daytime. There is little eagerness to work in industry and administration. In television, prayers take the place of movies and religious sensitivity increases. *Id es Seghir* (or *Id Fitr*): joyfully-celebrated festival of breaking the fast at the end of *Ramadan*. *Id el Kebir*: great sacrificial festival; in memory of Abraham's sacrifice and the sparing of Ishmael (Isaac, according to Christian tradition), millions of sheep are slaughtered on the tenth day of the pilgrimage month *doul hedschra*. The faithful distribute two-thirds of the meat to the needy. People buy themselves new clothes for the festival.

Moussems are pilgrimage celebrations at the graves of the most important *marabouts*, often having the character of a public festival. **Guelmim**: *moussem* at the grave of the Sidi Ahmed Amaro with a camel market at the beginning of June in Asrir. **Tan Tan**: pilgrimage festival in June with a camel sacrifice and *guedra* (knee dance). **Moulay Idriss**: largest *moussem* of the country in August in the holy city of Idriss I with *fantasia*. **Tiznit**: on the third Thursday in August, *moussem* of the Sidi Ahmed ou Mossa. **Meknes**: spectacular procession of the Aissaoua brotherhood on *mouloud* day (among other things, snakes and scorpions are eaten). **Moulay Bou Selham**: *moussem* in May (near Kenitra). **Fès**: candlelight procession in September in honor of the founder Moulay Idriss II. **Imilchil**: marriage market of Ait Haddidou in September. **Tamegroute**: festival of the Sidi Mohammed ben Nasser on *achoura* day.

Folklore festivals: Almond-blossom festival in **Tafraoute** (January/February). Mandarine festival in **Berkane** (December). Festival of horses in Tissa with *fantasia* (October). Rose festival in **El Kelaa M'Gouna** (May). Cherry festival in **Sefrou** (June). Date festival in **Erfoud** (October). Folklore festival in **Marrakech** (in spring). Many festival dates change from year to year: ask at tourist information offices!

Photography

Before you photograph individual people from close up, particularly women, you should ask their permission. The honor of a Moroccan can be injured if a stranger possesses a picture of his wife! The entertainers at the Jemaa el Fna in Marrakech live well from the obligatory tips given by photo-tourists (from DH 1 upwards). As part of your camera equipment, you should have at least one UV filter and ideally a polarizing filter and long lenses. The best light for photography is in the early morning and late afternoon; because of the lack of contrast it is almost impossible to take good landscape pictures in the middle of the day. Photography is not allowed at military installations and dams!

Shopping

Fixed prices are to be found only in the shops of the new city quarters and in governmental craft centers. You can get information about price levels there as well. Only then should you visit the bazaar (souk) in order to bargain: first offer one fourth of the price given and then yield in small steps. For mor information, see feature article on the art of bargaining.

Theft

The risk of being robbed by a pickpocket in the crowds of the bazaar or in croward city buses is by far not as great as in southern Europe. There are moped-driving handbag thieves in Morocco. Particularly in Tangier, Tetouan, Casablanca and Marrakech you should keep an eye on your valuables. Instead of having larger amounts of money, passport and tickets in handbags or shoulder bags, carry them directly on your body (but not in money bags around your neck, since thieves keep their eyes on them). When walking in the city, you can entrust your car to an official parking-lot attendant with a badge. Hotel safes should be used and, if there are no individual safe-deposit boxes, pay attention to the sealing of the safekeeping envelope.

Tips

The reasons for which tips are requested in Morocco are often beyond your wildest imagination. However, for many of those employed in the tourism sector (waiter, porter, receptionist, parking-lot attendant, guide, chauffeur, assistant driver and travel supervisor), tips are an indispensable supplement to the meagerly-calculated wages. An appropriate baksheesh – from DH 2 upwards – opens many doors; in hotels which are booked-up it may sometimes even open room doors.Always remember the little wisdom, that a tip is not for services rendered, but rather to ensure the efficient performance of services in the future.

Women traveling alone

Women traveling alone are relatively safe in this country if they are able to ignore tactless passes and observe some elementary rules of conduct. Western women are considered to be available at any time and easy prey. Films, magazines, RTL-plus via satellite, and bare-bossomed bathers in Agadir appear to confirm the prejudice. Eye contact, open hair, tight-fitting clothing and bare skin are interpreted by most Moroccan men as an invitation to make advances. A draped jellabah conceals the primary charms and a wedding ring suggests a protective man. Invitations to see a "Berber house" made by men should be refused. In case of necessity, a reference to AIDS, known as SIDA in Morocco, can work wonders. Moroccan women who feel themselves harassed yell *chouma* (shame) loudly or use their well-filed fingernails to scratch the face of the man who is too persistent.

ADDRESSES

Embassies in Rabat

(Area code 07) Algeria: Rue Tarik Ibn Ziad 46, Tel: 65591. **Germany**: Zankat Maddine 7, Tel: 69662. **Argentina**: Rue Mekki Bitaouri 12, Tel: 55120. **Austria**: Zankat Tididas 2, Tel: 64003. **Belgium**: Ave. de Marrakech 6, Tel: 64746. **Brazil**: Ave. de Marrakech 1, Tel: 65522. **Canada**: Rue Jaafar Essadik, Tel: 71375. **Denmark**: Rue de Khemisset, Tel: 69293. **Egypt**: Ave. d'Alger 31, Tel: 31833. **Finland:** Rue de Khemisset 16, Tel: 62312. **France**: Rue Shanoun 3, Tel: 77822. **Great Britain:** Bd. Tour Hassan 17, Tel: 20905. **Greece**: Rue d'Oujda 23, Tel: 23839. **Italy**: Zankat Idriss El Azhar 2, Tel: 66598. **Libya**: Rue Bouchaib Doukali 1, Tel: 67400. **Mauretania**: Rue Thami Lamdouar 6, Tel: 56817. **Netherlands**: Rue de Tunis 40, Tel: 33512. **Norway**: Charia As-Saouira 22, Tel: 61096. **Poland**: Zankat Oqbah 23, Tel: 71791. **Portugal**: Rue Thami Lamdouar 5, Tel: 56446. **Saudi Arabia**: Place de L'Unité Africaine, Tel: 30171. **Senegal**: Rue Cadi Ben Hamdi Senhagi 17, Tel: 54148. **Spain**: Zankat Madmir 3, Tel: 69481. Sweden: Ave. John F. Kennedy 159, Tel: 54740. **Switzerland**: Square de Berkane, Tel: 66974/67512.**Tunisia**: Ave. de Fès 6, Tel: 30636. **USA**: Charii Marrakech 2, Tel: 62265.

Airlines in Casablanca

(Area code 0) **Aeroflot**: Ave. des F.A.R. 27, Tel: 310521. **Air Afrique:** Place Zelaqa 57, Tel: 318379. **Air Algérie**: Rue Alla Ben Abdallah. **Air**

France: Ave. des F.A.R. 11, Tel: 224133. **Alia**: Ave. des F.A.R. 44, Tel: 311267. **Alitalia**: Ave. des F.A.R. 44, Tel: 222250. **British Airways**: Place Zellaqa 57, Tel: 307607. **Iberia**: Ave. des F.A.R. 44, Tel: 279600. **KLM**: Bd. El Hansali, Tel: 272729. **Lufthansa**: Ave. des F.A.R./ Tour des Habbous, 9th floor, Tel: 312371. **Sabena**: Ave. des F.A.R. 41, Tel: 313991. **Swissair**: Ave. des F.A.R. 28, Tel: 313280.

Inland Offices of Royal Air Maroc

Agadir: Ave. Général Kettani, 08-23145. **Al Hoceima**: Aéroport Côte du Rif, 098-2005. **Casablanca**: Ave. des F.A.R. 44, 0-311122/273211. **Fès**: Ave. Hassan II 54, Tel: 06-20456. **Laayoune**: Place Bir Anzarane 7, Tel: 224071. **Marrakech**: Ave. Mohammed V 197, Tel: 04-30939. **Oujda**: Bd. Mohammed V, Tel: 068-3963. **Rabat**: Ave. Mohammed V (train station), Tel. 07-69710. **Tangier**: Place Mohammed V, Tel: 09-34722.

Tourist Offices

Inland offices of the Office National Marocain du Tourisme (O.N.M.T.): **Agadir**: Place P.H. Sidi Mohammed, Tel: 822894. **Casablanca**: Rue Omar Slaoui 55, Tel: 271177. **Fès**: Place de la Résistance, Tel: 51709. **Marrakech**: Place Abdelmumen Bed Ali, Tel: 48906. **Meknes**: Place Administrative, Tel: 24426. **Rabat**: Main office of the O.N.M.T., Ave. d'Alger 22, Tel: 07-21252. Branch office: Rue Aguelmane Sidi Ali 43, Tel: 73644. **Tangier**: Boulevard Pasteur 29, Tel: 38239. **Tetouan**: Ave. Mohammed V 30, Tel: 64407.

Representation abroad. Australia: 2060 Sydney, 11 West Street North, Tel: 9576717. **Canada**: Montreal, Rue Université 2001, Tel: 8428111. **Great Britain**: London, 174 Regent Street. **U.S.A.**: New York, 20 East 46th Street, Tel: 5572520. Los Angeles, Beverly Hills, 421 North Rodeo Drive, Tel: 2718939.

Phrase Guide

French is often spoken in the cities; a basic knowledge of Moroccan-Arabic is necessary in the mountains.

hello, welcome	*merhaba*
peace be with you	*salam alaikum*
good morning	*saba alchär*
good evening	*msa alchär*
how are you?	*lebbes*
farewell	*bisslamma*
enjoy your meal	*ismillah*
with the help of God	*inchallah*
thank God	*hamdulilah*
thank you	*schukran (dialect),*
	barakallahufik
I beg your pardon	*sahmani*
please	*afak*
Mr	*sidi*
Mrs	*lalla*
yes	*ijeh or na'am*
no	*la*
none, nothing	*makasch*
money	*fluss*
How much?	*asch-hal*
too much	*beseff*
okay	*wacha*
beautiful	*msienn*
come here	*aschi*
go away	*sir, barra (coarse)*
bring, give	*schib*
careful!	*balek*
look here	*schuf*
where is?	*fain?*
is this the way to?...	*hadi trik...?*
right	*limin*
left	*lechmal*
far	*ba'id*
large	*kebir*
small	*seghir*
business	*hanud*
market	*souk*
gas station	*mhatta dlessans*
workshop	*mekhanik*
car	*arabiya*
water	*el ma*
bread	*khobz*
dates	*tmar*
egg	*bida*
fish	*huta*
meat	*leham*
vegetable	*chodra*
mutton	*kebch*
chicken	*dschasche*
coffee	*kahwa*
milk	*chalib*
oil	*sit*
orange	*limousse*
salt	*melha*
tea	*atai*
lemon	*lamun*
sugar	*sukar*
Sunday	*el had*
Monday	*el tnin*
Tuesday	*el tleta*
Wednesday	*el arba*
Thursday	*el khemis*
Friday	*el djemaa*
Saturday	*es sebt*
1	*wahed*
2	*tnin*
3	*tleta*
4	*arba*
5	*khamsa*
6	*setta*
7	*seba*
8	*tmenia*
9	*tse'ud*
10	*aschra*
11	*hadasch*
12	*tnasch*
13	*tletasch*
14	*arbatasch*
15	*khamstasch*
16	*settasch*
17	*sb'atasch*
18	*tmentasch*
19	*tsatsch*
20	*aschrin*
21	*wahed u aschrin*
30	*tletin*
40	*arbain*
50	*khamsin*
60	*settin*
70	*sbain*
80	*tmanin*
90	*tsa'in*
100	*mia*
1000	*alef*

AUTHORS

Berthold Schwarz studied geography as well as social and cultural anthropology. Since 1975 he has been traveling the Orient, Africa, and Asia both professionally and privately. In Morocco, he has been working since 1984, organizing trekking tours and leading study trips.

Dr. Anton Escher is a geographer, has a command of Moroccan-Arabic and researched traditional handicraft in Moroccan cities for his doctoral thesis. As a recognized expert on Fès, he knows all the artisan masters there and is one of the very few foreigners who can do without a guide in the labyrinthine alleys of Fès el Bali.

Walter Knappe studied biology and has led many study trips in areas of Islamic culture. He is the author of a number of books on Morocco and works as an assistant professor in adult education.

Rainer Leyendecker is a geologist and leads study and trekking trips in Morocco and Nepal.

Monika Müller is a travel service agent and specialist for horse-trekking in Morocco, Tunisia, Portugal and Turkey.

Dr. Ingolf Vereno is a chemist and Orientalist. He works for the F.A.O. as a development-aid expert and lived in Casablanca for four years.

Bernadette Vereno was born and raised in Casablanca and was a teacher for Italian and French there. She is therefore very familiar with the living conditions of Moroccan women.

Dr. Frank Welte studied Orientalism and learned Moroccan-Arabic. He spent a year in Meknes and wrote his doctoral thesis on Moslem brotherhoods there; his particular interest is in the trance techniques of the Aissaoua and Gnaoua.

PHOTOGRAPHERS

Becker, Frank S.	117
Bondzio, Bodo	76, 179
Bugdoll, Edmund	168, 202
Escher, Anton	45, 63, 177
Fischer, Peter	81
Frieser-Rex, Elke	38
Henninges, Heiner	28, 30, 43, 112
Hinze, Peter	155
Hühn, Holger	54, 103, 120, 172, 181
Janicke, Volkmar	55, 56, 66, 121, 175
Jung, Gerold	85, 88
Knappe, Walter	17, 65, 196
Leyendecker, Rainer	46/47, 212, 213, 234
Ranftl, Ursula	235
Reuther, Jörg	156
Rex, Peter	68, 70/71, 72, 108, 124, 216
Rohrbach, Carmen	138, 143, 146
Schwarz, Berthold	1, 12/13, 18, 24, 26, 27, 29, 31, 35,36, 40, 41, 64, 100, 106, 111, 113, 115, 126/127, 130L, 130R, 131, 133, 134, 136/137, 140, 144,158, 159, 161, 162L, 162R, 163, 164, 174, 180, 184, 185, 187, 189, 190, 204, 206, 207, 209, 224, 225, 227, 228, 230, 231, 237
Schwarz, Reiner	14, 82
Steinhardt, Jochen	cover, 8/9, 20, 22, 50, 59, 83, 87, 90, 91, 95, 98/99, 109, 114, 118, 148/149, 150, 154, 166/167, 194/195, 201, 218/219, 220/221, 223
Tetzner, Marina	34, 78, 178
Thiele, Klaus	10/11, 33, 44, 48/49, 232
Vereno, Ingolf	183, 205

INDEX